First World War
and Army of Occupation
War Diary
France, Belgium and Germany

31 DIVISION
Divisional Troops
Royal Army Medical Corps
94 Field Ambulance
1 March 1916 - 30 April 1919

WO95/2354/2

The Naval & Military Press Ltd
www.nmarchive.com
Published in association with The National Archives

Published by

The Naval & Military Press Ltd

Unit 10 Ridgewood Industrial Park,

Uckfield, East Sussex,

TN22 5QE England

Tel: +44 (0) 1825 749494

www.naval-military-press.com

www.nmarchive.com

This diary has been reprinted in facsimile from the original. Any imperfections are inevitably reproduced and the quality may fall short of modern type and cartographic standards.

© Crown Copyright
Images reproduced by permission of The National Archives, London, England, 2015.

Contents

Document type	Place/Title	Date From	Date To
Heading	WO95/2354/2		
Heading	31st Division Medical 94th Field Ambulance Mar 1916-1919 Apl		
Heading	No 94 Field Amt. March April 1916 Dec. 18		
Miscellaneous	Appendix A	03/04/1916	03/04/1916
Heading	94 F Amb Vol I		
War Diary	Kantara	01/03/1916	01/03/1916
War Diary	At-Sea	02/03/1916	05/03/1916
War Diary	Marseilles	06/03/1916	07/03/1916
War Diary	On Train	08/03/1916	08/03/1916
War Diary	Pontremy	09/03/1916	09/03/1916
War Diary	Huppy	10/03/1916	25/03/1916
War Diary	Wanel	26/03/1916	26/03/1916
War Diary	Flesselles	27/03/1916	27/03/1916
War Diary	Beauval	28/03/1916	28/03/1916
War Diary	Vauchelles	29/03/1916	31/03/1916
Miscellaneous		06/05/1916	06/05/1916
War Diary	Vauchelles	01/04/1916	03/04/1916
War Diary	Bus Les Artois	04/04/1916	30/04/1916
Heading	May 1916 B. 94 F. Amb.		
Miscellaneous		31/05/1916	31/05/1916
War Diary	Bus Les Artois	01/05/1916	31/05/1916
Heading	June 1916 B. 94 FA		
Miscellaneous	D.A.G. 3rd Echelon	04/07/1916	04/07/1916
War Diary	Bus Les Artois	01/06/1916	30/06/1916
Heading	War Diary Of 94th Field Amb. 1st July 1916 To 31st July 1916		
War Diary	Bus Les Artois	01/07/1916	06/07/1916
War Diary	Gezaincourt	07/07/1916	08/07/1916
War Diary	Calonne Sur Lys.	09/07/1916	31/07/1916
Heading	War Diary Of 94th Fd Ambulance Aug 1916		
War Diary	Colonne Sur Lys	01/08/1916	31/08/1916
Heading	War Diary 94th Field Ambulance 31st Division September 1916		
War Diary	Colonne Sur Lys.	01/09/1916	16/09/1916
War Diary	Mesplaux	17/09/1916	30/09/1916
Heading	War Diary 94th Field Ambulance 31st Division October 1916		
War Diary	Mesplaux	01/10/1916	03/10/1916
War Diary	White House	04/10/1916	04/10/1916
War Diary	Robecq	05/10/1916	08/10/1916
War Diary	Sarton	09/10/1916	16/10/1916
War Diary	Couin	17/10/1916	31/10/1916
Heading	31st Div. 94th Field Ambulance		
Heading	War Diary 94th Field Ambulance 31st. Division November 1916		
War Diary	Couin	01/11/1916	30/11/1916
Heading	War Diary 94th Field Ambulance 31st Division December 1916		
War Diary	Couin	01/12/1916	31/12/1916

Heading	War Diary 94th Field Ambulance. 31st Division January 1917		
War Diary	Couin	01/01/1917	10/01/1917
War Diary	Beauval	11/01/1917	22/01/1917
War Diary	Vacquerie	23/01/1917	31/01/1917
Heading	War Diary 94th Field Ambulance 31st Division February 1917		
War Diary	Vacquerie	01/02/1917	20/02/1917
War Diary	Beauval	21/02/1917	22/02/1917
War Diary	Couin	23/02/1917	28/02/1917
Heading	War Diary 94th Field Ambulance. 31st Division March 1917		
War Diary	Couin	01/03/1917	08/03/1917
War Diary	P176 19	09/03/1917	19/03/1917
War Diary	Orville	19/03/1917	20/03/1917
War Diary	Beauvoir	21/03/1917	21/03/1917
War Diary	Blangermont	22/03/1917	22/03/1917
War Diary	Pressy Les Pernes	23/03/1917	24/03/1917
War Diary	Flechinelle	25/03/1917	25/03/1917
War Diary	Robecq	26/03/1917	31/03/1917
Heading	War Diary 94th Field Ambulance 31st Division April 1917		
War Diary	Robecq	01/04/1917	07/04/1917
War Diary	Allouagne	08/04/1917	10/04/1917
War Diary	Bruay	11/04/1917	14/04/1917
War Diary	Ourton	15/04/1917	25/04/1917
War Diary	Guestreville	27/04/1917	30/04/1917
Heading	Summary Of Medical War Diaries For 94th F.A. 31st Divn. 13th Corps. 1st Army. 3rd Army From 11/4/17. Western Front. April-May. 17		
Miscellaneous	94th F.A. 31st Divn. 13th Corps. O.C. Lt. Col. H. Stewart. 1st Army. 3rd Army From 11/4/17	11/04/1917	11/04/1917
Heading	War Diary 94th Field Ambulance 31st Division May 1917		
War Diary	Anzin	01/05/1917	02/05/1917
War Diary	H.4 b.5.5	03/05/1917	06/05/1917
War Diary	Anzin	07/05/1917	21/05/1917
War Diary	Cambligneul	22/05/1917	31/05/1917
Heading	Summary Of Medical War Diaries For 94th F.A. 31st Divn. 13th Corps. 1st Army 3rd Army From 11/4/17. Western Front. April May. 17		
Miscellaneous	94th F.A. 31st Divn. 13th Corps. O.C. Lt. Col. H. Stewart. 3rd Army.		
Heading	War Diary 94th Field Ambulance 31st Division June 1917		
War Diary	Cambligneul	01/06/1917	10/06/1917
War Diary	Anzin	11/06/1917	20/06/1917
War Diary	Ecoivres	21/06/1917	30/06/1917
Heading	War Diary 94th Field Ambulance 31st Division July 1917		
War Diary	Ecoivres	01/07/1917	31/07/1917
War Diary	War Diary 94th Field Ambulance 31st Division August 1917		
War Diary	Ecoivres	01/08/1917	31/08/1917
Heading	War Diary 94th Field Ambulance 31st Division September 1917		

War Diary	Ecoivres	01/09/1917	30/09/1917
Heading	War Diary 94th Field Ambulance 31st Division October. 1917		
War Diary	Ecoivres	01/10/1917	07/10/1917
War Diary	Aubigny	08/10/1917	31/10/1917
Heading	War Diary 94th Field Ambulance 31st Division November 1917		
War Diary	Aubigny	01/11/1917	30/11/1917
Heading	War Diary 94th Field Ambulance 31st Division December 1917		
War Diary	Aubigny	01/12/1917	05/12/1917
War Diary	Aubigny	06/12/1917	11/12/1917
War Diary	ACQ	12/12/1917	21/12/1917
War Diary	Roclincourt	22/12/1917	31/12/1917
Heading	No. 94 F.A.		
War Diary	Roclincourt	01/01/1918	31/01/1918
Heading	No. 94. F.A.		
War Diary	Roclincourt	01/02/1918	28/02/1918
Operation(al) Order(s)	94th Field Ambulance Order No. 19 By Lieut. Col. Hugh Stewart, D.S.O., M.C., R.A.M.C., Commanding 94th Field Ambulance.		
Heading	92nd Field Ambulance		
War Diary	Roclincourt	01/03/1918	02/03/1918
War Diary	Mt. St. Eloi	03/03/1918	03/03/1918
War Diary	Bailleul Aux Cornailes	04/03/1918	21/03/1918
War Diary	Bailleulmont	22/03/1918	24/03/1918
War Diary	Gouy En Artois	25/03/1918	31/03/1918
Heading	94th Field Ambulance		
War Diary	Ivergny	01/04/1918	01/04/1918
War Diary	Houvelin	02/04/1918	08/04/1918
War Diary	Tincques	09/04/1918	10/04/1918
War Diary	Merris	11/04/1918	11/04/1918
War Diary	Strazeele	12/04/1918	12/04/1918
War Diary	Borre	13/04/1918	13/04/1918
War Diary	Lakreule	14/04/1918	18/04/1918
War Diary	Les Cinq Rues	19/04/1918	27/04/1918
War Diary	La Kreule	27/04/1918	30/04/1918
Heading	War Diary 94th Field Ambulance May. 1918 Vol 27		
War Diary	La Kreule	01/05/1918	24/05/1918
War Diary	Quiestede	25/05/1918	31/05/1918
Heading	94th F.a. June 1918		
War Diary	Quiestede	01/06/1918	15/06/1918
War Diary	Hondeghem	16/06/1918	17/06/1918
War Diary	Sercus	18/06/1918	20/06/1918
War Diary	Wallon Capelle	21/06/1918	30/06/1918
Heading	No. 94 F.A. June 1918		
War Diary	Wallon Capelle	01/07/1918	31/07/1918
Heading	94th. F. Amb. Aug 1918		
War Diary	Wallon Capelle	01/08/1918	23/08/1918
War Diary	Hondeghem	24/08/1918	31/08/1918
Heading	94th Fd. Amb. Sept. 1918		
War Diary	Hondeghem	01/09/1918	03/09/1918
War Diary	St. Sylvestre Cappel	04/09/1918	05/09/1918
War Diary	Bailluel	06/09/1918	07/09/1918
War Diary	Meteren	08/09/1918	30/09/1918
Heading	94th F. A. Oct 1918		

War Diary	Meteren	01/10/1918	01/10/1918
War Diary	Gough Lines	02/10/1918	15/10/1918
War Diary	Courte Dreve Farm	16/10/1918	17/10/1918
War Diary	Quesnoy	18/10/1918	18/10/1918
War Diary	Mouveaux	19/10/1918	20/10/1918
War Diary	Lannoy	21/10/1918	26/10/1918
War Diary	Cuerne	27/10/1918	27/10/1918
War Diary	Harlebeke	28/10/1918	31/10/1918
Heading	No. 94 F.A. Nov 1918		
War Diary	Harlebeke	01/11/1918	02/11/1918
War Diary	Roncq	03/11/1918	07/11/1918
War Diary	Sweveghem	08/11/1918	09/11/1918
War Diary	Rugge	10/11/1918	10/11/1918
War Diary	Renaix	11/11/1918	13/11/1918
War Diary	Heestert	14/11/1918	14/11/1918
War Diary	Bisseghem	15/11/1918	15/11/1918
War Diary	Wevelghem	16/11/1918	22/11/1918
War Diary	Menin	23/11/1918	23/11/1918
War Diary	Vlamartinge	24/11/1918	24/11/1918
War Diary	Steen Voorde	25/11/1918	25/11/1918
War Diary	Blendecques	26/11/1918	30/11/1918
Heading	94th F.A. Dec. 1918		
War Diary	Blendecques	01/12/1918	31/12/1918
Heading	No. 94 Field Ambulance Jan 1919 31st Div Box 2131		
War Diary	Blendecques	01/01/1919	04/01/1919
War Diary	Steenbecque	05/01/1919	31/01/1919
Heading	No. 94 Field Ambulance Feb. 1919		
War Diary	Steenbecque	01/02/1919	12/02/1919
War Diary	Steenwerck	12/02/1919	28/02/1919
War Diary	94th. F.A. Mar. 1919		
War Diary	Steenwerck	01/03/1919	20/03/1919
War Diary	St. Omer	21/03/1919	31/03/1919
Heading	No. 94. F.A. Apr. 1919		
War Diary	St. Omer	01/04/1919	30/04/1919

WO 95/23541/2

31ST DIVISION
MEDICAL

94TH FIELD AMBULANCE
MAR 1916 - DEC 1918
1919 APL

31ST DIVISION
MEDICAL

31st Div

Left Kantara
1.3.16.

March } 1916.
April

No 94 Field Amb.

Dec '18

31

COMMITTEE FOR THE
MEDICAL HISTORY OF THE WAR

Date   9- JUN. 1916

Copy forwarded
Officer i/c
    A. G.
        Base.

Herewith War Diary of
94ᵗʰ Field Ambulance for
March 1916.

262
3.4.16

Hugh Stewart Lt Col
   R.A.M.C.
O.C. 94ᵗʰ Field Amb.

94 F amb
Vol 1

WAR DIARY or INTELLIGENCE SUMMARY

(Erase heading not required.)

Army Form C. 2118

Place	Date	Hour	Summary of Events and Information	Remarks and references to Appendices
	MARCH 1916			
KANTARA	1st		Entrained at 2.15 this morning in open trucks for PORT SAID. Train very late leaving, arrived PORT SAID 7 a.m. Marched down to Docks. After breakfast then marched on board H.T. MINNEAPOLIS & allotted messes. Horses under L' STEADMAN arrived by late train & were got safely on board. Medical & Surgical equipment brought by train to docks thence by lighter to Ship & placed in No. 2 Hold. Ship sailed at 6 p.m.	
AT SEA	2.		Received orders re allotment of deck for "alarm" parade & boat stations. Alarm practised. Nothing to report.	
AT SEA	3.		Slightly rough. CO's parade at 10 a.m. Horses taken over duties as M.O. i/c Ship. Got FB taken over all sanitary duties on board. Went round with CO ship.	
AT SEA	4.		Much finer today. Passed MALTA at 1 pm.	
AT SEA	5.		Medical Inspection of all troops on board held today. No cases of Venereal or Infectious disease found.	

WAR DIARY or INTELLIGENCE SUMMARY

(Erase heading not required.)

Army Form C. 2118

Place	Date	Hour	Summary of Events and Information	Remarks and references to Appendices
MARSEILLES	6		Arrived here this afternoon but did not disembark. No one allowed on shore. R.	
MARSEILLES	7		Disembarked today and whole unit entrained at 2 p.m. en route for the North. All equipment loaded on train. Rations and forage for three days with us. Halted at ORANGE for one hour where tea was provided for the men by the French authorities. R.	
ON TRAIN	8		Halted at MACON & LES LAUMES for food on the way. Tea being provided by French authorities. Very severe frost during night. R.	
PONT REMY	9		Arrived here at 12.30 & detrained, received orders to march to HUPPY & be billeted there. After men had had dinner unit marched out, baggage being transported by motor lorries. Arrived at HUPPY about 4 p.m. & went into the billets shown to me by the Staff Captain 94th Inf. Bde. R.	
HUPPY	10		Snow during the night. Detailed "C" Section to take over charge of the dressing station. Rearranged the billets for the men & otherwise settled the places. R.	

WAR DIARY or INTELLIGENCE SUMMARY

Army Form C. 2118

(Erase heading not required.)

Place	Date	Hour	Summary of Events and Information	Remarks and references to Appendices
	MARCH 1916			
HUPPY	11.		Proceeded to ABBEVILLE to draw our first line transport. Drew all wagons and heavy and light draught horses also five riders, all good animals. R.	
HUPPY.	12.		No supplies having arrived for the transport units attached to us & rations I went to PONT REMY today to see the Officer i/c Supplies. On return found orders received to send N.C.O. & loaders to train to take over our train wagons. Detailed Sgt. the CLUBB. Sent Ambulance wagon to FORCEVILLE to collect one officer & one O.R. sick. R.	
HUPPY	13.		Routine work during day. Evacuated 3 cases to No. 2 Stationary Hospital Abbeville by Ambulances. A.D.M.S. came round & was pleased with arrangements made. R.	
HUPPY	14.		No supplies having arrived I sent Capt. McEWEN & Lt. JIBB to make enquiries then they were able to do and supplies now coming in regularly. R.	
HUPPY	15.		Capt. McEWEN proceeded to Headquarters today to demand the military & Communication department. R.	

WAR DIARY or INTELLIGENCE SUMMARY

(Erase heading not required.)

Army Form C. 2118

Instructions regarding War Diaries and Intelligence Summaries are contained in F. S. Regs., Part II. and the Staff Manual respectively. Title Pages will be prepared in manuscript.

Place	Date	Hour	Summary of Events and Information	Remarks and references to Appendices
	MARCH 1916			
HUPPY	16		Route march for men in the morning. Went to see ADMS in the morning to arrange various details of pt his contingent to small requisitions required. R	
HUPPY	17		Nothing to report routine work carried out. R	
HUPPY	18		Went to ABBEVILLE on duty today. Nothing to report. R	
HUPPY	19		Divine Service for R.Cs today in Chapel at 9.15. Lieut KING marched the party there. No arrangements made for holding any service for C of E. R	
HUPPY	20		Routine work in the morning. Went over to Headquarters to see ADMS re several matters. Route march for men in the morning. R	
HUPPY	21		Received telegram allowing three of all ranks to proceed on leave. Went to H.Q. to obtain leave for self and O.M. A H A B J IBB as everything running smoothly now. Received sanction. Proceeded to ABBEVILLE to for Harcourt to proceed via BOULOGNE & having received same returned & had to leave late that night to catch boat train London. Handing over to Capt T. McEWEN. R	

WAR DIARY or INTELLIGENCE SUMMARY

(Erase heading not required.)

Army Form C. 2118

Place	Date Hour MARCH 1916	Summary of Events and Information	Remarks and references to Appendices
HUPPY	22nd	Lieut Col. H. STEWART has gone on leave, also Lieut. Q.M. A.H ADDY-JIBB & one other rank. Lieut. Col. H. STEWART handed over command to Capt. T. McEWEN.	
HUPPY	23rd	The unit received its first payment in FRANCE. Received orders to hold the unit in readiness to move on the 26th inst.	
HUPPY	24th	Visited the A.D.M.S. at HALLENCOURT	
HUPPY	25th	Visited Head Quarters of the 94th Brigade for moving orders & was informed that I should receive them from A.D.M.S. At 4 p.m. having received no orders, proceeded to A.D.M.S. & found that orders had been forwarded to the unit. On returning found orders had been delivered. Lieut. M.B. KING & the interpreter proceeded to WANEL to arrange for billets for the night of the 26th	
WANEL	26th	The unit left HUPPY at 8.30 a.m. prompt — all sick having been evacuated to No 3 Casualty Clearing Station prior to departure as directed by A.D.M.S.	

WAR DIARY or INTELLIGENCE SUMMARY

(Erase heading not required.)

Army Form C. 2118

Place	Date	Hour	Summary of Events and Information	Remarks and references to Appendices
WANEL	MARCH 1916 26th (cont)		Proceeded via LIMEUX–HALLENCOURT to WANEL arriving there at 11.30 a.m. En route the unit was held up by movement of troops for 20 minutes. The distance from HUPPY to WANEL was 8 miles. At HALLENCOURT received from A.D.M.S. moving orders for tomorrow. At WANEL received orders for 2 officers & 3 N.C.Os. to proceed on 27th to 48th Division for the purpose of instruction in the front line of trenches.	
~~WANEL~~ FLESSELLES	27th		Lieut. J.H.C. WALKER & Lieut. W.R. HODGE with 3 N.C.Os. left for HALLENCOURT to join party proceeding for the above instruction. The unit moved out of WANEL at 7 a.m. according to instructions & proceeded to LONGPRE where it joined the 94th Brigade, marching behind the 210th Field Coy R.E. Before leaving WANEL the ambulance evacuated 18 sitting cases & at LONGPRE 15 sitting cases were evacuated by the motor ambulances to No 3 Casualty Clearing Station. The column then proceeded to VIGNACOURT via CONDE–HANGEST–BOURDON–POINT 77. On the way men who had fallen out were taken on the ambulances. At VIGNACOURT the 94th Field Ambulance left the	

WAR DIARY or INTELLIGENCE SUMMARY

Army Form C. 2118

(Erase heading not required.)

Place	Date	Hour	Summary of Events and Information	Remarks and references to Appendices
	MARCH 1916			
FLESSELLES	27th (cont)		column & proceeded on to FLESSELLES arriving at 3.30 p.m. where it went into billets which had been arranged for by Lieut D.T. FRASER & the interpreter who had been sent on early in the morning. The distance of this march was about 20 miles. 6 cases are detained in the Field Ambulance till tomorrow.	
BEAUVAL	28th		The above 6 cases were evacuated to No 3 Casualty Clearing Station at SAINT OUEN also, ambulances having been wired for, 22 cases were evacuated to the same C.C.S. from VIGNACOURT. According to orders received, the unit left FLESSELLES at 9.30 a.m. & proceeded in the rear of the 210th Field Coy R.E. to BEAUVAL via NAOURS & VERT GALLAND FARM arriving at the billets at 1.30 p.m. Billets had been arranged for by Lieut D.T. FRASER & the interpreter.	
VAUCHELLES	29th		The unit left BEAUVAL at 9 a.m. under orders for VAUCHELLES marching via BEAUQUESNE - MARIEUX & arrived there at 12.45 p.m. where they went into billets again arranged for by Lieut D.T. FRASER & the interpreter who travelled through early in the morning. Visited the A.D.M.S. at BUS-LES-ARTOIS advising him of the arrival of the 94th Field Ambulance at VAUCHELLES.	

WAR DIARY or INTELLIGENCE SUMMARY

Army Form C. 2118

Place	Date	Hour	Summary of Events and Information	Remarks and references to Appendices
VAUCHELLES	MARCH 1916 30th		Inspected the billets & issued orders to be observed in this village.	
VAUCHELLES	31st		LIEUT. A.H.A. TIBB & 10 other ranks arrived back this morning from leave. Unloaded wagons & greased axles etc. Proceeded to A.D.M.S. re delay in receiving telegrams. Lieut' J.H.C. WALKER & Lieut' W.R. HODGE & 3 N.C.O.s arrived back from instruction in the trenches.	

Rep Stewart Lieut Col
OC 94 Field Amb

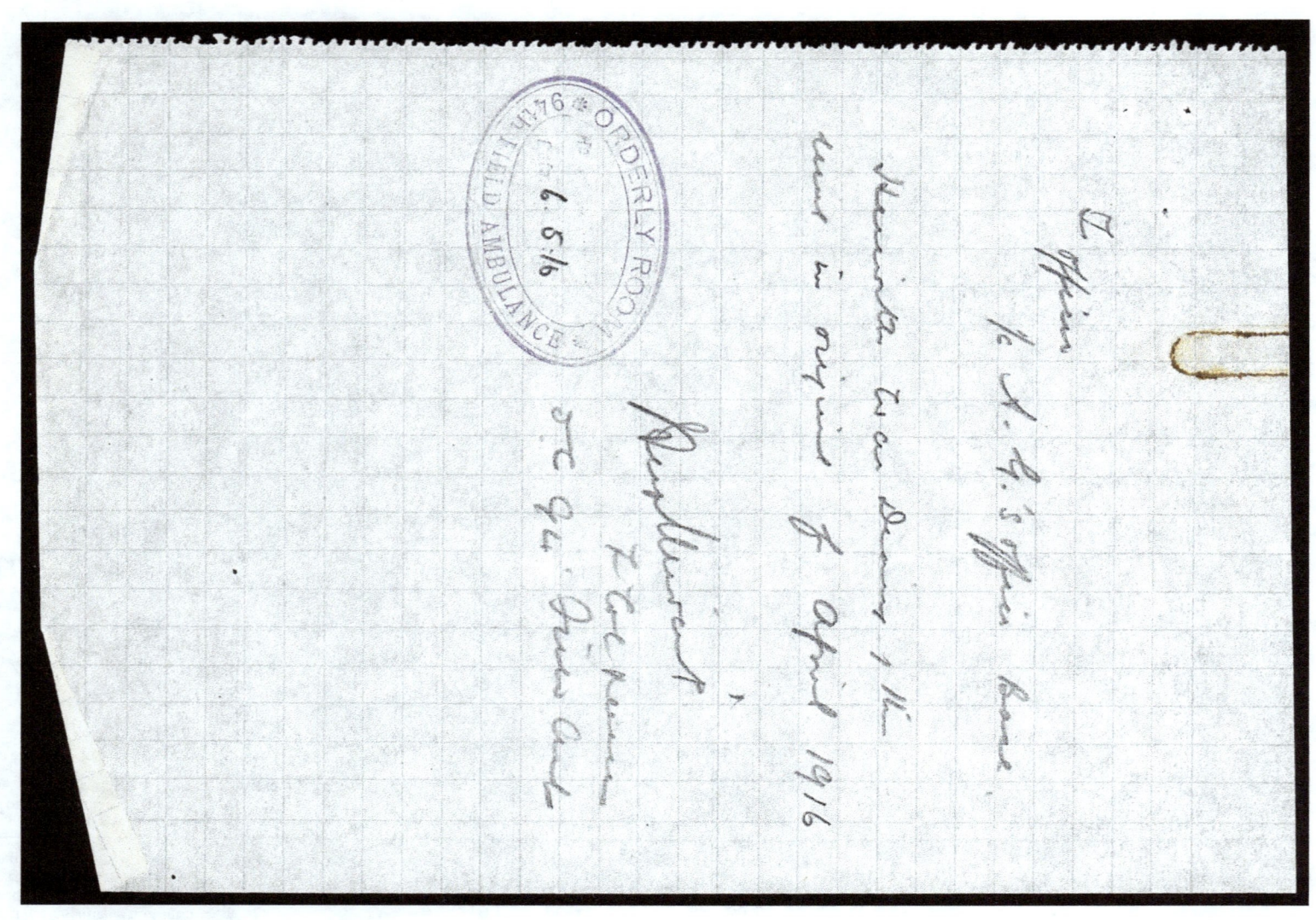

Officer ic N.Z.'s Officers Base

Herewith two dress i/c
enc in origin 7 April 1916

RMMunro?
Lieut
OC 9c Div Amb

[Stamp: ORDERLY ROOM 1/76 FIELD AMBULANCE 6.5.16]

WAR DIARY or INTELLIGENCE SUMMARY

Army Form C. 2118

94 7 Amb

Vol 2

Place	Date	Hour	Summary of Events and Information	Remarks and references to Appendices
VAUCHELLES	APRIL 1916 1st		Arrived back from leave of absence today & resumed command of unit. During my absence the motor Ambulances viz 5 SIDDELEY DEESY + 2 FORDS + 3 MOTOR Cycles arrived with 19 N.C.O's + men who were taken on the strength of the unit. Inspected billets of the men & the arrangements made, everything satisfactory. Reptsreadshtd R.	
VAUCHELLES	2d		Went thro' all the correspondence &c which had arrived during my absence. R.	
VAUCHELLES	3d		Received orders from A.D.M.S to send one officer to COLINCAMP to get in touch with the T.O.f. Advanced dressing Station there & to learn the arrangements as to evacuations &c for that part of the line with a view to taking over from them tomorrow. I detailed LIEUT STORMO for this duty & accompanied by him I went to COLINCAMP and visited all the Collecting posts & all the arrangements made. On my return I was informed that I would be required to vacate the billets here the next day & I proceeded to Headquarters to see the A.D.M.S re this. The A.D.M.S then informed me that arrangements had been made for my Ambulance to move the next day to BUS LES ARTOIS where billets in huts would be provided & where I would open an headquarters dressing station. R.	

WAR DIARY
or
INTELLIGENCE SUMMARY

(Erase heading not required.)

Army Form C. 2118

Instructions regarding War Diaries and Intelligence Summaries are contained in F. S. Regs., Part II. and the Staff Manual respectively. Title Pages will be prepared in manuscript.

Place	April Date 1916	Hour	Summary of Events and Information	Remarks and references to Appendices
BUS LES ARTOIS.	4		The party for COLINCAMP paraded at 9.15 am today under LIEUT. J.H. WALKER. The following marched at 9.30 am. 28 other ranks "A" Section with Motor Ambulance, two drivers & one orderly and three wheeled stretchers. Proceeded by car to BUS and arranged the billets. The Field Ambulance marched for VAUCHELLES to BUS arriving at 2.15 p.m. & took over the billets. Motor Ambulance parked near by, made all necessary arrangements. Took the motor ambulance which will be required to go to COLINCAMP up there to show the way. Found everything satisfactory and all posted. The Headquarters dressing station open & able to take in cases. FP.	
BUS LES ARTOIS.	5th		Some rain during night and much colder. Arranged the huts & tents in the Headquarters. Had all tents stained. Saw A.D.M.S. re establishing Divisional Baths, one to be at Colincamp, one BERTRANCOURT, & one at BUS. Selected sight for two latter. Went with A.D.M.S. to COLINCAMP and saw the arrangements for washing there. Inspected Advanced Dressing Station everything satisfactory.	
BUS LES ARTOIS.	6		General rearrangement of huts so as to accommodate more patients. Everything now working smoothly, I consider however that we should have many more huts as our accommodation is at present too limited	

WAR DIARY or INTELLIGENCE SUMMARY

Army Form C. 2118

Place	Date	Hour	Summary of Events and Information	Remarks and references to Appendices
BUS LES ARTOIS	APRIL 1916 7.		to be efficient. Informed A.D.M.S. General routine work in morning. Weather has become milder and drier. Went with A.D.M.S. round advanced dressing Station at COLINCAMP and from there round the Collecting post at ECZEMA AVENUE. I pointed out the difficulties of evacuation in the event of any rush of work and asked that inter-communicating trenches might be dug and traffic regulated in one direction so that Stretcher bearers with wounded might not be stopped by reinforcements which would necessarily be coming up. I also asked that a communication trench for bearers only over a certain area might be dug and that Shelters which would be at least Splinter proof be made at certain places for the accommodation of my bearers working in relief.	
BUS LES ARTOIS	8.		D.D.M.S VIII Corps came round & inspected Headquarters this morning. Suggested incineration of faeces, otherwise appeared satisfied. I pointed out the difficulties of obtaining any supply of wood, corrugated iron etc. necessary for the proper building of incinerators etc.	
BUS LES ARTOIS	9.		Divine Services today as follows { R.C's 9.30 am { Non Conf 10.0 am { C of E. 10.30	

WAR DIARY or INTELLIGENCE SUMMARY

Army Form C. 2118

Place	Date	Hour	Summary of Events and Information	Remarks and references to Appendices
BUS LES ARTOIS	APRIL 1916 10		Went to Advanced Dressing Station at COLINCAMPS to see the work on dug outs there. Suggested that the barn should be utilized for wounded. R.	
BUS LES ARTOIS	11		Very wet. Lieut JIBB went to BEAUVAL to get drugs etc. for the advanced medical stores. R.	
BUS LES ARTOIS	12		Went to see A.D.M.S. re the baths which it is proposed to run here and which he wishes us to supply men to work under the direction of the Sanitary section. There is to be a large disinfector attached to one billet with a plant of clean clothing and a small boiler for heating the steam. The baths are to be at the Mairie and the R.E. have been asked to put in a kind of Thresh bath arrangements. Spray & tubs are also to be used. Sent fatigue party to commence work on the farm to be used for the disinfector which need repair. R.	
BUS LES ARTOIS	13.	20:	Two men sent on leave. Pte PRICE granted special leave to the Went to COLINCAMPS & saw the work done there.	

WAR DIARY
or
INTELLIGENCE SUMMARY
(Erase heading not required.)

Army Form C. 2118

Place	Date	Hour	Summary of Events and Information	Remarks and references to Appendices
BUS LES ARTOIS	APRIL 1916 14		Went to AMIENS on duty today. Capt. T. McEWEN returned from leave. Pt. SHEPHEARD did not return. N.	
BUS LES ARTOIS	15		Went to COURCELLES to see if I could find a suitable place for a dressing station to be used for walking cases only. Two plans suggested themselves to me, either to have dug outs built on the side of a sunken road or to take a large farmhouse just on the outskirts of the town and use it as there were good stables & outhouses very suitable, also large cellar capable of holding at least 30, this last seemed most suitable. N.	
BUS LES ARTOIS	16		Divine Services R.C. at 8 a.m. C of E at 10.30 a.m. Nonconformist 10 a.m. Pt. Shepherd not yet returned Reported absence to R.D.V.S. and A.P.M. N.	
BUS LES ARTOIS	17		Lieut HODGE who has been troubled for some day with Otitis Media was worse today so I had him evacuated to	

WAR DIARY or INTELLIGENCE SUMMARY

Army Form C. 2118

(Erase heading not required.)

Place	Date	Hour	Summary of Events and Information	Remarks and references to Appendices
	APRIL 1916			
BUS LES ARTOIS	17 Cont		No 4 Casualty Clearing Station BEAUVAL. "C" Section (tent & bearer subdivision to number of 30) under Lieut McWILLIAMS proceeded to COLINCAMPS for duty as Advanced dressing station. Lieut STORMS & "A" section returned to Headquarters. Capt WALKER remained at COLINCAMPS as town commandant.	
BUS. LES ARTOIS	18.		Baths & disinfector now running smoothly. Tents being used and about 300 daily being bathed. Disinfection of clothing proceeding satisfactorily. Lieut Jibb went to BEAUVAL for drugs etc.	
BUS LES ARTOIS	19		LIEUT A. E STENNING reported his departure for England on completion of his period of service & is struck off the strength	
BUS. LES ARTOIS	20.		Dr WARD put under arrest by C.R.A for negligent driving of ambulance. Decided to send the case for trial by F. G. C. M.	

WAR DIARY or INTELLIGENCE SUMMARY

Army Form C. 2118

(Erase heading not required.)

Place	Date	Hour	Summary of Events and Information	Remarks and references to Appendices
BUS LES ARTOIS	APRIL 1916 21		Took summary of Evidence in the case of D. WARD today & put in application for a D.C.M. on this case. Capt T. McEWEN appointed prosecutor. D.D.M.S. VIII Corps went round COLINCAMP and the front line trenches. I accompanied him & showed him all the position, bearers etc. Very wet day rain without ceasing. D.	
BUS LES ARTOIS	22		Still very wet ordinary routine work D.	
BUS LES ARTOIS	23		Easter Sunday. Divine Services C of E 10.30 am R.Co 9.0 am Non Conf 10 am. Lieut H WALES reported his arrival for duty & is taken on the strength & posted to "C" Section. Capt KING has taken over duties as Transport officer vice LIEUT STENNING 4 men R.A.M.C arrived for duty, taken on the strength & posted to sections. D.	

WAR DIARY or INTELLIGENCE SUMMARY

Army Form C. 2118

Place	Date	Hour	Summary of Events and Information	Remarks and references to Appendices
	APRIL 1916			
BUS LES ARTOIS	24		Baths now doing 400 per diem. I was asked by the Division to go to PARIS and make arrangements about the purchasing & erection of Shower baths there. Left at AMIENS at 6.30. Capt. T. McEWEN officiating for me. R.	
BUS LES ARTOIS	25		Trial of Dr WARD took place today, the accused was found "Not Guilty" & honorably acquitted. A Section took over the duties at Headquarters for "B" Section today. LIEUT WALES temporary as M.O. i/c 11 E YORKS.	
BUS LES ARTOIS	26		Returned from PARIS today having made all arrangements & purchased the apparatus. Spent day in AMIENS making enquiries re the washing of the Clothes which is not very satisfactory. Reported to Headquarters the result of my journey. R. LIEUT FRASER temporarily as M.O. i/c 12. E.YORKS R.	
BUS LES ARTOIS	27		Went to COLINCAMPS. Dug outs at EUSTON not sufficiently large, reported same to A.D.M.S. 31 Div. Weather has become beautifully fine — warm R.	

WAR DIARY or INTELLIGENCE SUMMARY

Army Form C. 2118

(Erase heading not required.)

Place	Date APRIL 1916	Hour	Summary of Events and Information	Remarks and references to Appendices
BUS LES ARTOIS	28		D.D.M.S VII Corps expected today but did not come. Went to COLINCAMPS with D.A.D.M.S 31 Div & inspected Dugouts there and at EUSTON. R.	
BUS LES ARTOIS	29		Sent to BEAUVAL for medical stores which were reported ready. Weather very much improved. R.	
BUS LES ARTOIS	30		Divine Service today C of E. 10-30 am R.C. 9-30 am Non Conf 10 am "B" Section under the Command 2 Cap T. McEWEN proceed to COLINCAMPS for duty relieving "C" Section who returned to Headquarters. Lieut FRASER detailed as Town Commandant in place of Cap WALKER who returned to Headquarters. R.	

Stewart Lt-Col
OC 94 Field Amb

31st Div

May 1916

B. 9H 7. Amb.

COMMITTEE FOR THE
MEDICAL HISTORY OF THE WAR
Date 26 JUN. 1916

Seiner

2
D. O. E. 3. Eskdn.

Samuelis von Drüvig, Lt.
94. Feen Batterieum.

3.6.16.

Ben Ulmerich
Leutnant Reserve
O.E. 94. Feld Ark.

WAR DIARY or INTELLIGENCE SUMMARY

Army Form C. 2118

Place	Date Hour	Summary of Events and Information	Remarks and references to Appendices
BUS LES ARTOIS	MAY 1916 1st	Very fine but inclined to be thundery. The Disinfector is now working very satisfactorily and the Batts have had the showers erected but are waiting for a pump to complete the work. R.	
BUS LES ARTOIS	2nd	Sgt BUXTON who has been N.C.O. i/c Baths relieved today by Sgt HADDON. Sgt BUXTON proceeded to COLINCAMP for duty with B. Bearers. Inspected Advanced Dressing Station at COLINCAMPS today. R.	
BUS LES ARTOIS	3rd	Cap J.H.C WALKER granted 9 days leave to Ireland left this morning. Period of leave granted from 4th May – 12th inclusive. D.D.M.O Corps came in and inspected the new incinerator I am building. R.	
BUS LES ARTOIS	4th	Went to AMIENS to pay the bill for the laundry work in connection with the Baths. Proceeded from there to FLIXECOURT to get articles for Q Branch 31st Div. R.	

WAR DIARY
or
INTELLIGENCE SUMMARY
(Erase heading not required.)

Army Form C. 2118

Instructions regarding War Diaries and Intelligence Summaries are contained in F. S. Regs., Part II. and the Staff Manual respectively. Title Pages will be prepared in manuscript.

Place	Date MAY 1916	Hour	Summary of Events and Information	Remarks and references to Appendices
BUS LES ARTOIS		5.	A.D.M.S. 31 Div inspected the Camp, and saw all the arrangements for the disposal & care of wounded & sick. Expressed himself very pleased with the arrangements.	
BUS LES ARTOIS		6.	G.O.C 31 Div inspected the Dressing station today. Lt & Q Mr JIBB proceeded to BEAUVAL for Medical Stores. Lieut FRASER detached for temp'y duty with 12. E. Yorks as their M.O was still on leave.	
BUS LES ARTOIS		7.	Divine services as usual today	
BUS LES ARTOIS		8.	Lieut V.H. Mc WILLIAMS R.A.M.C T.C reports his departure for ENGLAND on completion of his period of contract & is struck off the strength. Went to COLINCAMPS and inspected there also the dug outs at that place & EUSTON which are nearing completion, also the collecting posts at the SUCERIE & ECZEMA AVENUE	

WAR DIARY or INTELLIGENCE SUMMARY

Army Form C. 2118

Place	Date 1916	Hour	Summary of Events and Information	Remarks and references to Appendices
BUS LES ARTOIS	MAY 9		Drew pay of the unit today and paid all at Headquarters. Sent the money of the Detachment at COLINCAMPS to the O.C. Advanced dressing station with acquittance rolls. Lieut HODGE who had been evacuated sick returned from the BASE today & resumed duty.	
BUS LES ARTOIS	10		Three drivers A.S.C and one driver A.S.C M.T reported their arrival today and are taken on the strength.	
BUS LES ARTOIS	11		Sent to BEAUVAL for drugs etc for the Advanced Depot of Medical Stores there.	
BUS LES ARTOIS	12		Went to COLINCAMPS & EUSTON & inspected them, everything satisfactory. Cpl DARBY Superintending Cook reported his arrival from No 3. C.C.S and is taken on the strength.	
BUS LES ARTOIS	13		Kit inspection today. All deficiencies to be paid for by individuals.	

WAR DIARY or INTELLIGENCE SUMMARY

Army Form C. 2118

(Erase heading not required.)

Place	Date	Hour	Summary of Events and Information	Remarks and references to Appendices
	MAY 1916			
BUS LES ARTOIS	14		Divine services to day as follows :— C of E. 10.30 am R.C. 9.30 am Non Conformist 10 am. D.	
BUS LES ARTOIS	15.		A Section under the command of Capt KING proceeded today to COLINCAMPS in relief of "B" Section who returned to Headquarters. Inspected the Collecting posts in ECZEMA & CHEEROH AVENUES today with the D.A.D.M.S. & Sanitary Officer. The Dump holes nearby are being used by working parties as latrines. Gave orders that these should be inspected daily and reported if kept dirty. The dug outs were clean. Issued written orders as to the disposal of refuse Etc in these dug outs & handed copy to each N.C.O or senior soldier in charge to be handed over whenever a change takes place. Inspected divisional station at COLINCAMPS everything satisfactory. D.	
BUS LES ARTOIS	16.		During night heavy bombardment of our left section took place. Number of casualties as reported by M.O. was 7. On receipt of this	

WAR DIARY or INTELLIGENCE SUMMARY

Army Form C. 2118

(Erase heading not required.)

Place	Date MAY 1916	Hour	Summary of Events and Information	Remarks and references to Appendices
	16 cont		information which was received at A.D.S at 10 a.m. CAPT KING took necessary steps to send extra bearers. Visited the collecting post at ECZEMA AVENUE & found three wounded men, who had been there about 3/4 hour waiting for the extra bearers, these having arrived they were removed. Inspected the Collecting post & found all satisfactory. A wire received at 1.30 p.m. saying more bearers were required O despatched 16 bearers at once in two cars. Capt KING at 3 p.m. reported all regimental aid posts & Collecting posts Clear of wounded. Sent in report to A.D.M.S. of the proceedings. All wounded were evacuated from the Headquarters of the Ambulance before 4 p.m.	
BUS LES ARTOIS	17		Siddeley Deasy motor Ambulance which has been at the Repair Shop since April 1st returns today in working order. Dr NOON replaced Dr KIRKMAN.	
BUS LES ARTOIS	18		Lieut WALES proceeded to COLINCAMPS in relief of LIEUT FRASER as town Commandant. Lt FRASER returns to Headquarters	

WAR DIARY or INTELLIGENCE SUMMARY

Army Form C. 2118

Place	Date	Hour	Summary of Events and Information	Remarks and references to Appendices
BUS LES ARTOIS	MAY 1916 19		LIEUT FRASER granted leave of absence to UK from 20 to 28 inclusive. D.D.M.S. VIII Corps visited & inspected the place today and expressed himself very pleased with the arrangements. R.	
BUS LES ARTOIS	20		Went to COLINCAMPS and inspected there. Everything satisfactory. Evacuation satisfactory. R.	
BUS LES ARTOIS	21		Divine Service C of E. 10.30 am R.C. 9.30 am R.	
BUS LES ARTOIS	22		Under instructions of ADMS 31 Div. I sent up two Field Medical Panniers and a large box of reserve dressings to be kept at ECZEMA AVENUE for the use of Regimental Medical Officers in emergencies. This afternoon I inspected ECZEMA, CHEEROH, SUCERIE & COLINCAMPS. The dug-outs are much cleaner and better kept in every way. I have had instructions & sent up	

WAR DIARY
or
INTELLIGENCE SUMMARY

(Erase heading not required.)

Army Form C. 2118

Instructions regarding War Diaries and Intelligence Summaries are contained in F. S. Regs., Part II. and the Staff Manual respectively. Title Pages will be prepared in manuscript.

Place	Date	Hour	Summary of Events and Information	Remarks and references to Appendices
BUS LES ARTOIS	22	Cont	large boxes with doors for use of the personnel of holding ford. Reported to the A.D.M.O. that the bearers have great difficulty in bringing a stretcher down TAUPIN TRENCH & ROMAN ROAD owing to the traverses of the trench being rather narrow & requested that they might be widened to allow a stretcher to be carried easily. Lieut BLACKMORE R.A.M.C.T.C reports his arrival for duty on relief of LIEUT McWILLIAMS and is taken on the strength.	
BUS LES ARTOIS	23		During the night the enemy blew in the front of our front line of trenches to some extent. Casualties to about the number of 70 arrived during the early hours of the morning & were dressed. Work of bearers quite efficient.	
BUS LES ARTOIS	24		LIEUT. H.D STORMS R.A.M.C.T.C reports his departure for England on completion of contract & is struck off the strength. Inspected the trenches and reported to the A.D.M.S. 31st Div that the traverses in TAUPIN TRENCH & ROMAN ROAD were	

WAR DIARY
or
INTELLIGENCE SUMMARY
(Erase heading not required.)

Army Form C. 2118

Place	Date	Hour	Summary of Events and Information	Remarks and references to Appendices
BUS LES ARTOIS	24 Cont		being made to narrow to permit of the shelters passing round them easily, thus preventing the easy evacuation of lying cases for CHEEROH AVENUE.	
BUS LES ARTOIS	25.		Today was very wet consequently nothing much was done everything very quiet. Lieut. HODGE & FRASER promoted Captain.	
BUS LES ARTOIS	26.		Reported to A.D.M.S. 31 Div that owing to having put my men under canvas to allow another lot of sick my men were overcrowded & requested four tents extra & permission to pitch them on ground behind the lines. Both these granted & work carried out.	
BUS LES ARTOIS	27.		COLINCAMPS shelled today. 5 men Machine gun Section killed in one billet. O/Lieut LYON R.F.A. brought in dead to A.D.S.	
BUS LES ARTOIS	28.		Visited COLINCAMPS and surroundings. CAPT HODGE proceeded to the Army School of Instruction of training in Antigas for Officers. Divisional observance of Sunday held as usual.	

WAR DIARY or **INTELLIGENCE SUMMARY**

Army Form C. 2118

(Erase heading not required.)

Place	Date MAY 1916	Hour	Summary of Events and Information	Remarks and references to Appendices
BUS LES ARTOIS	29		D.M.S. IV Army inspected the Ambulance this afternoon & the D.D.G. of G.H.Q. inspected this evening. No faults found by either.	
BUS LES ARTOIS	30		The O.C. Div Train inspected first line transport today & expressed himself satisfied with the condition of the horses and harness. Was President of a board on P.U. of P.B. men today.	
BUS LES ARTOIS	31		Lieut BLACKMORE detailed as M.O. /c R.E. temporarily during absence on leave of M.O. Went to AMIENS to buy padlocks for the lockers of G.S. wagons & Ambulance wagons. Handed over same to Drivers — obtaining signature of same.	

Duplluwait Lieut Col
Rame
O.C. 94 Field Amb

June 1916.
S

CB. 94 7a.

COMMITTEE FOR THE
MEDICAL HISTORY OF THE WAR
Date   5 AUG. 1916

D.a.9.
3. Eschelon

Henrich Kra Georg 2
k. 94' Field Ambulance
7 k. months 8 June 1916

[signature]
Lt [?]
k. 94' Field Amb

[top, rotated] Henrich

[stamp] ORDERLY ROOM 94TH FIELD AMBULANCE 2/627 4.-7.16

WAR DIARY or INTELLIGENCE SUMMARY

Army Form C. 2118

94. F Amb

Vol 4

Place	Date JUNE 1916	Hour	Summary of Events and Information	Remarks and references to Appendices
BUS LES ARTOIS	1		Visited and inspected Advanced Dressing Stations at COLINCAMPS today. Director General A.M.O inspected here today & expressed himself pleased with arrangements made. Lieut BLACKMORE detailed for temporary duty with the R.E.	
BUS LES ARTOIS	2		Inspected dugout at COLINCAMPS and reported to A.D.M.O that the work was being very slowly carried out	
BUS LES ARTOIS	3		Inspected dugouts at SUCERIE, ECZEMA & EUSTON everything satisfactory the latter are being used by working parties. Reporters came. Lieut HODGE reported his arrival for the 4 Army Anti Gas School. In view of the forthcoming raid tonight I sent up "A" section bearers under Capt KING and another car to COLINCAMPS to reinforce the bearers up there.	

WAR DIARY or INTELLIGENCE SUMMARY

Army Form C. 2118

Instructions regarding War Diaries and Intelligence Summaries are contained in F. S. Regs., Part II. and the Staff Manual respectively. Title Pages will be prepared in manuscript.

(Erase heading not required.)

Place	Date JUNE 1916	Hour	Summary of Events and Information	Remarks and references to Appendices
BUS LES ARTOIS	4		Raid made at 12 midnight. Germans shelled our front line trenches in retaliation. Wounded started coming to Dressing Station at about 4 a.m. All attended to and all got in by 11 a.m. Total casualties treated 3 officers and 83 men. Went to COLINCAMPS during evacuation to see how things were getting on. Good work done by Sections concerned. R.	
BUS LES ARTOIS	5		Very wet so that it was impossible to do very much work about the place. R.	
BUS LES ARTOIS	6		Still wet at intervals. CAPT BUCHAN reported his arrival for duty and is taken on the strength of the unit and posted to "A" Section. R.	
BUS LES ARTOIS	7		Received 3 section tents from the Town Major and moved the personnel in the tent large hut into them and shifted the	

WAR DIARY
INTELLIGENCE SUMMARY
(Erase heading not required.)

Army Form C. 2118

Place	Date Hour	Summary of Events and Information	Remarks and references to Appendices
BUS LES ARTOIS	7/8 Cont	hut into line with others to form an Officers ward. Received 25 beds for the B.R.C. room for use of Officers or O.R.	
BUS LES ARTOIS	8	Went to GEZAINCOURT with the A.D.M.S. and saw the 29. C.C.S.	
BUS LES ARTOIS	9	Lecture on Gas by the Chemical Adviser to Army today. All officers not on duty attended. Went to GEZAINCOURT with D.A.D.M.S. today re baths to be established there.	
BUS LES ARTOIS	10	Sent two G.S wagons to VAUCHELLES to 93 F.A to assist in moving their extra equipment to SARTON. Handed over 12 B.R.C Beds to S. Mid Div. F.A. by order D.D.M.S. VIII Corps	
BUS LES ARTOIS	11	Two G.S. wagons to VAUCHELLES to 93 F.A. Went to COLINCAMPS and inspected work at dug outs there. Not much progress being made.	

WAR DIARY or INTELLIGENCE SUMMARY

Army Form C. 2118

Instructions regarding War Diaries and Intelligence Summaries are contained in F. S. Regs., Part II. and the Staff Manual respectively. Title Pages will be prepared in manuscript.

(Erase heading not required.)

Place	Date	Hour	Summary of Events and Information	Remarks and references to Appendices
BUS LES ARTOIS	15		Informed A.D.M.S. that ECZEMA was very difficult to evacuate thus. A.D.M.S. informed me that on new plans this trench was only an out trench & could not be used for horse traffic. Proceeded with D.A.D.M.S. to trenches & went over all the new horse trenches and found them very fit for carrying stretchers down. Selected dugout near junction of TAUPIN & RAILWAY trench as suitable place to keep bearers for use between this point & EUSTON. Line of evacuation for front trenches now CATEAUX, JORDAN, RAILWAY & CENTRAL. Notice to A.D.M.S. re dugout. Q	
BUS LES ARTOIS	16		Went to COLINCAMPS today. Sent two wagons & ten men to get timber for R.E. to complete dugouts here. More work done. Dressing Station satisfactory. Q	
BUS LES ARTOIS	17		Took over large hut situated in next camp & horse station constructing 2 roadway in front of it in order that cars may be able to turn round in front. Obtained permission for C.R.E. to have necessary stores for the guards for the work there. Q	

WAR DIARY
or
INTELLIGENCE SUMMARY

(Erase heading not required.)

Army Form C. 2118

Instructions regarding War Diaries and Intelligence Summaries are contained in F.S. Regs., Part II. and the Staff Manual respectively. Title Pages will be prepared in manuscript.

Place	Date Hour	Summary of Events and Information	Remarks and references to Appendices
	JUNE 1916		
BUS LES ARTOIS	11	Rest in tents. At 12 Bde Bombers and 12 coys of Lewis gunners in CHEERO & SOUCRIE trenches. 2nd & O.C. 12 Bde inspected the lines & pay inspected the & enquired into all Guns and the & & & pass to relief by teams & No 12 in tactical line. It 11 at 2pm a relief by teams & EUSTON during this took place the front and frown & EUSTON during this the works. Q.	
BUS LES ARTOIS	12	Great work again at C.E. front at EUSTON in relief & assembly of CHEERO & SOUCRIE. Q.	
BUS LES ARTOIS	13	Front at COLINCAMPS & in front trenches Pts 7, Z ECENH. B. Baths under Cpt HODGE proceed to COLINCAMPS today relieving C. Castles who returned to Headquarters. Q.	
BUS LES ARTOIS	14	SOUCRIE & CHEERO trenches c No12 Coy proceed forward to EUSTON. Capt McEWEN proceed to COLINCAMPS & Tour Angles. LIEUT WALES returns & some. Q.

1875 Wt. W593/826 1,000,000 4/15 I.C.C.&A. A.D.S.S./Forms/C.2118.

WAR DIARY or INTELLIGENCE SUMMARY

Army Form C. 2118

Instructions regarding War Diaries and Intelligence Summaries are contained in F. S. Regs., Part II. and the Staff Manual respectively. Title Pages will be prepared in manuscript.

(Erase heading not required.)

Place	Date JUNE 1916	Hour	Summary of Events and Information	Remarks and references to Appendices
Bus les Artois	18		Proceeded to COLINCAMPS today in order to make arrangements for the bearer subdivisions to be billeted there during active operations. Decided to make a roadway between the following points K.25.d.2.6 and K.25.d.7.1. By this means cars can run down to EUSTON passing my Advanced dressing station COLINCAMPS without going thro the town. The ground will require a little smoothing first. Detailed 10 men to proceed there & do the work.	
Bus les Artois	19		Went to COLINCAMPS with A.D.M.S. to see how work at dug outs proceeding. Conference of A.D.Ms Officers of O.C. FAs to discuss final plans. Went to COLINCAMPS with OC 93 Field Ambulance to show him the billets there. Arranged to draw wood of the R.E. for the Construction of Shelters for lightly wounded cases. Arranged with Town Major to take over some new ground.	
Bus les Artois	20		Roadway in front nearly finished. Saw Claims Officer re ground. Drew 150 empty petrol tins for water. A.D.MS making	

WAR DIARY or INTELLIGENCE SUMMARY

Army Form C. 2118

(Erase heading not required.)

Place	Date June 1916	Hour	Summary of Events and Information	Remarks and references to Appendices
BUS LES ARTOIS	20 cont		Arrangements for the supply of more lamps. Indents for more Straw and Coal. Work on dugouts at COLINCAMPS proceeding. All deep dugouts etc. have been placed in position at EUSTON & COLINCAMPS. P.	
BUS LES ARTOIS	21		Went to COLINCAMPS today and inspected them. CAPT HODGE reported by LIEUT BLACKMORE as having suspicion of Incipient Pulmonary Tuberculosis. P.	
BUS LES ARTOIS	22		CAPT HODGE evacuated to 29. C.C.S. today. Information to A.D.M.S. asking for Reinforcement. P.	
BUS LES ARTOIS	23		Went to COLINCAMPS & EUSTON. Everything satisfactory down there. Arranged to draw 18 Hurricane lanterns & some 4 wicks to EUSTON & COLINCAMPS for use in dug outs. All men now in position. All medical stores & returns for ready. P.	

WAR DIARY
or
INTELLIGENCE SUMMARY
(Erase heading not required.)

Army Form C. 2118

Instructions regarding War Diaries and Intelligence Summaries are contained in F. S. Regs., Part II. and the Staff Manual respectively. Title Pages will be prepared in manuscript.

Place	Date	Hour	Summary of Events and Information	Remarks and references to Appendices
BUS LES ARTOIS	24		LIEUT BLACKMORE sent to EUSTON today for duty there. COLINCAMPS shelled slightly today. CAPT McEWEN reported that he had left the dressing station in favour of the Dugout. R.	
BUS LES ARTOIS	25		Divine service today as usual. D.D.M.S. VIII Corps inspected today. R.	
BUS LES ARTOIS	26		LIEUT BLACKMORE reported that the most southerly Dugout at EUSTON had received a direct hit which had burst the roof slightly. Reported to A-D.M.S with request that the R.E. might make necessary repairs. R.	
BUS LES ARTOIS	27		CAPT BUCHAN sent to EUSTON today in relief 2 LIEUT BLACKMORE who reported sick.	
BUS LES ARTOIS	28		CAPT WALKER proceeded to EUSTON today for duty. Inspected EUSTON & COLINCAMPS Dugout. R.E. have nearly finished the repairs at EUSTON. TRENCH Railway of EUSTON to COLINCAMPS completed. 17 miles available for wounded. R.	

WAR DIARY
or
INTELLIGENCE SUMMARY
(Erase heading not required.)

Army Form C. 2118

Place	Date	Hour	Summary of Events and Information	Remarks and references to Appendices
BUSLES ARTOIS	29		Work of permission for more shire to make paths thro' the camp to enable the Bearers to carry Stretchers for one ward to another as the rain has been very severe the land [is] fast deep and consequently the camp almost impassable. Wired for the Surgical advisor at Army to see Lieut Crosse. He arrived at 10 p.m. & advised both cases to be sent to the 35. C.C.S.	
BUSLES ARTOIS	30		Roadmaking today having couple obtained [?] of C.R.E. to draw stones. Issued orders for the Bearer subdivision to parade at 5 p.m. tonight under Cap FRASER for work in Front line. Cap KING sent to COLINCAMPS to relieve LIEUT BLACKMORE who is sick. Everyone in position for the following operations. Operation orders have already been issued. Copy attached. Hy Mewat Lt Colonel O.C. 9th Field Amb.	

Confidential   31st Division   Vol VII

War Diary

of

94th Field Amb:

July 1916

1st July 1916. to 31st July 1916.

COMMITTEE FOR THE
MEDICAL HISTORY OF THE WAR
Date   31 AUG. 1916

WAR DIARY or INTELLIGENCE SUMMARY

Army Form C. 2118

Vol 7   9th Field Ambulance

Place	Date 1916	Hour	Summary of Events and Information
BUS^{LES} LESARTOIS	July 1		The attack started at 7.30 this morning and we were soon getting wounded into Main Dressing Station. Disposition of F^d Ambulance at commencement as follows. Cap^{ts} KING & FRASER and Bearers, 3 sections in trenches. Cap^{ts} WALKER & BUCHAN at EUSTON, with 1 & 2 "C" sections. And Capt McEWEN & Lt BLACKMORE at COLINCAMPS with 1 & 4 'B' section. LIEUT WALES with Lt THOMPSON of 71 Sanitary section, Lt CRAIG M.O. of D.A.C. and Lt JOHNSON M.O. of R.E. were at Main dressing station. Work proceeded smoothly. At 9.30 I went to COLINCAMPS & then by motor to EUSTON. Cars were running there & taking cases back again at 3 p.m. & found congestion at COLINCAMPS, this was cleared by motors at once & then went to EUSTON & did the same there. Work continued thro' the night. P.—
BUS LES ARTOIS	2		Up to 12 today we had taken over 1200 cases including officers the cases have now slackened. The work has been excellent all round. Relieved the Bearers / B section 94.F.A. & 1 sect.

WAR DIARY or INTELLIGENCE SUMMARY

Army Form C. 2118

94th F A

Place	Date / Hour	Summary of Events and Information	Remarks and references to Appendices
	July 1916		
BUSLES ARTOIS	2	95 FA by two sections / 93 FA at 1 pm today. The wounded are now practically all clear.	
BUSLES ARTOIS	3	Relieved all bearers today leaving 1 Section at the Front & one at Euston. We are now only getting the cases lying outside the trenches which are not many. The whole bearer to be relieved tomorrow as the Division is coming out of the line. ~~Capt~~ LIEUT FREW reported his arrival P.	
BUSLES ARTOIS	4	Relieved Colincamps & Euston today by another Field Ambulance. We are under orders to move to another area to rest. Made all preparations for the move. Capt CHRISTIE & ANGLIN arrived. Capt ANGLIN posted to 11 E Lancs D.	
BUSLES ARTOIS	5	Received orders to proceed with 94 I. B. to GEZAINCOURT tomorrow leaving at 9.45 from starting point on the BUS LOUVERCOURT Road. Went to see Staff Captain 94 IB to arrange about billets. Capt CHRISTIE posted to 14 Y&L D.	
BUSLES ARTOIS	6	Capt ~~Frazer~~ & Interpreter BION sent on to billets. Units marched at 9.15. Capt McEWEN left behind to clear up. Arrived at GEZAINCOURT at 4.30 & went into Billets. P.	

WAR DIARY ~~or INTELLIGENCE SUMMARY~~

(Erase heading not required.)

Army Form C. 2118

9th F.A.

Place	Date July 1916	Hour	Summary of Events and Information	Remarks and references to Appendices
GEZAINCOURT	7		Received orders today to be prepared to move at short notice equipped as lightly as possible. Arranging everything & preparing to have dump made. Keay out at Acheux came down & told me. Capt. BUCHAN left for duty with the 3rd Army. G.	
GEZAINCOURT	8		Orders received today that unit would leave FREVENT by train for STEENBECQUE at 9.22 am tomorrow. To be at station three hours previous to this. Proceeded to FREVENT to see what arrangements were for loading. Everything satisfactory. Issued necessary orders for move. Capt. FRASER & Interpreter BION sent ahead in ambulance to arrange billets. Lt. & Qr. Mr. JIBB to take all the motors by road to new place. G.	
CALONNE SUR LYS	9		Left GEZAINCOURT today at 1.30 am & marched to FREVENT where we arrived at 6.10 am. Cook proceeded to prepare breakfast for the men. Entrained all personnel etc before 8 am. Train left at 8.22 am arrived STEENBECQUE at 12.30. Lt. & Q. JIBB	

WAR DIARY or INTELLIGENCE SUMMARY

Army Form C. 2118

Place	Date Hour	Summary of Events and Information	Remarks and references to Appendices
	JULY 1916		
	9	with motor joined us here and I proceeded by car to CALONNE SUR LYS to see what arrangements were made, Capt McEWEN to bring up the ambulances after men had had meals. On arrival at CALONNE I inspected billets & distributed the 4 sections with Capt FRASER who met me there. D.D.M.S. XI Corps came and told me about various details. Unit arrived at 5 pm having marched via S' VENANT. "C" section detailed to run the Hospital during our stay here or 14 days whichever occurs first. R.	
CALONNE SUR LYS.	10	Arranged various details. Went to S' VENANT to see Ardours. Saw B.Gen Commanding 94 Inf B.? re billets. Arranged with Staff Capt the allotting 2 same. Arranged for clean clothing. R.	
CALONNE SUR LYS.	11	Baths started, clean clothes to come tomorrow. Inspected everywhere everything satisfactory. Went to MERVILLE to see C.C.S. Weather continues very fine. R.	
CALONNE SUR LYS	12	Routine work. Section all checking deficiencies in their ordnance + Surgical + Medical Equipment. D.D.S.O. XI Corps came round & inspected the place	

WAR DIARY or INTELLIGENCE SUMMARY

Army Form C. 2118

Place	Date	Hour July 1916	Summary of Events and Information	Remarks and references to Appendices
		12 Cont	and gave various instructions to be observed & dealt with regard to the keeping of the A. & D. Book. The XI Corps Commander held a meeting to meet officers of the 9th Infantry Bd. & attached. Welcomed the brigade to the XI Corps. R.	
COLONNE SUR LYS	13.		Fine day. Usual morning rounds. Wagons all washed today. Kit inspection of all ranks. Clothing board and deficiencies indented for. Checked list of deficiencies for sections and indented for replacements. Went to MERVILLE to see O.C. Laundry and settle arrangements. Also saw Corps rest station. R.	
COLONNE SUR LYS.	14.		Received orders this morning at 2.40 am to have unit ready for a move at short notice. Ordered everyone up and wagons to be loaded up. Morning dark with thin drizzle which however left off before 11 a.m. Everything ready for moving at 7 am. Dump arranged for vide Divisional orders & site notified. At 9.30 went in to St VENANT to see A.D.M.S. and try and find out when move likely to take place	

WAR DIARY

~~INTELLIGENCE SUMMARY~~

(Erase heading not required.)

Army Form C. 2118

Instructions regarding War Diaries and Intelligence Summaries are contained in F. S. Regs., Part II. and the Staff Manual respectively. Title Pages will be prepared in manuscript.

94 F a

Place	Date	July Hour 1916	Summary of Events and Information	Remarks and references to Appendices
COLONNE SUR LYS		14 Cont.	Heard that previous orders cancelled and others were to follow. Made arrangements to evacuate all sick either to the Corps Rest Station or to Casualty Clearing Station. Received orders at 4.30pm that the Field Ambulances would remain in present location for the present. One tent subdivision would remain and two tent + three bearer subdivisions would be packed + ready to move at short notice. Issued necessary orders detailing "C" tent subdivision to remain behind. "C" tent subdivision unloaded wagons and took over the buildings again. A + B wagons to remain packed ready loaded. Received orders from A.D.M.S. 31st Division that two officers were to be sent of temporary duty to 93 Field Ambulance at ZELEBOS. Detailed LIEUT BLACKMORE + FREW of this unit with orders to proceed at 8 p.m. tomorrow. Can to return after leaving them.	
COLONNE SUR LYS.		15.	Fine morning. Ordered wagons to be washed one at a time. Made usual inspection. Ordered meat safe to be made, muslin to be purchased in MERVILLE. Received orders to have two horse	

WAR DIARY

(Erase heading not required.)

Army Form C. 2118

94th F.A.

Place	Date	JULY 1916 Hour	Summary of Events and Information	Remarks and references to Appendices
COLONNE SUR LYS	15 (Cont'd)		Ambulances ready to proceed with 94 Infantry Brigade. Detailed orders, hour of departure 12 noon. LIEUT BLACKMORE & FREW left to join 93 Field Ambulance for temporary duty.	
COLONNE SUR LYS	16.		Church Service for R.C.s in the Church at 10 am. No other services arranged. Fine morning but rain during day. Under instructions from A.D.M.S. 31 Div. Capt WALKER and Capt FRASER proceeded to 1st South MIDLAND FIELD Ambulance for temporary duty during the forthcoming offensive on the 61 Div Front. The ambulance is to be in reserve if required and to send up reinforcements if needed.	
COLONNE SUR LYS.	17.		Dull misty morning little or no wind. Slight drizzle cleared up about 11 am. Made usual inspection of lines etc. Went to LESTREM to see A.D.M.S. re several matters & have credentials signed. Under instructions A.D.M.S. 31 Div. Pte TEAL was detailed to proceed to Headquarters to relieve Pte MANNERS who was sent to the Ambulance. Transferred 7/Lieut R. THOMAS. 171st R.F.A. to Corps ... Tonsillitis (convalescent)	

WAR DIARY

Army Form C. 2118

(Erase heading not required.)

94th FA

Place	Date	Hour	Summary of Events and Information	Remarks and references to Appendices
	JULY 1916.			
	17 cont.		Capt WALKER and FRASER returned this evening from temporary duty with the 1st South Midland Field Amb. R.	
COLONNE SUR LYS.	18.		Proceeded to Headquarters 31st Div to draw pay of the unit. Drew 6200 francs. Capt McEWEN paid the unit. Sent Lt & Q.A.N.A. JIBB to MERVILLE to get Medical stores. Received orders fm A.D.M.S. 31 Div to detail an officer to take charge of the Forest Guard at LA FORET daily at 10 a.m. Detailed Capt McEWEN of this duty. Under instructions fm A.D.M.S 31 Div Capt KING & LIEUT WALES detailed to proceed tomorrow morning to report for temporary duty to the A.D.M.S 61st Div to arrive before 10 a.m. Morning cold but improved in afternoon which was much warmer. R.	
COLONNE SUR LYS.	19.		Very fine warm morning. Capt KING & Lieut WALES left at 8.30 am for temporary duty with 61st Div with orders to report to A.D.M.O. 61 Div. Made usual inspection. Investigated loss of Iron rations. Inspected water carts & tested water. At 9.30 pm received instructions fm A.D.M.O	

WAR DIARY

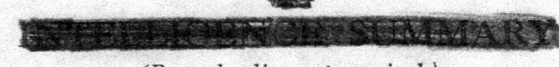

(Erase heading not required.)

Army Form C. 2118

Instructions regarding War Diaries and Intelligence Summaries are contained in F. S. Regs., Part II. and the Staff Manual respectively. Title Pages will be prepared in manuscript.

Place	Date	Hour	Summary of Events and Information	Remarks and references to Appendices
COLONNE SUR LYS	JULY 1916. 19	Cont	31 Div* that the Bearer Division & The Ambulances were to be prepared to move on receipt of wire from D.D.M.O. XI Corps. Issued necessary orders & received nominal rolls of men. Capt FRASER to proceed — Command.	*A.D.&S 31 Div 18° M3277
COLONNE SUR LYS.	20		No orders for bearers received during night. Fine morning. Paraded 2 a.m. Bearers paraded in marching order for inspection. Made usual inspection of billets etc. Received orders at 3.45 pm from A.D.M.O 31 Div* that the bearers would not now be required. Capt KING and Lt WALES returned at 6 pm.	*A.D.&S 31 Div No M770.
COLONNE SUR LYS.	21		Usual inspection today. Bright fine morning little wind. Proceeded to LESTREM to Div Headquarters & saw A.D.M.O. Submitted names of Officers and other ranks of the unit whom I wished to recommend for good work especially during the recent operations. Lt BLACKMORE & Lt FREW returned from temporary duty at 93 Field Ambulance this morning at 11 a.m.	
COLONNE SUR LYS.	22.		Usual inspection. Fine bright day. Report of section No Gas drill had been carried out during the week.	

WAR DIARY or INTELLIGENCE SUMMARY

Army Form C. 2118

(Erase heading not required.)

Place	Date	Hour	Summary of Events and Information	Remarks and references to Appendices
COLONNE SUR LYS	JULY 1916 23		Sunday. Day fine. No inspection today. Church service for R.C's at 10 a.m. in the Church. Open air service for C. of E. in Field at 3 p.m. Made out roll of men recommended for advancement to next higher rate of Corps pay. P.	
COLONNE SUR LYS	24		'B' Section relieved C Section in charge of the Dressing Station today. Capt. WALKER took over the duties of M.O i/c Front Patrol for Capt. McEWEN. Clothing issued to men as replacements. Made usual inspection of billets etc. P.	
COLONNE SUR LYS	25		Made usual inspection today. Weather continues fine but much cooler. C.O's parade of all ranks today at 11. a.m. Saw all Sections officers with reference to the D.D.M.S XI Corps letter with regard to the dirty condition of the Clothing etc. of Medical units. Issued stringent orders re this. Received one Acting L/Cpl. as reinforcement, sent to A.D.M.S with reference to his A.B. 64 not completed. LIEUT WALES to proceed to ARQUES tomorrow with patients to see the Eye Specialist. P.	

WAR DIARY or INTELLIGENCE SUMMARY

Army Form C. 2118

(Erase heading not required.)

Place	Date	Hour	Summary of Events and Information	Remarks and references to Appendices
COLONNE SUR LYS	July 1916 26		LIEUT WALES with 9 patients of Eye specialist left for ARQUES at 6.15 a.m. today. Fine morning, warmer than yesterday. Made usual inspection of billets. Route march under command of Capt. KING of all available ranks. Issue of clothing made to men today. 'A' section instruction in Gas Helmet drill. R.	
COLONNE SUR LYS	27		Commanding officers parade today of all ranks now actually on duty. Fine morning, dress clean, warmer. Interpreter BION fronted time of absence by French Mission 51 Div. 'B' section instruction in Gas Helmet drill. LIEUT WALES returned from ARQUES this afternoon. Obtained permission of ground of flying field for men and grazing of horses. Hot one stopped by Major. R.	
COLONNE SUR LYS	28		Beautifully fine day, very warm. Made usual inspection of all billets. Route march during morning of all sections. Inspection of all iron rations during afternoon. R.	

WAR DIARY ~~or INTELLIGENCE SUMMARY~~

(Erase heading not required.)

Army Form C. 2118

94 F.A.

Place	Date Hour July 1916	Summary of Events and Information	Remarks and references to Appendices
COLONNE SUR LYS	29	Very hot fine day. Made usual inspection. Capt. CHRISTIE returned last night for temporary duty with the 1st York & Lancs. C section receiving instruction in Gas helmet drill today. Inspected water carts & saw water tested all correct. Capt. FREW detailed to proceed under instructions of A.D.M.S. 31st Div to 47 Reserve Park A.S.C. Went to LESTREM & saw A.D.M.S. Went to R.E. Stores at LA FOSSE & got some lime & sandbags. P.	
COLONNE SUR LYS.	30	Parade services today as follows. Non Conformist ... 9.30 under Capt. CHRISTIE R.Cs 10 am under Capt. KING. C of E. 10 am under Capt. McEWEN. Another very hot day. P.	
COLONNE SUR LYS.	31	Made usual inspection. Kit inspection of "B" section at 10.30 a. C & A route march of two hours. A.S.C. instruction in Gas helmet today & helmets inspected.	Hugh Stewart Lieut Col comma OC. 94 Field Amb.

Confidential   <u>31st Div</u>   Vol VIII

<u>August 1916</u>

War Diary

of

<u>94th. Fd. Ambulance</u>

Aug 1916.

COMMITTEE FOR THE
MEDICAL HISTORY OF THE WAR
Date   -9 OCT. 1916

WAR DIARY or ~~INTELLIGENCE SUMMARY~~

(Erase heading not required.)

Army Form C. 2118

94 Field Ambulance

Place	August Date 1916	Hour	Summary of Events and Information	Remarks and references to Appendices
COLONNE SUR LYS.	1		Bright fine day no wind. Despatched War Diary for July to A.D.M.S. 31 Div. and copy for April to Officer i/c R a.m.c. Records Aldershot for custody. Made usual inspection of all billets etc. Commanding Officer parade. Went to LESTREM to see A.D.M.S. 31 Div. Gas drill & instruction 'A' section. Kit inspection by o/c section.	
COLONNE SUR LYS.	2		Fine morning slight wind. Made usual inspection of billets etc. Water in water carts tested and report rendered by sections. Section drill in morning. Inspection of horses and transport by O.C. Headquarter Coy A.S.C 31 Div Train. Dr DABELL A.S.C. granted leave to U.K. for 8 days on special grounds. 8 Reinforcements arrived today and taken on strength. One case of inspected C.D.M. was admitted this evening. Examined case and considered that he should not be sent to MALASSISE. Transferred case to No 2 C.C.S. Car & orderly to be isolated until disinfected. Reported action taken at once to A.D.M.S. 31 Div.	
COLONNE SUR LYS	3		Fine morning Wind N.E. Paraded reinforcements separately & allotted them to sections. Kit inspection of each of the held. Commanding officer parade at 11 a.m. Gas Helmet drill &	

WAR DIARY
or
INTELLIGENCE SUMMARY
(Erase heading not required.)

Army Form C. 2118

A4 Field Ambulance

Place	Date / Hour	Summary of Events and Information	Remarks and references to Appendices
	AUGUST 1916		
	3 (cont)	instruction to "B" section. Kit inspection A.S.C. & M.T. Forwarded applications of Capts T. McEWEN, J.H.C. WALKER & M.D. KING for permanent commissions in the R.A.M. Corps. Car conveying C.S.M. came disinfected. Orderlies clothes also disinfected.	
COLONNE SUR LYS	4.	Wind much stronger today N.E. Much cooler but still very fine. Made usual inspection. Seen the Officer for 7th and 38 Div came to take over here. Received instructions from D.D.M.S. XI Corps to hand him over the mill. Arranged with him as to transport lines etc. Went over to LESTREM to see A.D.M.S. about same. Drill in morning of sections. Capts McEWEN, WALKER & KING went over to be interviewed by A.D.M.O. as to their fitness for permanent Commissions in the R.A.M.C.	
COLONNE SUR LYS	5.	Much cooler wind as before. Made usual inspection & billets etc. 97th Field Ambulance arrived here at 12.5 a.m. and went to the mill. Saw LIEUT COL BURKE Commanding and settled details with him with regard to demolition etc. Unit went for a Route March in morning. Gas helmet drill for "C" section.	

WAR DIARY

Army Form C. 2118

94 Field Ambulance

Place	Date August 1916	Hour	Summary of Events and Information	Remarks and references to Appendices
COLONNE SUR LYS	6		Sunday. Divine Service as follows:- R.C's 10 a.m. parade under Capt. KING. C of E. 11.30 a.m. No other parades during day. R.	
COLONNE SUR LYS	7		Warm day. Wind still strong. Made usual inspection. Went to LESTREM to see A.D.M.S. Detailed Capt. KING to take over medical charge of the Forest Control at LE FORET today. A Light tent subdivision took over the work at the dressing station from "B" Section today. LIEUT FREW reported his arrival from the 47th Reserve Park on completion of temporary duty. Under instructions from A.D.M.S. of Div. LIEUT BLACKMORE was detailed to proceed to the Divisional Bombing School & School of Instruction at PACAUT as M.O i/c & reported his departure this evening. Unit had Company drill under Section Officers today. R.	
COLONNE SUR LYS	8		Warm day, wind much less. Commanding Officers parade at 10.45. Army act read to unit by Capt. McEWEN & Went	

WAR DIARY
or
~~INTELLIGENCE SUMMARY~~
(Erase heading not required.)

Army Form C. 2118

94. Field Ambulance

Place	Date	Hour	Summary of Events and Information	Remarks and references to Appendices
COLONNE SUR LYS	AUGUST 1916. 8		to LESTREM to draw pay for the unit from the Field Cashier XI Corps. Paid unit at 2. p.m. Gas helmet drill & instruction to "A" section. Issue of P.H.G helmets to all instead of the P.H. Helmet which is to be returned.	
COLONNE SUR LYS.	9		Very warm day practically no wind. Made usual inspection of all billets etc. Withdrew all Steel helmets issued to the men viz 100 which are to be handed over to the 93 Infantry Brigade under instructions for 31st Division Headquarters. Route march for whole unit under the orders of Capt. WALKER during morning.	
COLONNE SUR LYS.	10		Misty morning much cooler little wind some rain in forenoon. Made usual inspection of all billets. Commanding officers parade at 11.0 a.m. Inspected all gas helmets & unit on parade.	
COLONNE SUR LYS	11		Much brighter & warmer, no wind. Made usual inspection. Company drill of all sections during morning. Saw Branch	

WAR DIARY

Army Form C. 2118

94 Field Ambulance

(Erase heading not required.)

Place	Date Hour	Summary of Events and Information	Remarks and references to Appendices
COLONNE SUR LYS	AUGUST 1916 11th (Cont)	Requisitioning Officer with regard to the rent to be paid for the Mill & outhouses used as a location Hospital and Billets. Had formal plan prepared showing area occupied. Under instructions from A.D.M.S. 31st Div. O sent one water Cart with horses & driver complete to the Divisional School of Instruction on temporary loan, received receipt of same.	
COLONNE SUR LYS	12th	A much warmer day & no wind. Made usual inspection of billets. Route march of Unit under Command of Capt. McEWEN. Sgt MULLIGAN dispenser "B" section evacuated to C.C.O. with METATARSALGIA. He is unable to march & in my opinion unfit to be with a Mobile unit. Went down to Div Headquarters to see A.D.M.S re Capt. CHRISTIE who is due to proceed to England on the 15th on completion of his second term of contract.	
COLONNE SUR LYS	13.	Sunday. Divine services as follows:— R.C's at 10 a.m. under Command of Capt. FRASER. Non Conf at 9.30 a.m. under Command of Lieut FREW C of E at 11.30 a.m. under Command of Capt. WALKER	

WAR DIARY

Army Form C. 2118

Instructions regarding War Diaries and Intelligence Summaries are contained in F. S. Regs., Part II. and the Staff Manual respectively. Title Pages will be prepared in manuscript.

~~INTELLIGENCE SUMMARY~~
(Erase heading not required.)

94 Field Ambulance

Place	Date / Hour AUGUST 1916	Summary of Events and Information	Remarks and references to Appendices
COLONNE SUR LYS	13 Cont.	Capt. CHRISTIE having been granted permission to proceed to ENGLAND on duty for the W² reported his departure this day and proceeded via BETHUNE. Dr. DABELL A.S.C. granted leave of absence to U.K. on the 2nd had not returned yesterday reported his absence to the A.D.M.S. and to the Officer i/c A.D.C Records WOOLWICH. Ordered Court of Enquiry to assemble to report on his absence and to assess the value of the kit taken by him, Capt. KING appointed president. D.	
COLONNE SUR LYS	14	An outbreak of Glanders having taken place in the Division all horses were malleined by the Veterinary Officer today. Much cooler windy day some rain. Made usual inspection of all billets. Returned all 36 & 36A maps to H.Q. Issued necessary orders for the Unit Dump to be formed in the event of an advance. Pt. PROST detailed in Charge. D.	
COLONNE SUR LYS	15	Colder inclined to rain, heavy showers during day. Commanding Officers parade at H.Q. Made usual inspection of all	

WAR DIARY

Army Form C. 2118

94. Field Ambulance

Place	Date	Hour	Summary of Events and Information	Remarks and references to Appendices
	AUGUST 1916			
COLONNE SUR LYS	15.		Billets today. A.D.V.S. 31 Division inspected horses today. "A" Carried out tests with the LUCE MONOWHEEL CYCLE CARRIER today. A.D.M.S. 31 Division inspected Dressing station, Billets & transport today. Three reinforcements R.A.M.C. arrived & reported & one A.S.C. M.T. driver reported arrival. D". DABELL having been returned sent to station by M.O.	
COLONNE SUR LYS	16.		Dull morning, brighter later on, no rain. Some rain during night. Usual inspections today. D. BLACK A.S.C. 31 Div Train was brought in yesterday evening with a fracture of Tibia & Fibula due to an accident on admission he was drunk. Reported to O.C. Div Train. Squad & Company drill today during morning.	
COLONNE SUR LYS	17.		Some rain during night. Fine morning, much cooler. Showers during day. Cap". McEWEN WALKER & KING proceeded to Headquarters 31st Div in order to be interviewed by the G.O.C. having applied for permanent Commissions in the R.A.M.C. Commanding officers parade at 11 a.m. after which made usual inspection of billets etc. O.C. 221 Coy A.S.C. 31 Div train inspected transports this afternoon. Gas helmet drill & inspection of gas helmets by "B" section. Kit inspection for "C" section.	

WAR DIARY or ~~INTELLIGENCE SUMMARY~~

(Erase heading not required.)

Army Form C. 2118

94 Field Ambulance

Place	Date	Hour	Summary of Events and Information	Remarks and references to Appendices
COLONNE SUR LYS	August 1916 18.		More heavy rain during night much cooler morning. No wind. Heavy rain mid-day & afternoon. Held board of examiners on two cooks to justify of next higher rate of pay. D. BLACK transferred to C.C.S accompanied by report by Lieut WALES.	
COLONNE SUR LYS	19.		Cooler rain during morning but clear in afternoon. Route march of all sections under Capt McEWEN. Went with interpreter and arranged billets of the A.S.C. and G.S.C.M.T. Made usual inspections. D.D.M.S XI Corps came round & inspected. Suggested marking horse lines with faggots & stakes.	
COLONNE SUR LYS	20.		Divine Services as follows. R-Cs at 9.30 under Capt KING. C of E at 11.30. Received orders for A.D.M.S 31 Div to hold heavier subdivisions ready to move at a few hours notice on orders of D.M.S. 1st army. Detachd bearers the ready. CAPT. KING & Capt FRASER to accompany them.	
COLONNE SUR LYS	21.		Brighter day rain during night little wind. Made usual inspection of billets etc. No orders for bearers yet received. Made enquiries re faggots at LA FORET. Sent Capt McEWEN to arrange of filling shale particulars. S. M. Cobbett sent with 5 wagons of same. These wagons to go daily for the future.	

WAR DIARY or INTELLIGENCE SUMMARY.

Army Form C. 2118.

94 Field Ambulance

Place	Date	Hour	Summary of Events and Information	Remarks and references to Appendices
COLONNE SUR LYS	AUGUST 1916 22.		Fine day no rain. Went over to Headquarters of the Division to draw money for the Field Cashier & also to see the A.D.M.S. re application for special leave submitted by Capt. McEWEN on account of his wife's health. Wagons went to ANNEZIN and for stores all night. Received orders that bearers who are standing by need not be confined to barracks. Received instructions from A.D.M.S. 51st Div to detail 1 Corporal 2 Lance Corporals and 20 orderlies to go to XI Corps Rest Station BOSNES tomorrow. Detailed the men & ordered them to parade tomorrow at 9.30 for inspection under Corporal SOPP. Issued iron rations to men who were deficient. R.	
COLONNE SUR LYS.	23		Rain during night fine day. Made usual inspection of all billets etc. Paraded 23 men for BOSNES under Corporal SOPP. and they left at 12.30. p.m. Capt. CHRISTIE having reported sick he was not reengaged for a third period was struck off the strength of the unit under instructions from A.D.M.S. 51st Div. R.	
COLONNE SUR LYS.	24		Very fine morning but more wind. Made usual inspection of all billets	

WAR DIARY or INTELLIGENCE SUMMARY

Army Form C. 2118.

94 Field Ambulance

Place	Date	Hour	Summary of Events and Information	Remarks and references to Appendices
	AUGUST 1916			
COLONNE SUR LYS	24		Capt PARKINSON. D.A.D.M.S. (Sanitary) 1st Army made a Sanitary inspection of all billets, Conservancy etc. and expressed himself very pleased with all arrangements. R.	
COLONNE SUR LYS	25.		Rain during night, fine morning. Made inspection of all billets in the place. Measured the proposed new Cookhouse & latrine and indented thro' A.D.M.S. 31 Div for the amount required. Capt T. McEWEN granted Special leave for 7 days from the 25th. Corpml ROWLEY granted special leave on account of the serious illness of his father for the 25 to 31st. Very promising day with a little rain in evening. R. Return instituted for A.D.M.S. 31 Div. One Ford & one Sidcar Ambulance sent to XI Corps Rest Stn.	
COLONNE SUR LYS	26.		Fine morning much wind. Route march of men today for two hours under the command of Capt McEWEN. arranged with Senior Chaplain of Services Commn. granted pass to M.T. drivers to attend the 31. Divisional Supply Column Sports at MERVILLE this afternoon. R.	
COLONNE SUR LYS	27.		Divine service arranged as follows.	

Army Form C. 2118.

WAR DIARY ~~or INTELLIGENCE SUMMARY~~

94 Field Ambulance

(Erase heading not required.)

Instructions regarding War Diaries and Intelligence Summaries are contained in F. S. Regs., Part II. and the Staff Manual respectively. Title pages will be prepared in manuscript.

Place	Date AUGUST 1916	Hour	Summary of Events and Information	Remarks and references to Appendices
COLONNE SUR LYS	27 cont.		R-C- at 10 a.m. in Church. Cof E at 11.45 in Mill. Rain fell heavily during the morning. Capt. McEWEN granted special leave of absence to the U.K. from 28 to 4 September inclusive reported his departure today. R.	
COLONNE SUR LYS	28.		Fine morning no rain. Low wind. Marked out new horse standings to be made and detailed party to start work this morning. Had Corkhouse at the mill taken down and enlarged. Corkhouse at the Dressing Station also the stables. Made usual inspection of all billets & found all correct. R.	
COLONNE SUR LYS	29.		Drizzling rain little & no wind. Sent Capt. KING to enquire for C.R.E. as the decision of the horse standing as we would require 200 to make a complete flooring of same. R.	
COLONNE SUR LYS	30.		Work on standing stopped until definite instructions as regards the	

WAR DIARY
or
INTELLIGENCE SUMMARY.
(Erase heading not required.)

Army Form C. 2118.

94. Field Ambulance

Place	Date 1916	Hour	Summary of Events and Information	Remarks and references to Appendices
	August		amount of fumes allowed is ascertained. Wrote to Adams to enquire about same. Under instructions from A.D.M.S. 31st Div Capt WALKER & KING proceeded to XI Corps Headquarters to be interviewed by the D.D.M.S. XI Corps with regard to their application for permanent Commissions in the R.A.M.C. Today has been very wet almost continual downpour with high wind. Outside work difficult. R.	
COLONNE SUR LYS	31st		Fine morning no rain wind light S.W. Made usual inspection of all billets etc. Sent Sgt BUXTON to LE PERK for sawdust. Granted an extension of leave by wire to Corpl ROWLEY until 4th (A.D.M.S. 31st Div Sanction). Made up Imprest Accounts & sent bills etc to Headquarters of Contingencies. Blankets (200) were sent yesterday to be disinfected preparatory to returning same to Ordnance. Received 300 bundles of repairing hurse standings.	

AusStewart
Lieut/Col Comm
O.C. 94 Field Amb.

Confidential

140/134

Vol 9

War Diary.

94th Field Ambulance 31st Division

September 1916.

COMMITTEE FOR THE
MEDICAL HISTORY OF THE WAR
Date 30 OCT. 1916

WAR DIARY or INTELLIGENCE SUMMARY

Army Form C. 2118.

94th Field Ambce

Place	Date	Hour	Summary of Events and Information	Remarks and references to Appendices
	SEPTEMBER 1916			
COLONNE SUR LYS	1st		Fine morning. Westerly wind. No rain. Started repairing the kick horse standings. Work on cook houses completed. 2 hours physical drill during morning. L/Cpl W Martin A.H.a Jibb proceeded to No 1 Advanced Depot Medical Stores for medicine & to return empty cases. 200 blankets returned to Ordnance Officer at Railhead under instructions from A.D.M.S 31st Div. Dispatched War Diary for August to A.D.M.S 31st Div and the duplicate copy for May to Officer i/c R.A.M.C records Aldershot.	
COLONNE SUR LYS	2nd		Fine morning. Wind W. Made arrangements of Divine Service tomorrow. Made usual inspections of all billets. Reconstructed the entire outside Yard behind Dressing station.	
COLONNE SUR LYS	3.		Fine morning no rain. Divine Services today as follows. R C. at 10 am under Capt KING. C of E at 11.45 am. 10 am nonconformist	

WAR DIARY or **INTELLIGENCE SUMMARY**.
(Erase heading not required.)

Army Form C. 2118.

94th Field Ambce

Place	Date	Hour	Summary of Events and Information	Remarks and references to Appendices
	SEPTEMBER 1916			
COLONNE SUR LYS	4.		Under instructions fr A.D.M.S 31 Div Cap" M B KING & Cap" J.H.C WALKER proceeded to LILLERS to be interviewed by D.M.S 1st Army on application for permanent commissions. Cap" McEWEN reported his arrival from leave of absence to the United Kingdom. Under instructions fr A.D.M.S 31 Div Cap" M B King was detached to proceed to take over medical charge of the 13th B" East YORKS as a temporary measure in relief of Cap" CAMPBELL who joined the unit for duty. LIEUT MORRIS reported his arrival for duty & is taken on the Strength of the Ambulance for this date. R.	
COLONNE SUR LYS	5.		Wet drizzling rain all day. Made complete inspection of all lines & billets. D.M.S. 1st Army made an inspection today and found all satisfactory. R	
COLONNE SUR LYS	6.		Cap" CAMPBELL placed on the sick list today suffering from Asthma. Fine day no rain bright sun.	

WAR DIARY or INTELLIGENCE SUMMARY.

Army Form C. 2118.

94th Field Ambce

Place	Date	Hour	Summary of Events and Information	Remarks and references to Appendices
			Made usual inspection of the lines etc. Drew money for Orders and men paid by Capt Fraser.	
COLONNE SUR LYS.	7.		Fine day bright sun. No wind. Made usual inspection of all billets etc. Horse lines being completed. Capt McEWEN went over to XI Corps Headquarters to be interviewed by D.D.M.O XI Corps.	
COLONNE SUR LYS	8.		Fine day Wind West. Went over to Headquarters 31st Division for a conference by the A.D.M.S. 31 Div on medical arrangements to be made for the projected attack on this front. My ambulance to be in reserve ready to move there if necessary.	
COLONNE SUR LYS.	9.		Fine bright morning no rain. Made arrangement of divine service tomorrow. Made inspection of all billets etc. Capt W.B. KING rejoined on completion of temporary duty with the 13th East YORKS. Capt CAMPBELL took off sick list.	
COLONNE SUR LYS	10.		Divine service today as follows	

WAR DIARY or INTELLIGENCE SUMMARY.

Army Form C. 2118.

94th Field Ambce

Place	Date	Hour	Summary of Events and Information	Remarks and references to Appendices
	SEPTEMBER 1916			
COLONNE S.R LYS.	10		R.C. at 10 a.m. C of E. 11.45 a.m. & Voluntary Holy Communion afterwards. Non Conf. 6. p.m. Dull day mainly no rain. R.	
COLONNE SUR LYS.	11		Fine day no rain little wind. Made usual inspection of billets etc. Horse standings being completed. New Latrines, Urinal & wash bench complete in billets. Cookhouse, Tailors & Shoemakers shop completed. R.	
COLONNE SUR LYS.	12		Fine day. no rain. Made usual inspection. 5 men returned fr Officers XI Corps rest station. Went to Headquarters & drew pay. Saw A.D.M.S. re extent for work etc required to complete work which the D.M.S. 1st Army had ordered to be done. R.	

WAR DIARY or INTELLIGENCE SUMMARY.

Army Form C. 2118.

94th Field Ambce

Place	Date SEPTEMBER 1916	Hour	Summary of Events and Information	Remarks and references to Appendices
COLONNE SUR LYS.	13.		Fine day. Usual work proceeded with. Nothing unusual to report. Capt MCEWEN proceeded to LILLERS to be interviewed by D.M.S 1st Army. R.	
COLONNE SUR LYS.	14.		Fine day Bright sun, no wind or rain. Held C.O inspection of all ranks full marching order everything satisfactory. Made an inspection of all billets etc after parade. R.	
COLONNE SUR LYS.	15		Fine day. Made usual inspection. In afternoon A.D.M.S 31 Div came round and told me we were to move to MESPLAUX on 17 sending advance parties on 16 to take over. We were also to have two advanced dressing stations at RUE DU BOIS & MARAIS. Accompanied by Capt MCEWEN I proceeded to all these places and saw what the arrangements were. On return worked out the details of the parties to take over. R.	

WAR DIARY or INTELLIGENCE SUMMARY.

Army Form C. 2118.

94th Field Ambce

Place	Date September 1918	Hour	Summary of Events and Information	Remarks and references to Appendices
CALONNE SUR LYS	16		Went to LESTREM to see A.D.M.S. about the following (1) the return of ambulances which were sent temporarily to Corps Rest. (2) relieving personnel sent there (3) return of water cart to the Div School of Instruction (4) neutralizing of traffic on certain roads. Went on then to MESPLAUX & arranged officers billets. On return detailed party to go this evening under Capt McEWEN and issued all necessary orders for the move (copy attached) Capt McEWEN and party left at 2 p.m. Went to Headquarters to see A.D.M.S. about the officer who is sent daily to LAFORET & to report that one ambulance had been at the workshop 7 weeks. No orders yet received as to their Cars or personnel returning. Sent despatch rider to Headquarters at 9.45 p.m. to get any orders. G.	
MESPLAUX	17		Fine morning. Reveille at 5 a.m. Unit marched under the Command of Capt WALKER from CALONNE SUR LYS to MESPLAUX leaving at 7.10 a.m. Left in Motor Ambulance at 8 a.m.	

WAR DIARY or INTELLIGENCE SUMMARY.

Army Form C. 2118.

94th Field Amb[ulance]

Place	Date SEPTEMBER 1916	Hour	Summary of Events and Information	Remarks and references to Appendices
	17		and left LIEUT MORRIS Rowe at 93 Field Ambulance proceeding to join the 3rd Div. & struck off the strength of this unit accordingly. Arrived at MESPLAUX and proceeded to take over everything at 9. a.m. Capt McEWEN reported that all men posted in accordance with my orders. Proceeded to make all arrangements for the company no 7 the work and made out the list, work requiring completion. Reported by wire to A.D.M.S. that I had taken over. CAPT McEWEN proceeded to A.D.O at RUE DU BOIS. R.	
MESPLAUX	18.		Very wet cold day. down pour continued through the whole day until 6 p.m. when it cleared. After morning inspection, I proceeded with Sgt WATSON & 2 men to "Unit" Horses dressing station and took it over to be held only, from there I went to BETHUNE & left the office of the 98 Field Ambulance at his headquarters, then proceeded to MARAIS a.O.D & saw Capt FRASER and inspected	

WAR DIARY
~~INTELLIGENCE SUMMARY.~~
(Erase heading not required.)

Army Form C. 2118.

94th Field Amb[ulance]

Place	Date	Hour	Summary of Events and Information	Remarks and references to Appendices
	SEPTEMBER 1916			
MESPLAUX		18	[illegible], arranged with Cap FRASER to [relieve?] four bearers at one Aid post and put them at the butts at BORRE under L/Cpl CALLIGAN, the bearers to be relieved by bearers of RUE DU BOIS. Went to RUE DU BOIS A.D.S. arranged with Capt McEWEN for him to run the canteen there, L/[F?] working order. Work on the Dug-outs being proceeded with. 2 afternoon A.D.M.S. made an inspection. LIEUT BLABER arriving[?] [illegible].	R.
MESPLAUX		19	Made a complete inspection this morning and arranged for various alterations to be made [illegible]. Went to see A.D.M.S. written report, special leave referred to G[eneral] [illegible] who said it was not possible. Arranged with D.A. [Cavalry?] [Section?] for an interchange of duties from 21st to 24th. Leave was granted [illegible] from the 21st to the 30th inclusive. The A.D.M.S. came round and was pleased with everything and remarked on the amount of work already done. [illegible] have been will attend.	R.

WAR DIARY
or
INTELLIGENCE SUMMARY.
(Erase heading not required.)

Army Form C. 2118.

94th Field Amb[ce]

Place	Date	Hour	Summary of Events and Information	Remarks and references to Appendices
	SEPTEMBER 1916			
MESPLAUX	20		Very wet during night but cleared about 9 a.m., but was misty all day. Went to White House and from there went to A.D.S. Rue du Bois. Capt WALKER relieved Capt McEWEN at the A.D.S. Capt McEWEN returned to headquarters. Went into MERVILLE to No 1 Advanced Depot of Medical Stores. Handed everything over to Capt McEWEN as I was proceeding on leave early tomorrow. Everything satisfactory. B. Bulliwant Lt Col R___	
MESPLAUX	21		Took over command of the 94th Field Ambulance last night as Lt Col STEWART was going on leave early this morning. Weather dull & cloudy with heavy showers in the morning but it cleared up in the afternoon though looking very unsettled. In the morning inspected all billets at Main Dressing Station & visited WHITE HOUSE Dressing Station arranging with the owner the amount to be paid for billets there. In the afternoon visited the A.D.S. at RUE DE BOIS meeting the A.D.M.S. We inspected this A.D.S. & found improvements & work going on satisfactorily.	

WAR DIARY
or
INTELLIGENCE SUMMARY.
(Erase heading not required.)

Army Form C. 2118.

94th Field Ambulance

Place	Date	Hour	Summary of Events and Information	Remarks and references to Appendices
	SEPTEMBER 1916			
MESPLAUX	21(cont)		I then went to the A.D.S. at MARAIS & found all correct. IN2.	
MESPLAUX	22nd		Weather clear & bright. Inspected the whole of the Main Dressing Station. In the afternoon visited the baths & canteen at LE TOURET which are situated close to the A.D.S. at RUE DE BOIS & afterwards went to BETHUNE to the Expeditionary Force Canteen for stock for canteen. IN2.	
MESPLAUX	23rd		Beautiful September day. Made the usual morning inspection. Visited the A.D.S. at MARAIS & arranged for a tank to hold drinking water. IN2.	
MESPLAUX	24th		Continuation of fine weather. Inspected billets. Divine service (C of E) at 11 a.m. D.A.D.M.S. visited this Dressing Station & inspected it, then we proceeded to the A.D.S. at RUE DE BOIS inspecting it, the baths & canteen. Afterwards we went to A.D.S. at MARAIS & then to the baths at GORRE which are under the supervision of this A.D.S. IN2.	
MESPLAUX	25th		Sharp September morn. During the day clear & bright.	

WAR DIARY
or
INTELLIGENCE SUMMARY.
(Erase heading not required.)

Army Form C. 2118.

94th Field Ambce

Instructions regarding War Diaries and Intelligence Summaries are contained in F. S. Regs., Part II. and the Staff Manual respectively. Title pages will be prepared in manuscript.

Place	Date SEPTEMBER 1916	Hour	Summary of Events and Information	Remarks and references to Appendices
MESPLAUX	25th (cont)		Inspected Dressing Station. Went to see the A.D.M.S. re the Interpreter as he had informed me that he was probably freeing this unit to go to the 93rd Infantry Brigade. In the afternoon visited the A.D.S. at RUE DE BOIS. Received notice from O.C French Mission, 31st Div. that Interpreter R. BION had been attached to the 93rd Inf. Brigade. J.W.E.	
MESPLAUX	26th		Weather clear & bright. Inspected billets. Went & saw A.D.M.S. re leave for Lieut & Quartermaster A.H.A.JIBB. J.W.E.	
MESPLAUX	27th		Weather continues fine. Southerly breeze. Lieut & Quartermaster A.H.A.TIBB went on leave early this morning. D.A.D.M.S. Corps. visited concerning drainage of land surrounding Dressing Station. Indented for roofing for horse standings the floor of which is nearing completion. Visited A.D.S. RUE DE BOIS, also baths & canteen at LE TOURET. J.W.E.	
MESPLAUX	28th		Weather crisp & bright. Wind Southerly. Held daily inspection of billets etc. Visited A.D.S. at RUE DE BOIS	

WAR DIARY or **INTELLIGENCE SUMMARY.**

Army Form C. 2118.

Instructions regarding War Diaries and Intelligence Summaries are contained in F. S. Regs., Part II. and the Staff Manual respectively. Title pages will be prepared in manuscript.

(Erase heading not required.)

94th Field Amb[ulance]

Place	Date	Hour	Summary of Events and Information	Remarks and references to Appendices
	SEPTEMBER 1916			
MESPLAUX	28th (cont)		also baths at GORRE. Sent a report to A.D.M.S. with regard to repairs & alterations required at these baths & also at baths at LE TOURET. JWS.	
MESPLAUX	29th		Dull Day with occasional drizzling rain. Inspected billets. Went to BETHUNE for stores for Canteen at LE TOURET. Inspected baths & canteen there. Received secret communication that 31st Division were to be relieved by the 5th Division & that preparations were to be made for a move. The interpreter M. BION left for duty with the 93rd Inf. Brigade. Visited A.D.S. at MARAIS. JWS.	
MESPLAUX	30th		Weather clear & bright again. Wind-Westerly. Inspected Main Dressing Station & the swimming baths. Equipment of 'A' & 'B' sections checked. Lieut Colonel STEWART expected from leave tonight so arranged for car to meet him at BETHUNE when leave train arrives. JWS. Returned from leave & took over Command. [signature] Lt Colonel	

Confidential   Volume X

Oct 1916

War Diary.

94th Field Ambulance   31st Division

October 1916.

COMMITTEE FOR THE
MEDICAL HISTORY OF THE WAR
Date — 9 DEC. 1916

WAR DIARY or INTELLIGENCE SUMMARY

94th Field Ambulance

Army Form C. 2118.

Place	Date / Hour	Summary of Events and Information	Remarks and references to Appendices
MESPLAUX	October 1916 — 1st	Made an inspection of whole place. Went to A.D.M.S. to report my return from leave. Received orders to hold ourselves in readiness to move at short notice as the Division was proceeding to join the Reserve Army. Completed War Diary for September & sent same to A.D.M.S. 51 Div. for disposal. Also sent duplicate copy of War Diary for June to Officer i/c Records Aldershot for safe custody. Fine day with little or no wind. Lt. BLACKMORE returned to H.Q.	
MESPLAUX	2nd	Very wet morning and wet all day. Section wagons packed ready for move. Lieut. FREW detailed to relieve Capt. KEAY as M.O. of 137 F.A. as a temporary measure during latter's absence on leave. Received instructions for disposal of surplus stores etc. Received orders to move, on 4th, on being relieved by a Field Ambulance 5th Div., to White House and remain there until we receive our entraining orders. Capt. McEWEN	

WAR DIARY or INTELLIGENCE SUMMARY.

Army Form C. 2118.

94th Field Ambce

Place	Date October 1916	Hour	Summary of Events and Information	Remarks and references to Appendices
MESPLAUX	2	Cont	proceeded to advanced dressing stations and completed all billeting arrangements.	
MESPLAUX	3		Made all arrangements for leaving over. Lt Col HANAFIN came here today and our arrangements here the Field Ambulance No 13 are taking over tomorrow. Sent Capt McEWEN to the Advanced dressing Stations with him to show him the place. Went to ADMS office + saw him on the move. (All ambulances (motor are to be handed over to the incoming Field ambulance and also all the medical stores at MESPLAUX) the unit moving as lightly equipped as possible.	
~~MESS~~ WHITE HOUSE	4		Wet drizzly morning sent party early to White House to get place ready. Handed over at 12 noon to OC 13 Field Ambulance. Capt McEWEN to hand over A.D.S. Party marched to White House transport to remain at MESPLAUX except some vehicles which are to go down. Saw ADMS about [illegible] noon, & then recommended of good work & promised to send some tomorrow. Capt McEWEN reports ADS handed over all men [illegible].	

WAR DIARY
or
INTELLIGENCE SUMMARY.
(Erase heading not required.)

Army Form C. 2118.

94th Field Amb.

Place	Date	Hour	Summary of Events and Information	Remarks and references to Appendices
ROBECQ		5.	Sent Capt FRASER & Interpreter to Robecq early to arrange about billets. Unit moved under the command of Capt McEWEN by road to ROBECQ leaving at 1.30. Proceeded in Ford cars and took over allotted billets. All men billeted by 5 pm. Saw Staff Captain 94 Inf Bde about sick. Sent names of officers to A.D.M.S. B section opened during morning for sick. P.	
ROBECQ		6.	Fine day. Inspected billets. Routine work. Nothing to report. P.	
ROBECQ		7.	Received entraining orders today. Sent Capt McEWEN over to Whitehouse to hand over to 13 F.A. at 10 am but no one turned up. Message at 4 from O.C. that he did not know where Whitehouse was and to send representative to report to him. Sent word to say I was unable to do this & gave map reference. P. Got orders to recall all men from leave wires to Lieut BLACKMORE & Dr HOLMES. P.	

WAR DIARY or INTELLIGENCE SUMMARY.   9th Field Amb[ulance]

Army Form C. 2118.

4

Place	Date	Hour	Summary of Events and Information	Remarks and references to Appendices
ROBECQ		8.	Preparations for departure. Reconnoitred the road and station. Entraining at 12.40 am. 9th to be at station at 9.40 pm on 8. Orders parade at 6.30. March off at 6.45. On arrival wagons loaded on train, men entrained and horses. Train left punctually.	
SARTON		9.	Arrived at DOULENS at 6 am, detrained and marched to SARTON where we were billeted. Billets bad. Officers in tents. Reported arrival to A.D.M.S. A.D.M.S. visited us and gave instructions. B section to own the Dressing Station. Fine day. Lt. Gill arrived from leave.	
SARTON		10.	Beautifully fine morning. Lieut. BLACKMORE arrived back from leave on being recalled. Went over to A.D.M.S. and found out all medical arrangements.	
SARTON		11.	Fine morning. Made full inspection 2 places. Received orders that the bearer Division was to be ready to move into the 94th B[riga]de and that Division to	

WAR DIARY or INTELLIGENCE SUMMARY.

94th Field Amb^ce

Army Form C. 2118.

Place	Date OCTOBER 1916	Hour	Summary of Events and Information	Remarks and references to Appendices
			be ~~ready~~ packed ready to move. Made all necessary arrangements	
SARTON	12		A.D.M.S. made an inspection today. Inspected baths at SARTON and proposed to take them over and start them going. Indented for material for the construction of a new latrine here.	
SARTON	13		Indented for stoves tubs and coal for baths & informed Brigade that I would be able to start bathing tomorrow. Got wood & canvas for latrine. Site selected & work begun.	
SARTON	14		Work well in hand. Started baths running today but very few men turned up. Sent 7 men to VARENNES	
SARTON	15		~~Pass~~ Routine work proceeded with. Latrine almost completed, baths working well. Church Parade C of E at 11	
SARTON	16		Received orders from A.D.M.S. that my Ambulance was to take over the Corps Rest station at COUIN by 12 noon tomorrow. Sent Capt McEWEN to COUIN to see about the	

WAR DIARY or INTELLIGENCE SUMMARY

9 H.T. Field Amb[?]

Army Form C. 2118

Place	Date	Hour	Summary of Events and Information	Remarks and references to Appendices
			arrangements there. Had everything packed ready to move. Parade ordered for 9.30 a.m.	
COUIN		17	Parade at 9.30 this morning & left at once. Capt WALKER detailed to remain behind and hand over to Town Major & then rejoin. March slow. At Authie transport held up so I proceeded with the personnel to Couin & took over from the 1/2 Highland field Ambulance 51st Div. Rest station attached to huts and marquees. Reported to A.D.M.S 31st Div 2 very having taken over. Saw D.D.M.S XVII Corps who told me what he wants done here.	
COUIN		18	Work started. The Ambulance took over 70 sick of the outgoing and 2 there were fit to return to duty. A.D.M.S came round & saw the place. He informed me that I would receive 230 cases from 95 Field Ambulance tomorrow which were to take over & hut. Accompanied A.D.M.S down to baths here & saw the arrangements. Fine wet during day.	
COUIN		19	Cases from 95 Fd Ambulance came in during morning the majority belonged to other Divisions notably 51st & 19th there was a very	

WAR DIARY or INTELLIGENCE SUMMARY

9H" Field Ambce

Place	Date	Hour	Summary of Events and Information	Remarks and references to Appendices
			large proportion of scabies cases. All the transferees were put into the marquees. Work started on making the fumigating box for scabies cases. Drew a large quantity of wood & completed view of work to be carried out in the Corps Rest Station. Handed over 20 marquees complete to the Officer Commanding 133 Field Ambulance under instruction of D Dir XIII Corps.	
COUIN	20.		After very heavy rain yesterday & today the evening turned out fine and hard frost succeeded. Obtained permission to utilize the wood & iron for making the huts warmer by putting corrugated iron sides to them. Started fitting & making stoves of the various wards and started work on the officers wards.	
COUIN.	21.		R.E. officer inspected today & said that the roofs required certain timbering, measurements made & indented for it. Frost still continues. Opined that I have not for large proportion of the stoves. Insisted on Division & reported that if unable to be viewed I might buy some. Received the permit to buy.	

WAR DIARY or INTELLIGENCE SUMMARY

Army Form C. 2118

94th Field Ambce

Place	Date October 19/16	Hour	Summary of Events and Information	Remarks and references to Appendices
COUIN	22		Sunday. Divine Service held at 11.30 and Celebration at 10. Voluntary Service held in Marquee. Work still being carried out. Frost succeeded by rain. Very unpleasant weather	
COUIN	23		Received orders to lessen the number at present in the Corps Rest Station (nearly 400), then can only be done by sending cases to C.C.S. as there are a lot not yet fit for discharge. There is a very big admission list daily. Went this even to see re number for discharge & to C.C.S. Lieut F Reed granted leave to U.K. for 10 days.	
COUIN	24		Very wet bleak day. Officers ward finish & occupied yesterday. This afternoon the Corps Commander came round & told me he wanted try & get piping for stoves for wards. All tents have now got conveyors inside. Stoves have been fitted in same. Also in dining hall & patients.	
COUIN	25.		Received D.D.M.S. operation orders and Assan. 31st Div. Orders. Wiring re the number of cases to start hospital at 5 pm. Went with the O.C. 31 M.A.C. to see A.D.M.S. 31 Div	

WAR DIARY or INTELLIGENCE SUMMARY

97th Field Ambulance

Place	Date	Hour	Summary of Events and Information	Remarks and references to Appendices
			all work being completed.	
COUIN	26		Wet day. Went to Amiens to buy stove piping for the stoves. Nothing unusual occurred during my absence. Made out all Allowance Claims & sent them in for payment.	
COUIN	27		Wet cold day. Stores put into Quartermasters store and 3 wards. Sulphur dioxide box finished and now seems to work well and does not leak.	
COUIN	28		Another wet day. Not much work done. Went round the whole camp & settled the method of dealing with the Gas & Shell Shock Cases. These cases are to be under the charge of Capt WALES and worked by the personnel of "A" Section. Got load of Ashes.	
COUIN	29		Sunday. Divine Services held. C of E 11.30 in Church hut Non Conformists at 3. Voluntary Service C of E at 6.	
COUIN	30		L. & Q. Martin a. H. a. Jibb went to Doullens with Indents of Medical Stores. Very wet both bicycles broke down. Wrote to O.C. operating centre Warloy asking him to relieve p-	

WAR DIARY or INTELLIGENCE SUMMARY

Army Form C. 2118.

94th Field Amb[ulance]

Place	Date October 1916	Hour	Summary of Events and Information	Remarks and references to Appendices
COUIN	31		Lambert & Bogan. Sic[k] Sent Lieut Jibb to Doullens & Beauval for medical stores. Car which took him to Doullens brought back Dentist who saw all cases and then returned Car taking him back to Doullens brought Lt Jibb back with stores. Went into Amiens to see if I could get pianos for the Division who are anxious to open forrest[?] house but could not get any. Day much finer, little or no rain very mild.	

Durthwait[?]
Lt Col R.A.M.C.
O.C. 94 F.A.

Nov 1916

31st 1D

140/1862

S.

94th Field Ambulance

COMMITTEE FOR THE
MEDICAL HISTORY OF THE WAR
Date -3 JAN. 1917

Confidential — Volume XI

Vol 9

War Diary.

94th Field Ambulance — 31st Division

November 1916.

WAR DIARY or INTELLIGENCE SUMMARY

Army Form C. 2118.

94 Field Ambulance

Place	Date November 1916	Hour	Summary of Events and Information	Remarks and references to Appendices
COUIN	1		Rather wet day. Completed work of strengthening the roofs of all buildings. Went to Beauval & Doullens for drugs etc. Very wet whilst there. Went to 62 Cas: Div H.Q. to see D.A.D.M.S.	
COUIN	2		Again wet. Routine work. All new ration tins in. Starts work on new Ward No 7 at present used as a linen store. 2yc Lieut Orr to Amiens. Car returned same day.	
COUIN	3		Work on buildings continued. Capt J.H.C WALKER Offr returned to Headquarters of Ambulance on completion of temporary duty with 165 Bde R.F.A. on being relieved by Lieut MERYON. On return Capt WALKER proceeds to the 15 D.L.I. for temporary duty relieving Lieut MacFarlane who was admitted to the Ambulance sick with a septic foot.	

WAR DIARY or INTELLIGENCE SUMMARY

Army Form C. 2118.

94 Field Amb.

Place	Date	Hour	Summary of Events and Information	Remarks and references to Appendices
COUIN	NOVEMBER 1916 4		Received orders that F. State was in the 5th. Made out details of same. D.D.M.S. XIII Corps arrived & visited the place. Routine work proceeding.	
COUIN	5		Sunday. Divine Services as follows. R.C. service by King at 8.30 C of E service by Fraser at 11.30. Voluntary services in afternoon. Weather remains very wet. Date of operation postponed until Nov 6th.	
COUIN	6		Lieut MACFARLANE now well discharged from the Ambulance & under instructions from A.D.M.S. at our station temporarily on the strength of the unit, with a view to his subsequent transfer to 170 B. R.F.A. Date of operation postponed until 7th.	
COUIN	7		Still very wet. Everything in a damp condition. Stoves now working satisfactorily in officers ward & chapel. Work started on the construction of a new tent lotrine for	

WAR DIARY or INTELLIGENCE SUMMARY

94 Field Amb.

Place	Date	Hour	Summary of Events and Information	Remarks and references to Appendices
	November 1916		patients exclusive of the 3 seat latrines at present in use. Lieut Blackmore reports his arrival fr 93 Field Ambulance & is taken on the strength of this unit & proceeds to the B.D.S. as temporary M.O.i/c in relief of Capt J.A.C. WALKER who has returned to Headquarters. Operation performed successfully. Still raining.	
COVIN	8		Routine work in camp proceeding. Still very wet. Rations not now lacking. Latrines finished & in use. Number of patients in increasing daily. Sick wastage however is small.	
COVIN	9		Eye cases sent to Amiens today in two cars. One car returned but other car was detained the night. L. PARKIN 12 R.O.F.A. sent in for eye trouble this afternoon. Sent in dispatch rider to Eye Specialist to ask for an appointment for him. Received appointment for 10 am tomorrow. Officer came in to Hospital this evening. Still wet. Pte McFarlane left for duty 17/4 B.W. attached 9 B.	

WAR DIARY
or
INTELLIGENCE SUMMARY

(Erase heading not required.)

9, Field Ambulance

Army Form C. 2118.

Place	Date / Hour	Summary of Events and Information	Remarks and references to Appendices
COUIN	NOVEMBER 19/16 10	Weather very mild. Car proceeded to Amiens with Lieut PARKIN. Both cars returned in afternoon. Received orders that operations will not take place on the 13th. Ward 7 completed. Our extra cmt attached arrived up today. Much hard work to face. G.	
COUIN.	11.	Wet day. Routine work. Arranged service of terrain with chaplain. Received orders that operations would commence on the 13th at 5.45 am. Made all necessary arrangements. Received permission for A.D.M.S. 31st Div to send up car to Bethune to bring back stores left there. G.	
COUIN	12.	Went with car to Bethune today (Capt. McEwen acting for me) for all stuff left behind. Replaced P. Smart by P. Hope. Received orders to send 2 Medical Officers & 17 other ranks to Walking Wounded Collecting Station. Detailed Capt. Walker + Capt. Frew. Under instruction for A.D.M.S. Leaving under Capt. King + Capt. Fraser. Left Repot TC 95. 2a. at Coigneux. G.	

WAR DIARY or INTELLIGENCE SUMMARY

94th [Field Amb?]

Army Form C. 2118.

Place	Date November 1916	Hour	Summary of Events and Information	Remarks and references to Appendices
Couin	13		Attack starts this morning. Fine morning with fog. No wounded being sent in here. 98 cases sick received yesterday. Owing to operations our urgent cases are being evacuated to C.C.S. Opened two new wards to relieve congestion. One shell shock case absolutely dumb recovered after inhalation of Ether returned to duty. O. went to Coigneux to see if bearers reported anything. P.	
Couin	14		Still operations but not on this front practically, no wounded now coming in. Sick still increasing, but only evacuating serious cases. Capt Pollard of the 31 M.A.C. is lending horse to direct cars. Went to Coigneux and on return sent up rations to Hebuterne by R & W under Jibb. P.	
Couin	15		Bearers reported their return this morning at 2-30 am. Capt King reports that P. Johnston G. was wounded & had been evacuated. Pt. Treadwell, Machon, Ashworth & Simons were also wounded very slightly but continued working after	

WAR DIARY or INTELLIGENCE SUMMARY

Army Form C. 2118.

94 Field Amb.

6

Place	Date	Hour	Summary of Events and Information	Remarks and references to Appendices
COUIN	November 1916 15		being dressed. Surgeon General MacPherson came here but finding that the wounded were being taken in have left.	
COUIN	16		Operations finished on this front for the present. All the Officers + other ranks for the Walking Wounded Collecting Station returned today. Evacuation of sick recommenced relieving the congestion. P.	
COUIN	17		Routine work proceeding. Have removed old bathhouse from old site & placed in front in camp. Made drawing room + 8 spray bath. Under instructions fr D.D.M.S. XIII Corps I am constructing a large disinfecting house for use with Clayton Disinfector. P.	
COUIN	18		Arranged services of tomorrow. Routine work being carried out. D.D.M.S. XIII Corps came round here + made suggestion which will be carried out. P.	

WAR DIARY or INTELLIGENCE SUMMARY

Army Form C. 2118.

7.

Place	Date	Hour	Summary of Events and Information	Remarks and references to Appendices
COUIN	November 1916 19		Sunday. Services as follows:- C of E at 11.30 a.m. R.C. at 8.30 a.m. P.	
COUIN	20		Bath house finished. Have arranged with D.A.D.S.&T. that I can draw clean clothing for patients in exchange for dirty, without previous notice. Patients who bathed are to have Hospital clothing until clean clothing arrives. Disinfector however being completed slowly owing to lack of materials. B. Capt CONNELL arrived & taken on Strength	
COUIN	21		A.D.M.S. XIII Corps made an inspection today. He told me the limits for the Walking Wounded Collecting Station were to draw here. Sent party of men under Sgt Weeks to take down all tents and huts & bring them here. Lorry provided for this purpose. Capt French received wire to say his wife had died suddenly. Went to Div H.D. and got him leave to proceed home at once. P.	
COUIN	22.		Tents etc for Walking Wounded Collecting Station arriving here.	

WAR DIARY or INTELLIGENCE SUMMARY

Army Form C. 2118.

Place	Date November 1916	Hour	Summary of Events and Information	Remarks and references to Appendices
COUIN		22	Capt. Tapcott Gill reported his arrival for duty, his name was taken on the strength of the unit. Orders came round with O.C. 71st Sanitary Section. Received permission for Town Major to move large latrine from another camp to this place for use of patients &c.	
COUIN		23	Under instructions from A.D.M.S. 31st Div Capt Cornwell J. left for duty with 93 Field Ambulance. Lieut Blake from temporary duty with 18 West Yorks returned to Headquarters today. S. Sjt Derry and remaining men of Walking Wounded Collecting Station returned to Headquarters today.	
COUIN		24	Sent Car to Amiens with patient for eye treatment. Had single fly marquee erected for patients dining & sitting room. Propose to join huts together with a store between them. Capt. Tapcott Gill left under instructions from A.D.M.S. 31st Div. for temporary duty with the 31st Div.	

WAR DIARY or INTELLIGENCE SUMMARY

Army Form C. 2118.

9

Place	Date	Hour	Summary of Events and Information	Remarks and references to Appendices
COUIN	November 1916 25		Very wet day. Almost impossible to carry out any out door work. Room of disinfection taking up much time. One hut has been changed to turn into preparation of tents in other enclosure. R.	
COUIN	26		Sunday no outdoor work. Divine Services as follows. C of E. 11-30. R-Co 8-30. R.	
COUIN	27		Finer day today. Two Marquees for Walking Wounded (Clink) Station erected as Dining Hall & Reception room for patients in A. Block. Fireplace built between them. Old dining room turned into ward and a separate ward of 20 beds set aside for Sergeants & W. Officers. Marquee erected as store of blankets etc in lieu of hut which has been turned into ward. R.	

WAR DIARY or INTELLIGENCE SUMMARY

94 ~~Field Ambulance~~

Army Form C. 2118.

10.

Place	Date November 1916	Hour	Summary of Events and Information	Remarks and references to Appendices
COUIN	28		Went to see A.D.M.S. re granting leave to Capt. J.H.C. Walker. Clayton Disinfecting horse finished but supplies has not yet sent Sulphur ordered on 18th inst. Sent urgent memo to them re same.	
COUIN	29		Capt. J.H.C. WALKER proceeded on leave, absence to U.K. D.A.D.M.S. came round ~~and~~ with Div Sanitary Officer. Hard frost during night. ~~[struck through]~~	
COUIN	30		Sent Car to Amiens with ~~men~~ for coal today, very large number this week & am sending in on Thursday & Friday & Saturday. Very hard frost. Outdoor work carried on. Making roads for horse lines but no flint available.	

Bulstwart L.Col R.A.M.C.
O.C. 94. Field Amb.

Confidential 140/1903   Volume XII

Dec. 1916

Vol 10

War Diary.

94th Field Ambulance.   31st Division

December 1916.

COMMITTEE FOR THE
MEDICAL HISTORY OF THE WAR
Date   31 JAN. 1917

WAR DIARY or INTELLIGENCE SUMMARY

94 Field Amb.

Army Form C. 2118.

Place	Date	Hour	Summary of Events and Information	Remarks and references to Appendices
COUIN	December 1916 1		Hard frost during night. Ordinary outdoor work being carried out. Saw D.A.D.M.S. re working the baths at COUIN party at ROSSIGNOL farm to be relieved by 95 Field Ambulance. Lieutenant & Col came	
COUIN	2		Freezing still. Went up to see Staff Captain 93 Bde to arrange some things. Work on Officers mess started, roof to be raised & windows put in. Sent two Cars to Amiens today with eye cases. I have had to send two cars daily with these cases instead of sending all one day. D.A.D.M.S. came round & inspected R.	
COUIN	3		Sunday. No work except routine. Services as follows. C of E at 10.am R.Cs at 8.3 Received orders to send an officer to relieve the M.O. of 18 D.L.I	

WAR DIARY or INTELLIGENCE SUMMARY

94 Field Ambulance

Place	Date 1916	Hour	Summary of Events and Information	Remarks and references to Appendices
			detailed Capt Walker for this duty. Lieut Blackmore admitted here with temperature. P.	
COIGN		4°	A.D.M.S. made an inspection today, he expressed himself pleased with the numerous improvements here. Clayton Disinfector in full working order doing all the blankets & clothing of the patients in Hospital. Officers Mess completed today. Weather now muggy with inclination to rain. Received orders from A.D.M.S. 31 div that under instructions from D.D.M.S. XIII Corps 50 men were to be sent to COIGNEUX for work at the main dressing station there. I wrote to A.D.M.S. asking if half this number could be sent as the large number of cases here kept all my men fully occupied. P.	
		5	Lieut Blackmore much better. Arranged with A.D.M.S. that he should be sent to the 7th Division and that on return ?	

WAR DIARY or INTELLIGENCE SUMMARY

94 Field Amb

Army Form C. 2118.

Place	Date 1916	Hour	Summary of Events and Information	Remarks and references to Appendices
COUIN	Decr	5	Lieut Lipsett Gill, the latter should be posted to 18 D.L.I relieving Capt Walls this bring my strength to 8 medical officers which is the war strength for field ambulances. P.	
COUIN		6	Pte TREADWELL was today presented with the ribbon of the Military Medal which he won for exceedingly good work on the 13 November continuing stretcher bearing after being wounded. The GOC 31 Divn distributed the ribbons. Lieut	
COUIN		6	Blackmore now quite fit marched discharged & left for 7th Divn. P.	
COUIN		7	Went to A.D.M.S office to see him on several matters. Capt Frew reported his arrival from leave today, he had been three days getting up from Havre and on going had been kept two days at the base. Capt Frew will take over wards for Lieut Blake when this officer goes on leave. P.	
COUIN		8	Capt Frew in bed with Influenza. Arranged with O.C. 93 Fld	

WAR DIARY or INTELLIGENCE SUMMARY

Army Form C. 2118.

94 Field Amb.

Place	Date December 1916	Hour	Summary of Events and Information	Remarks and references to Appendices
	8		Ambulance to exchange duties of horse So as to permit Lieut BLABER getting away on the 12th. Instructions endent to floring all the hutt lines — P.	
COUIN	9		Capt Frew Dinvel letter up to take over L Blaber's wards tomorrow. Received orders to send a qualified dispenser to Special Hospital Warley in relief of Pte Curran. Detailed Sgt Watson for this duty with instructions to proceed next day. P.	
COUIN	10		Received letter from O.C. Special Hospital Warley to say that all my men there had been sent for temporary duty to 49 C.C.S. Sent a D.M.S. as to whether I was now to send Sgt Watson & he said I should do so. Sgt Watson left at 2 pm on return & can I received verbal message to say Pte Curran had left for to 49 C.C.S. & that Sgt Watson was being retained there. Advised a D.M.S. of the — Usual Sunday service held all obligatory. P.	

WAR DIARY or INTELLIGENCE SUMMARY.

Army Form C. 2118.

Place	Date	Hour	Summary of Events and Information	Remarks and references to Appendices
COUIN	December 1916 11		Attended at A.D.M.S office as member of a medical Board with Capt FRASER on an officer for Commission. Capt J.H.C WALKER returned from leave of absence. LIEUT BLABER left on leave from 12th to 21st inclusive	
COUIN	12		Forwarded application for Capt Fraser for duty with the Expeditionary Force in Salonika, Mediterranean. Issued again fresh orders re fires in billets	
COUIN	13		Routine work carried out. Nothing to note	
COUIN	14		25 men who were working at 95 Field Ambulance returned to headquarters under instruction from A.D.M.S 31st Div.	

WAR DIARY
or
INTELLIGENCE SUMMARY.

Army Form C. 2118.

6

Place	Date December 1916	Hour	Summary of Events and Information	Remarks and references to Appendices
COUIN	15		Cap? J. UPPCOTT GILL reported his return to Headquarters on completion of temporary duty with the 31 Div.	
COUIN	16		Routine work. Cap? FRASER receives a wire to say his father was very ill. Applied for 42 days leave to go to Canada. Forwarded same to A. H. & D. for transmission to the D.M.S. 5 Army. R.	
COUIN	17		Sunday. Voluntary services held. Cap? J. UPPCOTT GILL proceeded under instructions for A.D.M.S. 31 Div. for duty with the 18. D. L. I. relieving Cap? H. WALES who returned to Headquarters.	
COUIN	18		Relieved the two men at the baths here and the 3 men 293 F.A. & the 4 men 295 F.A. at the baths at	

WAR DIARY
or
INTELLIGENCE SUMMARY.
(Erase heading not required.)

9 L? Field Amb.

Army Form C. 2118.

7

Place	Date 19 16	Hour	Summary of Events and Information	Remarks and references to Appendices
	Desyh		AUTHIE + ROSSIGNOL FARM respectively by hanging unfit men who were sent under instructions for A.D.M.S. 31st Div.	
COUIN		19	Sgt WATSON who had been detained at WARLOY reported his return last evening without any means or explanation. Received orders to detail the name of an officer who will when required proceed of duty at the Div School at BEAUQUESNE. Capt FREW detailed for this duty	
COUIN		20	Ordinary work being carried out. Sapper Pilling admitted very cyanosed and in bad condition diagnosis broncho-pneumonia. Put into special ward with special orderly	
COUIN		21	Sapper Pilling died 6. am this morning reported same. Lieut	

WAR DIARY or INTELLIGENCE SUMMARY

Army Form C. 2118.

Place	Date 1916	Hour	Summary of Events and Information	Remarks and references to Appendices
	December		BLABER wired that he was sick on leave & had applied E.W.D for extension	
COUIN	22		Routine work. Saw A.D.M.S 31 Div re Loving men working at COIGNEUX returned for xmas day. C' + Q M.S. GIBB forwarded to medical stores	
COUIN	23		Nothing to record.	
COUIN	24		Received intimation that Lt. BLABERS leave was extended to 29'inst. Cap FRAZER granted special leave of 6 weeks to go to CANADA for the 26' inst. As men had not returned for COIGNEUX Cau Holmes who wired for them to return at once & they returned at 8p.m. They are to rejoin 95 on afternoon of 26". Funeral ... services held	

WAR DIARY or INTELLIGENCE SUMMARY.

Army Form C. 2118.

Place	Date	Hour	Summary of Events and Information	Remarks and references to Appendices
COUIN	25		Xmas day. No work except [illegible]. Men dinner at 5.30. G.O.C. 3? Div [illegible] also A.D.M.S. Furlough leave for the 27? of 10 days. Application of 14 days to be sent to Corps. [illegible] is granted.	
COUIN	26		Handed over to Capt. McEWEN on going on 10 days leave. [illegible signature]	
COUIN	27		Inspected whole Camp. Gave orders for [illegible] boards on pathways to be lifted & re-laid. ME.	
COUIN	28		Two reinforcements arrived — one being attached to "D" section, the other to "C" section. ME.	

WAR DIARY or ~~INTELLIGENCE SUMMARY~~.

(Erase heading not required.) 94th Field Ambulance.

Army Form C. 2118.

10.

Place	Date December 1916	Hour	Summary of Events and Information	Remarks and references to Appendices
COUIN	29		Application of Capt. Weber R.A.M.C. for Special Leave has been granted provided this officer can be spared. Orders received from A.D.M.S. to detail one officer to proceed to 165th Brigade R.F.A. on the 1st Jan 1917 for temporary duty for 14 days. J.M.S.	
COUIN	30		Inspected whole camp. Usual work carried out. J.M.S.	
COUIN	31		Church Services were held at 11 a.m & 6 p.m. By orders of A.D.M.S. 1 N.C.O. & 24 men of this unit returned at 5 p.m. from 95th Field Ambulance at COIGNEUX. They return there on the morning of the 2nd Jan 1917. J.M.S.	

J. McEwen
Capt. R.A.M.C. S.R.
a/O.C. 94th Field Ambulance

Confidential 140/1943 Volume XIII

Jan. 1917

S

Vol XI

War Diary.

94th Field Ambulance, 31st Division

January. 1917.

COMMITTEE FOR THE
MEDICAL HISTORY OF THE WAR
Date 13 MAR. 1917

WAR DIARY or INTELLIGENCE SUMMARY

94th Field Ambulance

January 1917

Place	Date	Hour	Summary of Events and Information	Remarks
COUIN	1		The Corps Commander having desired that all work be suspended as far as possible on New Year's Day this was done. Capt. KING R.A.M.C.S.R. left for temporary duty with 165th Brigade R.F.A. Capt. FREW, who was detailed for this, was unable to go owing to being in bed with Influenza.	JME
COUIN	2		At 8 a.m. 1 N.C.O. & 24 O.Rs (who returned from COIGNEUX on the 31st Dec. 1916) left for that place. Inspected Camp.	JME
COUIN	3		Nothing to report.	JME
COUIN	4		Received notice of forthcoming move of 31st Division	JME
COUIN	5		Capt. WALES left on special leave of 14 days. Surgeon General SKINNER D.M.S. Fifth Army inspected Divisional Rest Station.	JME

WAR DIARY or INTELLIGENCE SUMMARY

Army Form C. 2118.

Place	Date January 1917	Hour	Summary of Events and Information	Remarks and references to Appendices
COVIN	5 (cont).		Lieut BLABER returned from leave of absence having been granted extension owing to personal illness. Received Operation Orders regarding the move in Rest Area. The 94th Field Ambulance will move into BRETEL.	McE McE
COVIN	6.		Visited BRETEL to arrange billets for officers & men. Had to go to GEZAINCOURT to find the Town Major.	McE
COVIN	7.		Returned from leave today. Capt. KING on leave relieved by Capt FREW returned to Headquarters today.	P
COVIN	8.		Received orders that the unit was to proceed to BEAUVAL instead of BRETEL. Capt McEWEN sent to arrange billets, reported Town Major did not know of the change. Reported to A.D.M.S. 31 Div. who gave me written orders re the change & location.	P

WAR DIARY
or
INTELLIGENCE SUMMARY.

Army Form C. 2118.

3.

(Erase heading not required.)

Instructions regarding War Diaries and Intelligence Summaries are contained in F. S. Regs., Part II. and the Staff Manual respectively. Title pages will be prepared in manuscript.

Place	Date 1917	Hour	Summary of Events and Information	Remarks and references to Appendices
COUIN	January 9		Sent Capt. McEWEN with written orders. Saw and arranged for the billets of the men. Had everything checked & transferred to 59th Field Ambulance who are to relieve us tomorrow. Issued instructions of the move.	
COUIN	10		Capt. McEWEN and main body with transport left today for BEAUVAL at 9-30. I remained with Lt. & D.M.S. A.H.A. JIBB to hand over. Handed over everything correct to O.C. 59th Field Ambulance & obtained receipt. Proceeded with Cars at 5 minute intervals to BEAUVAL. Men arrived at 5 p.m. all billets inspected. First orders issued and all necessary precautions taken to prevent an occurrence.	

WAR DIARY
or
INTELLIGENCE SUMMARY

Army Form C. 2118.

Place	Date January 1917	Hour	Summary of Events and Information	Remarks and references to Appendices
BEAUVAL	11		Under instructions of A.D.M.S. 31 Div Capt WALKER proceeded on temporary duty to 14 York & Lancs in relief of Capt BELAY who reports sick.	
BEAUVAL	12		A.D.M.S. came round today, he wishes me to have accommodation for 50 other ranks here, this was done by readjusting the billets. A Section detailed to take over charge.	
BEAUVAL	13		Received instructions from A.D.M.S. 31 Div that during the period of rest men are to be trained by Route Marches & lectures. Drew out programme of same. 50 men are to go daily to 95 F"? Amb for fatigues	

WAR DIARY or INTELLIGENCE SUMMARY

Army Form C. 2118.

Place	Date	Hour	Summary of Events and Information	Remarks and references to Appendices
BEAUVAL	14		~~[struck through]~~	
			P' HEATHFIELD detailed for duty with the Flying Corps at CANDAS proceeded there today and is struck off the strength. S.M. Campbell granted leave of absence to U.K. for the purpose of being married. Services held today as under C of E. 10.3.0 R.C. 9.am	
BEAUVAL	15		Route March under Cap' McEWEN. Sentence of 1 year J.H.L. passed on N° 60746 P' MIDDLETON R.A.M.C by a F.G.C.M. was today remitted by the Brig Gen Comm° 94th Inf B'de	
BEAUVAL	16		Route march and lecture by Cap' KING. LIEUT BLABER detailed under instruction for A.D.M.O	

WAR DIARY or INTELLIGENCE SUMMARY

Army Form C. 2118.

Place	Date	Hour	Summary of Events and Information	Remarks and references to Appendices
			31 Div. for duty temporarily with the 5 Army School of Instruction reported his departure thence today on relief of Capt. PO POOLEY granted leave. D-	
BEAUVAL	17		Routine work carried out. Route march daily. Nothing to report. D-	
BEAUVAL	18		Routine work. Nothing unusual to report. D-	
BEAUVAL	19		Under instructions of A.D.M.S. 31 Div. Holding party consisting 2 Sgt. BUXTON and 4 men have been sent to VACQUERIE to which place we are to move on leaving here about the 22nd Inst. D-	

WAR DIARY
or
INTELLIGENCE SUMMARY.

Army Form C. 2118.

Place	Date	Hour	Summary of Events and Information	Remarks and references to Appendices
BEAUVAL	20		Capt McEWEN proceeded to VACQUERIE to pay men there and also to take over & sent working party of 57 F.A. back to their unit. Orders received fr A-D-M-S to move on 22nd. D-	
BEAUVAL	21		Issued necessary instructions of move tomorrow. Sent all cases remaining to XIII Corps Rest Station. Checked and handed over all standing equipment to Officer ¼ S.M. Field Ambulance. D-	
BEAUVAL	22		Unit left at 10 a.m. & march to VACQUERIE. Lorry f blankets ordered f 8 o'clock had not arrived by 11 a.m. reported to A.D.M.S. Unit arrived Vacquerie & moved into billets. Issued fire notices and took all necessary precautions. D-	

WAR DIARY or INTELLIGENCE SUMMARY

Army Form C. 2118.

Place	Date 1917	Hour	Summary of Events and Information	Remarks and references to Appendices
VACQUERIE	23		Cap: Frew reports his arrival for temporary duty with 165 B'de R.F.A. on the 20. Cp: KING granted leave to U.K. 22 - 1 Feb. Work proceeded here making accounts of billets 250 other ranks. D.	
VACQUERIE	24		Routine work. New latrines constructed. Route march for men. D.	
VACQUERIE	25		Places now settled. Two buildings used for Hospital purposes. Officers ward of 4 beds settled. All arrangements settled. D.	
VACQUERIE	26		A.D.M.S. came round today and expressed himself pleased with the arrangements. Route march for men. Made out return of men who are willing to transfer to Railway units etc. D.	

WAR DIARY or INTELLIGENCE SUMMARY.

Army Form C. 2118.

94 Field Amb.

9

Place	Date	Hour	Summary of Events and Information	Remarks and references to Appendices
	January 1917			
VACQUERIE	27		Route march in morning. 3 carpenters detailed by A.D.M.S. 31 Div proceeded to Corps Rest station to build a Clayton Disinfecting hut for 95 Field Ambulance. Weather F.	
VACQUERIE	28		Divine service held. No other work except routine done. F.	
VACQUERIE	29		Route march. Parade at 10 a.m. for inspection. Lecture given by Capt McEWEN on Discipline	
VACQUERIE	30		Route march. Lecture by Capt WALES on Surgery & wound infection. F.	
VACQUERIE	31		Route march	(illegible) of 94 Field Amb

Confidential   140/1991   Volume XIV

Feb 1917

War Diary

94 Field Ambulance. 31st Division

February 1917.

COMMITTEE FOR THE
MEDICAL HISTORY OF THE WAR
Date   4 APR. 1917

WAR DIARY or **INTELLIGENCE SUMMARY**

Army Form C. 2118.

Place	Date February 1917	Hour	Summary of Events and Information	Remarks and references to Appendices
VACQUERIE	1st		Inspected all billets. Issued further orders as to fire precautions to be taken. Improvement work slow owing to lack of labour. Three Carpenters having been sent under instructions of A.D.M.S. 31st Div. to the XIII Corps Rest Station to erect a Clayton Hut Disinfector there.	
VACQUERIE	2		Inspection of all gas helmets held today.	Ayrshire L'Estrange R.
VACQUERIE	3		Lieut & Q.Mr A.H. GIBB granted leave to U.K. from 3/2/17 - 13/2/17. Lieut P.L. BLADER reports his arrival from 5th Army School of Instruction.	R.
VACQUERIE	4		Parade service held today. C of E 10-30 a.m. R.C. 8-15	R.

WAR DIARY or INTELLIGENCE SUMMARY

Army Form C. 2118.

Place	Date	Hour	Summary of Events and Information	Remarks and references to Appendices
VACQUERIE	5		Capt WALES proceeded to 12 KOYLI for temporary duty in relief of Capt FORBES proceeding on leave	
VACQUERIE	6		Capt T. McEWEN granted leave of absence to U.K. 6.2.17 - 16.2.17. Capt KING returned from leave on the 4th inst having been held up at BOULOGNE	
VACQUERIE	7		Received one reinforcement from 31 Div Train today. D. HOPPER whose character was very bad reported matter to A.D.M.S. 31 Div with request for a change to be made	
VACQUERIE	8		Three reinforcements received from train today	
VACQUERIE	9		Inspected unit today & made detail list of clothing to be obtained	

WAR DIARY or INTELLIGENCE SUMMARY

Army Form C. 2118.

Place	Date 1917	Hour	Summary of Events and Information	Remarks and references to Appendices
VACQUERIE	10		Nothing to report	
VACQUERIE	11		Divine Service C of E 10.30 am R Cs 10 - am	
VACQUERIE	12		With reference to my objection to S- HOPPER ASC, S. HEY was sent today to relieve him. Sgt ANDREWS ASC who had been evacuated to the Base returned today fr 29. C.C.S.	
VACQUERIE	13		One reinforcement received fr Base today	
VACQUERIE	14		Nothing to report	

WAR DIARY or INTELLIGENCE SUMMARY.

Army Form C. 2118.

Place	Date	Hour	Summary of Events and Information	Remarks and references to Appendices
VACQUERIE	February 1917 16		"B" Section chosen to represent the Ambulance in the forthcoming Corps competition to take place on the 22nd Feb. Capt McEWEN will command. Lt. Q. Martin R.H.A. field returned from leave to U.K. on 15 inst.	
VACQUERIE	17		Capt McEWEN reports his arrival from leave of absence. The ambulance has been chosen to represent the Division in the forthcoming Corps Competition. Major Ware D.A.D.M.S. inspects them today. Competition on the 19th Feb at BEAUVAL.	
VACQUERIE	18		Orders having been received that the Division will take over the 19th Div area at HEBUTERNE moving on 19th 20th & 21st. Went to LOUIN with A.D.M.S. to make arrangements. "B" Section left for BEAUVAL under Capt. K.M.F. Capt McEWEN to follow on morning of 19th.	

WAR DIARY or INTELLIGENCE SUMMARY

Army Form C. 2118.

Place	Date 1917	Hour	Summary of Events and Information	Remarks and references to Appendices
VACQUERIE	19		Cap McEWEN went to BEAUVAL. Evacuated all cases to Corps Rest Station. Capt FREW evacuated to Officers Hospital 29 C.C.S. today with gastritis. Made all arrangements for move tomorrow. Issued all necessary orders. One horse wagon to accompany 94 Inf Brigade tomorrow & two on the 20th.	
VACQUERIE	20		Paraded at 9 a.m. ready to move. Weather very wet. Moved off at 10.30 & proceeded via FIENVILLIERS – CANDAS – BEAUVAL road. Going very heavy especially just outside CANDAS. Unit arrived about 2.15 p.m. Capt McEWEN showed me billets & camp. Hot meal ready for men. Reported arrival to A.D.M.S. No sick to be treated here.	

WAR DIARY
or
INTELLIGENCE SUMMARY.

Army Form C. 2118.

94 Field Ambulance.

Place	Date 1917	Hour	Summary of Events and Information	Remarks and references to Appendices
BEAUVAL	February 21		"C" Section under the command of Capt McEWEN proceeded without transport to COUIN this morning with instructions to take over from 59 Field Ambulance. No other work done.	
BEAUVAL	22		Unit left under command of Capt KING for COUIN by road. After seeing all billets etc correct I left with ambulances, & arrived at COUIN at 11.30. I found Capt McEWEN had posted everyone. Went round with Lt Col MACKENZIE ROWE O.C. 59 Field Ambulance whilst Lt & Q. JIBB checked all stores being handed over. Unit outgoing left at 1.p.m. and the incoming arrived at 3.30 p.m. Capt KING reported that going had been very heavy in places but horses had done very well.	

WAR DIARY
or
INTELLIGENCE SUMMARY.
(Erase heading not required.)

Army Form C. 2118.

Instructions regarding War Diaries and Intelligence Summaries are contained in F. S. Regs., Part II. and the Staff Manual respectively. Title pages will be prepared in manuscript.

Place	Date February 1917	Hour	Summary of Events and Information	Remarks and references to Appendices
COUIN	23		Made inspection of buildings etc. Found dirty. Fatigue parties to clean up everywhere. Issued necessary fire precautions. R	
COUIN	24		Rearranged bath house making dressing & undressing rooms with clean clothing store at one end. Scabies cases and the fever bathed in separate building. All cases and the bathed & given clean change as soon as possible after admission. R	
COUIN	25		Church service arranged but no parade. Fatigues in morning free after dinner. Capt FREW returned from Officers Hospital GEZAINCOURT. R	
COUIN	26		New dining tent for personnel erected & in use. New NISSEN hut has been fitted with lavatories & orderlies	

WAR DIARY or INTELLIGENCE SUMMARY

Place	Date 1917	Hour	Summary of Events and Information	Remarks and references to Appendices
			bunk at one end. Paths have been settled. I am going to erect marquees when time & men available.	
COVIN	27		Capt. WALKER posted permanently to 14th F.A. in as struck off the strength of the unit of this date.	
COVIN	28		Work on marquees commenced. Work on other parts progressing satisfactorily; nothing further to report.	

Dunkerwart
L. be Kaine
O.C. 94 Field Amb.

Confidential
Mar 1917

140/2042   Volume XV

Vol 13

War Diary.

94th Field Ambulance.   31st Division

March 1917.

COMMITTEE FOR THE
MEDICAL HISTORY OF THE WAR
Date 11 MAY 1917

WAR DIARY or INTELLIGENCE SUMMARY.

Army Form C. 2118.

Instructions regarding War Diaries and Intelligence Summaries are contained in F. S. Regs., Part II. and the Staff Manual respectively. Title pages will be prepared in manuscript.

(Erase heading not required.)

Place	Date March 1917	Hour	Summary of Events and Information	Remarks and references to Appendices
COUIN	1		Routine work. Received orders to send one officer at once to report to O.C. 4 C.C.S. Capt FREW detailed for this duty. Excellent road.	
COUIN	2		Went to A.D.M.S on duty. Received orders to send 1 bearer subdivision & one officer to take over A.D.S. N. HEBUTERNE of 93 F.A. Capt KING and A sect bearers detailed & left at 3-30. Inspected all before leaving.	
COUIN	3		Nothing doing. Routine work handicapped by shortage of men.	
COUIN	4		Divine Services held as usual.	

WAR DIARY or **INTELLIGENCE SUMMARY.**

Army Form C. 2118.

Place	Date	Hour	Summary of Events and Information	Remarks and references to Appendices
	March 1917			
COUIN	5		Routine work. Went to A.D.M.O. Office to board with Lt. BLABER 'A' Section bearers returning having handed over to 95 F.A.	
COUIN	6		Capt KING unable to return with bearers on account of having fever. Came down in lorry with temperature & all appearance of Influenza.	
COUIN	7		Went to A.D.M.O. Office with Capt McEWEN as member of medical board. D.D.M.O. VI Corps telephoned, detailing one tent SubDiv to remain at COUIN & the remainder to proceed to P.17.t.12. Corps Main Dressing Station & take over there being	

WAR DIARY
or
INTELLIGENCE SUMMARY.

Army Form C. 2118.

94 Field Amb.

3.

Place	Date 1917	Hour	Summary of Events and Information	Remarks and references to Appendices
P.			Joined there by 2 tent sub Divisions of an Ambulance T Div. Move to take place as soon as possible. I was detailed to command. Went at once to D.D. ms X Corps for instructions, received same. Capt KING in bed with Influenza. Issued all orders A & B Sections to move with me C Section under Capt WALES to run ~~down~~ Rest Station COUIN. P.	
COUIN	8.		Went to Corps main Dressing Station & took over. Lt. & Q.M. JIBB accompanied me. Left him in charge as Ambulance not moving until tomorrow. Returned to COUIN P.	

WAR DIARY
or
INTELLIGENCE SUMMARY

Army Form C. 2118.

(Erase heading not required.)

Place	Date	Hour	Summary of Events and Information	Remarks and references to Appendices
P 17 L 19	March 1917	9	Proceeded this morning to ? Corps Dressing Station & took over command. Capt. McEWEN to hand over. Capts. MACKIE & BUCKLEY & Lts. STORDY & BALL reported their arrival with two tent subdivisions 2/5 F.A. Capt. McEWEN arrived about 1-30. Detailed all duties. Reported arrival A.D.M.S.	
"		10	Inspected everything & detailed work. Capt. WALES posted to command C Section. Capt. ALEXANDER posted as reinforcement & take in charge.	
"		11	Went to O.D.M.S. V Corps for further instructions. Marquees require repitching. Latrine accommodation inadequate. Pit system to be started.	

WAR DIARY
or
INTELLIGENCE SUMMARY.
(Erase heading not required)

Army Form C. 2118.

Place	Date	Hour	Summary of Events and Information	Remarks and references to Appendices
P.17b	March 1917	12.	Started work on first room Maquiers. Ground very wet after thaw. Officers latrine built. S.	
"		13.	Went over to COUIN on duty. Routine work here. S.	
"		14.	Attack made last night. Casualties this time very few. D.A.D.M.S. V Corps came round. S.	
"		15.	D.D.M.S. V Corps came round. Under instructions for him went as far as SERRE + selected site for proposed Main Dressing Station. Wrote report on same. Received instructions that the Division was to proceed to 2 Army & to be in the ~~Corps~~ T BOUQUEMAISON	

WAR DIARY
or
INTELLIGENCE SUMMARY
(Erase heading not required.)

Army Form C. 2118.

Place	Date	Hour	Summary of Events and Information	Remarks and references to Appendices
P.176 +9	March 1917		area by 20" inst. Capt KING returns to 124 Yorks for temporary duty vice Capt WALKER sent L.C.O. with Measles.	
		6.30	received orders that we were the 3 rendering to move in 4 hours. G.S. & L.S. wagons packed and all preparations made. R.	
"		16	Went to COUIN made necessary preparation there & issued orders. Saw Adams. Later received orders that the move to 2nd Army was postponed, starting probably on 18th. R.	
"		17	Routine work. all necessary arrangements made for coming tomorrow. R.	
"		18	Handed over to 21 F.A. and unit moved by	

WAR DIARY or INTELLIGENCE SUMMARY.

Army Form C. 2118.

Place	Date	Hour	Summary of Events and Information	Remarks and references to Appendices
P.17b			road to COUIN.	
ORVILLE	19	19°	Handed over the Divisional Rest Station and unit moved out and marched to ORVILLE	
ORVILLE	20	20°	Collected all cars in area (92 B") and proceeded with cars to next camp at BEAUVOIR. Capt McEWEN accompd brought up rear. Capt Walker proceeded in advance to get billets.	
BEAUVOIR	21		Marched to BLANGERMONT. Roads very bad. One horse had to be shot. Shut down at intervals.	
BLANGERMONT	22		Marched to PRESSY-LES-PERNES here we remain	

WAR DIARY or INTELLIGENCE SUMMARY.

Army Form C. 2118.

Place	Date	Hour	Summary of Events and Information	Remarks and references to Appendices
PRESSY LES PERNES			two days. R.	
	23		Resting R	
"	24		Moved to FLECHINELLE. Have all the men were able to have a much needed bath.	
FLECHINELLE	25		Moved to Robecq where we went into billets previously occupied by us last October. Opened temporary wards 'C' Section in charge	
ROBECQ	26		Capt KING returned for duty at 14 Yorks Capt Walker being returned to C.C.S.	
"	27		Routine work. All wagons being cleaned.	
"	28		Sections checking equipment all indents for replenish	

WAR DIARY or INTELLIGENCE SUMMARY

Army Form C. 2118.

Place	Date	Hour	Summary of Events and Information	Remarks and references to Appendices
ROBECQ	29		Strength 20". Continue work. Granted leave to 9th April. Handed over to Capt. McEWEN	
ROBECQ	30		Another Volume. Section equipment fully checked & indents for replacements made out. Received secret communication re disposal of stores in the event of move of Division. Went to see A.D.M.S. concerning certain matters. ME.	
ROBECQ	31		Inspected all billets & transport lines. Capt. D.T. FRASER M.C. having been reported by a Medical Board in Canada as unfit for duty, is struck off the strength of this unit from 7th Feb 1917.	J.B. McEwan Capt. R.A.M.C. S.R. O.C. 94th Field Amb.

Confidential 140/2086 Volume XVI

Vol 14

War Diary.

94th. Field Ambulance 31st. Division

April 1917.

COMMITTEE FOR THE
MEDICAL HISTORY OF THE WAR
Date −6 JUN. 1917

WAR DIARY of INTELLIGENCE SUMMARY

Army Form C. 2118.

(Erase heading not required.) 94th Field Ambulance

Place	Date	Hour	Summary of Events and Information	Remarks and references to Appendices
	April 1917			
ROBECQ	1		Church Services held for C. of E. men & Roman Catholics	
ROBECQ	2		Went with A.D.M.S. to the New Area visiting the Main Dressing Station at LES QUATRES VENTS on road from ARRAS to BRUAY & obtained information with regard to Advanced Dressing Stations & mode of evacuation of wounded. Received D.D.M.S. XIII Corps No. 549/3 Medical Arrangements XIII Corps Operations No. 5.	
ROBECQ	3		Inspected all billets & horse lines etc. The men sent on a Route march.	
ROBECQ	4		The cleaning of the wagons completed, & equipment being arranged for the Tent Subdivision which is moving with the Bearer Division.	

WAR DIARY or INTELLIGENCE SUMMARY

Army Form C. 2118.

94th Field Ambulance

Place	Date	Hour	Summary of Events and Information	Remarks and references to Appendices
ROBECQ	April 1917 5		The unit went for a route march. Attended meeting of O.C.'s ambulances & Medical Officers of regiments at A.D.M.S.'s office. Received D.D.M.S. XIII Corps No 549/11 Medical Arrangements XIII Corps Operations No 6.	
ROBECQ	6		Received movement orders of 92nd Inf. Brigade No 112 re impending move. 13 reinforcements arrived today. "B" section wagons packed ready to move with Busnes Division. Lt. Col. STEWART returned from leave this evening.	
"	7		Returned from leave yesterday having been recalled by Div. Went to A.D.M.S. with reference to move. All completed await necessary orders.	

WAR DIARY
or
INTELLIGENCE SUMMARY.

Army Form C. 2118.

Instructions regarding War Diaries and Intelligence Summaries are contained in F. S. Regs., Part II. and the Staff Manual respectively. Title pages will be prepared in manuscript.

(Erase heading not required.)

Place	Date April 1917	Hour	Summary of Events and Information	Remarks and references to Appendices
ALLOUAGNE	8		Left ROBECQ this morning & proceeded by road to ALLOUAGNE. Cap. FREW proceeded in front to arrange billets. On arrival units went into billets. We are under four hours notice to move.	
"	9		Inspected billets, all correct.	
"	10		Wagons all cleaned and settled. Nothing to report. Received orders to move to BRUAY tomorrow.	
BRUAY	11		Moved to BRUAY. Cap. KING went on as billeting officer. Snow came down heavily all day. Billets very dirty.	
"	12		Raining & blowing hard. Nothing to report.	
"	13		Weather better, wagons all cleaned & greased.	
"	14		Moved to OURTON today, short march, trouble about billets, close billets for officers.	

WAR DIARY or INTELLIGENCE SUMMARY

Army Form C. 2118.

Instructions regarding War Diaries and Intelligence Summaries are contained in F. S. Regs., Part II. and the Staff Manual respectively. Title pages will be prepared in manuscript.

Place	Date April 1917	Hour	Summary of Events and Information	Remarks and references to Appendices
OURTON		15	Wagons all cleaned & routine work	
"		16	Capt Frew left this evening for duty with the XIII Corps Heavy Siege park.	
"		17	Nothing to report	
"		18	All motor vehicles have now been handed over to the 5" Div & we have received in exchange Daimlers & Fords. Motor cycles not yet changed. Sgt Elliot, Cpl Roberts & L/Cpl Chandler returned with three cars for duty with this unit.	
"		19	Nothing to report	
"		20	Wagons have all been repainted & have repaired. Water Carts inspected & one condemned by Ordnance Officer. Capt Frew & Lt BLABER reported their return for duty	

WAR DIARY or INTELLIGENCE SUMMARY

Army Form C. 2118.

Place	Date	Hour	Summary of Events and Information	Remarks and references to Appendices
	April 1917			
		7	duty with 11 E. Yorks & 13 E Yorks respectively	
OURTON	21		Nothing to report	
"	22		Divine Services held today. C of E at 9.45 am R.Co at 10.30 am Non Conf at 10.15 am Capt King reported his departure to Headquarters XIII Corps for instruction as D.A.D.V.S. On our arrival Andrews 31 Div Two draculier + one Ford proceeded to duty with 63. R.N. Div.	
"	23		Routine work. Nothing to report	
"	24		Nothing to report. Went to GUESTREVILLE to look for billets	
"	25		Moved to GUESTREVILLE today. Moved completed without difficulty. Billets satisfactory but dirty.	

WAR DIARY or **INTELLIGENCE SUMMARY.**

Army Form C. 2118.

Place	Date April 1917	Hour	Summary of Events and Information	Remarks and references to Appendices
GUESTREVILLE	27		Cleaning billets etc. Wagons overhauled. S.	
"	28		Nothing to report S.	
"	29		Received orders to move into line & to go to ANZIN. Went with D.A.D.M.S to ARRAS and ANZIN to see & issued necessary orders for move S.	
"	30		Paraded at 8 a.m. & left at once. Marched to ACQ where we arrived at 11. Waited here while men had meal & horses watered. Reached ANZIN at 2 p.m. Field ambulance not being ready tomorrow Quarter Tent. Cpt THOMPSON had arranged for billets. Place very dirty.	

Signed Lt Col
O.C. 94th Fld Amb

B.E.F.

SUMMARY OF MEDICAL WAR DIARIES FOR 94th F.A. 31st Divn. 13th Corps.
1st Army.
3rd Army from 11/4/17.

WESTERN FRONT. April_May. '17.

O.C. Lt. Col. H. Stewart.

SUMMARISED UNDER THE FOLLOWING HEADINGS.
Phase "B" Battle of Arras- April- May. 1917.

1st Period Attack on Vimy Ridge April.

2nd Period Capture of Siegfried Line May.

B.E.F.

94th F.A. 31st Divn. 13th Corps.   WESTERN FRONT.

O.C. Lt. Col. H. Stewart.   April. '17.

1st Army.

3rd Army from 11/4/17.

Phase "B" Battle of Arras April- May. 1917.

1st Period Attack on Vimy Ridge April.

1917.

April. 8th.   Headquarters. at Robecq.
11th.   Moves: To Allouagne.
                "   To Bruay.
              Transfer. 3rd Army.

1.

B.E.F.

94th F.A. 31st Divn. 13th Corps.   WESTERN FRONT.

O.C. Lt. Col. H. Stewart.   April. '17.

3rd Army.

Phase "B" Battle of Arras- April- May. 1917.
1st Period Attack on Vimy Ridge April.

1917.

April. 11th.   Transfer. 3rd Army.

14th.   Moves: To Ourton.

18th.   Transport. All motor vehicles handed over to 5th Divn. Daimlers and Fords being received in exchange.

22nd.   Two Daimlers and 1 Ford proceeded for duty with 63rd R.N. Divn.

25th.   Moves: To Guestreville.

30th.   " To Anzin.

94th F.A. 31st Divn. 13th Corps.　　　WESTERN FRONT.

O.C. Lt. Col. H. Stewart.　　　April. '17.

3rd Army.

Phase "B" Battle of Arras - April - May. 1917.
1st Period Attack on Vimy Ridge April.

1917.

April. 11th　Transfer. 3rd Army.

14th.　Moves: To Ourton.

18th.　Transport. All motor vehicles handed over to 5th Divn. Daimlers and Fords being received in exchange.

22nd.　Two Daimlers and 1 Ford proceeded for duty with 63rd R.N. Divn.

25th.　Moves: To Guestreville.

30th.　"　To Anzin.

B.E.F.

94th F.A. 31st Divn. 13th Corps.　　WESTERN FRONT.

O.C. Lt. Col. H. Stewart.　　April. '17.

1st Army.

3rd Army from 11/4/17.

Phase "B" Battle of Arras April- May. 1917.

1st Period Attack on Vimy Ridge April.

1917.

Headquarters. at Robecq.

April. 8th.　Moves: To Allouagne.
11th.　　"　To Brusy.

Transfer. 3rd Army.

1.

Confidential Volume XVII

May.97 14 140/2200 Vol 15

S War Diary

94th Field Ambulance 31st Division

May 1917.

COMMITTEE FOR THE
MEDICAL HISTORY OF THE WAR
Date -7 AUG. 1917

WAR DIARY
or
INTELLIGENCE SUMMARY

Army Form C. 2118.

Place	Date	Hour	Summary of Events and Information	Remarks and references to Appendices
ANZIN	May 1917 1st		Field Ambulance, the 63 Div left this morning. Cap KING & Lt GATT with bearers Division proceeded to the line, they are to work under the direction of the O.C. 93 F.A. who is responsible for the front line evacuations. I went up to the A.D.S. and with Lt Col POLLARD went over the evacuation line of the Right sector i.e. the GAVRELLE Sector and went to the Bearer Collecting Post situated in Gunpits still housing two german Howitzers. Cap KING is to work the R' sector & Lt GATT the left.	
ANZIN	2nd		Went to A.D.M.S. office today. Received orders that the attack will take place tomorrow morning at 4.30 a.m. The A.D.M.S. considered & advised that I should take over complete charge of the evacuation Rt sector. I therefore moved my advanced headquarters to the Gunpits H.4.b.55. & took with me further 8 bearers and 1 small tent subdivision under the command of Cap WALES. Capt McEWEN was left in charge at ANZIN. 30 tent subdivision under CAPT THOMPSON proceeded to the main Dressing Station at St CATHERINE. On arrival at Gunpits I made all necessary arrangements with Capt KING & arranged for the ambulances to take up positions. Cap KING & Lt GATT to remain at Gunpits for night & leave at 4 a.m. tomorrow morning for line	Sheet 51 B N.W

WAR DIARY or INTELLIGENCE SUMMARY

Army Form C. 2118.

Place	Date 1917	Hour	Summary of Events and Information	Remarks and references to Appendices
H.4.b.5.5.	May 3		Capt KING & Lt GATT & bearers went up at appointed hour. Wounded come in slowly at 11 am. Received report fm Capt KING asking for more bearers, sent last reserve so sent urgent message to A.D.M.S 31 Div asking for 30 additional bearers, these were sent up in cars & arrived by 2 pm. Wounded coming in fairly regularly. At 5 pm Capt KING reported aid post clear. Lt GATT at 7 pm reported all clear. Capt KING was in touch with the 16th West Yorks which Lt GATT kept in touch with the 15th & 18th W Yorks. At 10.30 pm received message fm A.D.M.S 31 Div saying 15th W Yorks had many casualties. This was dated 4 pm. A.D.M.S could give no location or numbers. He asked me to send 20 bearers & M.O. if possible to their aid. At this time as I had no reserve bearers and as I knew that Lt GATT was with the 15 WEST YORKS who were clear at 7 pm I could not send up any more as reported same to A.D.M.S by special messenger. Night very quiet. R.	Sheet 51B N.W
H.4.b.5.5.	4		Things very quiet, went to see A.D.M.S. nothing further to report. Capt KING & Lt GATT returned & 30 bearers were rested in reserve. R.	

WAR DIARY or INTELLIGENCE SUMMARY

Army Form C. 2118.

Place	Date 1917	Hour	Summary of Events and Information	Remarks and references to Appendices
H4b55	May 5		Bearers for 95 Field Ambulance returned to their unit. Everything quiet, nothing particular to do. Went round all the R.A.Ps. P'HACK was killed this morning in the trenches whilst watching to carry in a wounded man. Body sent to 95 F.A. for burial. Received instructions from ADMS. I returned with my headquarters to ANZIN leaving Capt KING in charge of the evacuation R' Sector with bearer Division & 3 ambulances.	Sheet 51 B N.W
"	6		Divine Service held today. Had to go to A-D-M-S O for further orders. He wishes me to relieve 93 F.A at the A.D.S on the 9th. P'HACK buried today.	
ANZIN	7		Orders Changed. I am to remain at ANZIN & treat sick & work the evacuation R' Sector. 93 F.A working the left. Nothing to report.	
"	8		Ordinary routine work today. Nothing to report.	
"	9		Went up to GUN PITTS today. Everything correct & working satisfactorily. Capt KING reported all well.	

WAR DIARY or ~~INTELLIGENCE SUMMARY~~

Army Form C. 2118.

(Erase heading not required) 94 Field Amb

Instructions regarding War Diaries and Intelligence Summaries are contained in F. S. Regs., Part II. and the Staff Manual respectively. Title pages will be prepared in manuscript.

Place	Date	Hour	Summary of Events and Information	Remarks and references to Appendices
ANZIN	10th		Have constructed a new pit latrine with flap top as per Army model. Inspected everywhere. A.D.M.O came round and I suggested that we should get accommodation & hut sick here, he agreed to ask the Corps.	
ANZIN	11		Nothing to report. Sgn Major has given me an extra billet to be used if sick if necessary.	
ANZIN	12		Lieut S. COUPER R.A.M.C posted to the Ambulance today for duty & taken on the strength.	
ANZIN	13.		Moved officers mess. Changed cookery arrangements, drew two Marquees from F.III Corps Main Station for use of sick and had them erected. Relieved 30 bearers in the line. Evacuation to hospital.	

WAR DIARY or INTELLIGENCE SUMMARY.

Army Form C. 2118.

Place	Date	Hour	Summary of Events and Information	Remarks and references to Appendices
ANZIN	14		Nothing to report.	
ANZIN	15		A.D.M.S. Came round today.	
ANZIN	16		Went up to Gunpits today. Everything satisfactory. Made necessary arrangements with Capt KING re Medical Arrangements for forthcoming Small Show.	
ANZIN	17		30 bearers sent up as reinforcements to Capt KING for forthcoming attack this evening.	
ANZIN	18		Nothing to report.	
ANZIN	19		Received orders that unit was to move on the 21st to CAMBLIGNEUL. Went over with Col POLLARD and saw the C.O. of ambulance 2/63 Div who are relieving us and also saw the billets we were to occupy.	

WAR DIARY or INTELLIGENCE SUMMARY.

Army Form C. 2118.

Place	Date	Hour	Summary of Events and Information	Remarks and references to Appendices
ANZIN		20	Difficulty having arisen as to Billets at Camblignuel owing to the Officers billets at present held by No 1 Field Ambulance being taken by the A.D.M.S. 31 Div I went over with Orders. O D. and arranged for billets for officers elsewhere. The bearers under Capt. KING were relieved at 6 pm this evening and returned to Headquarters. The ambulances also returned	
ANZIN		21	Paraded at 8 am & marched at that hour. Capt. McEWEN and 6 men were left behind to clean up and hand over. Capt THOMPSON & 4 O.R. left yesterday evening to CAMBLIGNEUL to take over from No 1 F.A. thence. Arrived at CAMBLIGNEUL at 11-30 am after good march. Orders are that the unit is to remain packed. G.	
No 1 CAMBLIGNEUL		22	Inspected all billets. Made arrangements of parades etc daily. Billets clean. G.	
CAMBLIGNEUL		23	Nothing to report. L. & Q. mess AHA TIBB from have C U R on Special parade.	

WAR DIARY or INTELLIGENCE SUMMARY.

Army Form C. 2118.

Place	Date	Hour	Summary of Events and Information	Remarks and references to Appendices
CAMBLIGNEUL	24		Capt KING proceeded to D.D.M.S. XIII Corps for duty. Lt GATT proceeded in relief of Capt FREW to MARDEUIL an M.O. 1/c Amm Siege Park.	
CAMBLIGNEUL	25		Nothing to report.	
CAMBLIGNEUL	26		Received order that Capt J.A.R. THOMPSON R.A.M.C. was to hold himself in readiness to proceed to the C.R.E. for duty as M.O. 1/c R.E. for the Li Gunne, in relief of Capt JOHNSON R.A.M.C.	
CAMBLIGNEUL	27		Nothing to report	
CAMBLIGNEUL	28		Capt FREW granted leave to U-K for the 29th inst and reports his departure today.	
CAMBLIGNEUL	29		Nothing to report	
CAMBLIGNEUL	31		Nothing to report	

B.E.F.

SUMMARY OF MEDICAL WAR DIARIES FOR 94th F.A. 31st Divn. 13th Corps.
1st Army.
3rd Army from 11/4/17.

WESTERN FRONT. April-May. '17.

O.C. Lt. Col. H. Stewart.

SUMMARISED UNDER THE FOLLOWING HEADINGS.
Phase "B" Battle of Arras- April- May. 1917.

1st Period Attack on Vimy Ridge April.

2nd Period Capture of Siegfried Line May.

B.E.F.

94th F.A. 31st Divn. 13th Corps.   WESTERN FRONT.
O.C. Lt. Col. H. Stewart.   May. '17.
3rd Army.

Phase "B" Battle of Arras April- May. 1917.
2nd Period Capture of Siegfried Line May.

1917.

May.1st. Medical Arrangements: Br. Divn. proceeded to the line working under direction O.C. 93rd Field Ambulance.
"R" Section- Gavrelle.
Coll. Post in gunpits still housing 2 German Howitzers.

2nd. Advanced Headquarters- gunpits H.4.b.5.5. (Sheet 51B N.W.) with small tent sub- Divn.
M.D.S. at St. Catherine.

3rd. Operations: Attack at 4.30. a.m.
Casualties. wounded came in slowly at 11 a.m.
Urgent message for 30 additional Brs.-these sent up in cars by 2.p.m.- wounded coming in fairly regularly At 5. p.m. A.P. clear.

5th. Casualties R.A.M.C. O and 1 killed.
Moves: Returned to Anzin.

21st. 94th Field Ambulance relieved by Ambulance of 63rd Divn. and moved to Cambligneul. Sheet 36B. W.15.c.2.5.-

B.E.F.

<u>94th F.A. 31st Divn. 13th Corps.</u>   <u>WESTERN FRONT.</u>
<u>O.C. Lt. Col. H. Stewart.</u>   May. '17.
<u>3rd Army.</u>

<u>Phase "B" Battle of Arras April- May. 1917.</u>
<u>2nd Period Capture of Siegfried Line May.</u>

1917.

May.1st. <u>Medical Arrangements:</u> Br. Divn. proceeded to the line
working under direction O.C. 93rd Field Ambulance.
"R" Section- Gavrelle.
Coll. Post in gunpits still housing 2 German Howitzers.

2nd. Advanced Headquarters- gunpits H.4.b.5.5. (Sheet 51B N.W.)
with small tent sub- Divn.
M.D.S. at St. Catherine.

3rd. <u>Operations:</u> Attack at 4.30. a.m.
<u>Casualties.</u> wounded came in slowly at 11 a.m.
Urgent message for 30 additional Brs.- these sent up
in cars by 2.p.m.- wounded coming in fairly regularly
At 5. p.m. A.P. clear.

5th. <u>Casualties R.A.M.C.</u> O and 1 killed.
<u>Move:</u> Returned to Anzin.

21st. 94th Field Ambulance relieved by Ambulance of 63rd Divn.
and moved to Cambligneul. Sheet 36b. W.15.c.2.5.-

Confidential   Volume XVIII

June 1917.   140/2230   Vol 16

War Diary.

94th Field Ambulance 31st Division

June 1917.

COMMITTEE FOR THE
MEDICAL HISTORY OF THE WAR
Date -7 AUG. 1917

WAR DIARY or INTELLIGENCE SUMMARY.

Army Form C. 2118.

Place	Date	Hour	Summary of Events and Information	Remarks and references to Appendices
CAMBLIGNEUL	1st 1917		Routine work carried out and training of men. Route march in afternoon.	
"	2.		Lectures to men on work. Capt. J.A THOMPSON. R.A.M.C having been posted as M.O. to 31 Div R.E. left today and is struck off the strength of the unit.	
"	3.		Divine Services as follows C. of E. 9.30 parade 9.15. Lt. & Qmaster N.H.A. JIBB returned from leave, absence to the United Kingdom today.	
"	4.		Nothing to report. Capt WALES appointed Town Major from today.	
"	5.		Under instructions from Divisional Headquarters Pt. MADDOCKS who has acted as trader to the Divisional Train returned to the unit today having been replaced by a permanent labour man.	
"	6.		Capt WALES having been granted leave to the U.K from 7 to 17 left today. He handed over the duties of Town Major to Capt SUTTON 95 Field Ambulance. Capt M.B KING. M.C R.A.M.C granted a bar to his Military Cross.	

WAR DIARY or INTELLIGENCE SUMMARY

Army Form C. 2118.

Place	Date 1917	Hour	Summary of Events and Information	Remarks and references to Appendices
CAMBLIGNEUL	6		N° T/4/64351 S. THOMPSON. A.S.C. & N° 60545 S. DREWITT. R.A.M.C. proceeded [on] furlough of 14 days to 1st Army Rest Camp. R.	
"	7		Nothing to report. R.	
"	8		Cap' HALLAM. R.A.M.C. posted for duty vice Cap' THOMPSON arrived & taken on the strength of the unit of to-days date. R.	
"	9		Received orders that the 31st Div was to take over the line from the 63rd Div on the 10/11 June. The ambulance is to be responsible for the evacuations from the left sector with the A.D.S. on the BAILLEUL Road, H.1.C.3.8. and the collecting post situated at B.29.a.2.8. from the 2nd R.N. Div Field Amb. this to take over on the afternoon of the 10th June. The remainder of ambulance to move to ANZIN-ST-AUBIN on Monday 11 June. Cap' FREW returns from leave. R.	Reference map 51 B N.W. 1:20,000
"	10		Went over to ANZIN and arranged with Town Major there for necessary accommodation. Bearers & tent subdivision of B Section under the Command of Cap' McEWEN with Cap' FREW	

WAR DIARY or INTELLIGENCE SUMMARY

Army Form C. 2118.

Place	Date	Hour	Summary of Events and Information	Remarks and references to Appendices
CAMBLIGNEUL			& Capt HALLAM were to have left in busses at 2 p.m. today. No busses arrived at this hour, waited until 2.30 p.m. & reported to A.D.M.S. Div Headquarters reported that the lorries had fight to seek them but that they were now coming, busses eventually arrived at 5.30 p.m. & party got away.	
ANZIN	11		Pouring wet day. Bn Paraded at 6.30 am left by route everyone wet through before arriving at 9.30 am. Went into assigned billets. Rain stopped about 12 noon & a fine afternoon resulted. We are to remain closed until further orders.	
"	12		Went up to A.D.S. today. Capt McEWEN reported that everything was very quiet in the line and casualties very few. Preparations being made for Divisional Horse Show which is to take place on the 18 inst. The ambulances entraining Ambulances & Water Cart Complete.	
"	13		Nothing to report.	

WAR DIARY or INTELLIGENCE SUMMARY

Army Form C. 2118.

Place	Date	Hour	Summary of Events and Information	Remarks and references to Appendices
ANZIN	15		Rearranged the Sections today forming Headquarter section & bearers, B Tent sub-div & bearers, C Tent sub-div & bearers. A Senior N.C.O. being placed in charge of the various departments of the Ambulance, & all employed men being placed in Headquarter Section instead of being distributed among the other sections. This will I consider work for greater efficiency in every way & is necessary owing to the reduction of officers.	
"	16.		No 69436 P. CROWDER sent to 62 Sanitary Section today	
"	17		Divine Services today as follows:- R.C. at 9.30 am. C.of E. at 11.30 am.	
"	18.		Under instructions of Officer i/c A.S.C. section Pte No T4/058906 Driver Service TYSON. B. is promoted to the rank of Corporal and posted to 31 Div Train as a replacement demanded for OC 31 Div Train today.	
"	19.		Capt BROWN late M.O. of 16.G.B. R.F.A. being become surplus	

WAR DIARY or INTELLIGENCE SUMMARY

Army Form C. 2118.

Place	Date	Hour	Summary of Events and Information	Remarks and references to Appendices
	1917		Owing to the breaking up of 16.9 B⁰ was posted to me for duty today. N⁰ 60751 Sgt HADDEN & N⁰ 61727 P. SHAW proceeded for 14 days to 1ˢᵗ Army Rest Camp. Received orders that the Ambulance was to take over the XIII Corps Rest Camp at ECOIVRES on the 21ˢᵗ inst.	
ANZIN	20		Went over to ECOIVRES to make arrangements re moving and took over at 2 p.m. today. Capt WALES & 'C' section to run the place until arrival of unit to take over.	
ECOIVRES	21		Marched to ECOIVRES today and took over 6ᵗʰ Field Ambulance left at 8 a.m. today. Wet day. Not much the lines.	
"	22		The Rest station which had been closed reopened today about 100 cases transferred of the 3 Division. Inspected everything. Issued instructions as to work to be carried out.	
"	23		Inspection today. 7 reinforcements arrived & taken on the strength. D.D.M.S. XIII Corps came round. He wishes me to go with D.A.D.M.S to MINGOVAL on Tuesday & see new site of the Rest Station there	

WAR DIARY or INTELLIGENCE SUMMARY

Army Form C. 2118.

Place	Date 1917	Hour	Summary of Events and Information	Remarks and references to Appendices
			it is proposed to build a new one with Hutted Nissen Huts	
ECOIVRES		24	Sunday, C of E service for men & patients at 10.30 a.m. Non C of E service at 6 p.m. Inspected whole camp	
"		25	Nothing to report. Routine work.	
"		26	T6/7906 Farrier Corpnl HARRISON transferred to 31 Div Train. T5/9613 A/Farrier Cpl QUINLAN transferred from 31 Div Train	
"		27	Routine work. Received A Forms 31 Div Operation Orders No 20 relating to the forthcoming operations. Details "B" + "C" became to be in readiness to proceed if required. Went over to A Forms with reference to leave to Capt McEWEN leave granted from 2nd July to 12th July inclusive. Capt BROWN saw A Forms with regard to expiry & renewal of contract for third period. Capt WALES signified his intention of not renewing his contract on completion of second year.	
"		28	Received orders detailing officer to Sanitary Course 30 June	

WAR DIARY ~~INTELLIGENCE SUMMARY~~

Army Form C. 2118.

Place	Date	Hour	Summary of Events and Information	Remarks and references to Appendices
ECOIVRES	1917		to 6 July. Detailed Lt COUPER for this duty. Capt WALES went to ADMS office to be interviewed. Saw D.A.D.M.S. XIII Corps with reference to sending down Impetigo cases which were not improving, received authority to do so. Very severe thunderstorm at about 6.30. Continuing for about 2½ hours place flooded.	
ECOIVRES	29		Fine morning but colder. Pte ASHWORTH who has been struck off the strength of the unit under instructions of D.M.S. 1st Army, on proceeding to 21 Labour Corps returning today. Informed A.D.M.O. 31 Div. & taken on strength.	
"	30		Capt M.R. KING returned for temporary duty with 95th Field Amb. Lt S. COUPER proceeded to ANZIN for Sanitary Course. Sgt HOOK - A.S.C. detailed for course of instruction at 12 Veterinary Hospital for 30 June to 6 July left today. Bearers now relieved, standing to. Capt KING detailed for duty with D.D.M.S. XIII Corps for the 2nd July.	

Butterworth
Lt Col R.A.M.C.
Comm. 94 F.A.

Confidential   Volume XIX

July 1917   140/2298   Vol 17

War Diary

94th Field Ambulance   31st Division

> COMMITTEE FOR THE
> MEDICAL HISTORY OF THE WAR
> Date   10 SEP. 1917

July 1917

WAR DIARY or INTELLIGENCE SUMMARY.

Army Form C. 2118.

9th Field Ambulance

Place	Date	Hour	Summary of Events and Information	Remarks and references to Appendices
ECOIVRES	1917 July 1		Sunday Services C of E at 10 am Patients and personnel under the command of Capt. T. McEWEN R.C. at 10 am in the Church. Non C of E (voluntary) at 6.30 pm. Made inspection of the camp. Inspected harness & found all satisfactory. Lieutenant A. LOCKE R.A.M.C.	
"	2		Made inspection of camp wards. All biscuits of iron rations turned over. Capt. McEWEN granted leave to U.K. 2/7/17 to 12/7/17.	
"	3		Usual inspection. Capt. M.B King R.A.M.C reported his departure for duty with D.D.M.O XIII Corps. Capt FREW R.A.M.C reported his return for temporary duty with the 9th Field Amb.	
"	4		Usual inspection. 8 reinforcements arrived & taken on the strength.	

WAR DIARY or INTELLIGENCE SUMMARY

Army Form C. 2118.

Place	Date	Hour	Summary of Events and Information	Remarks and references to Appendices
ECOIVRES	July 1917 5.		Casual inspection of lines & patients wards. Held full marching out parade of "C" Section under the Command of Capt. WALES.	R.
"	6		Usual inspection. Inspected transport. Nothing to report.	R.
"	7		Usual inspection. LIEUT. COUPER reports his return to Headquarters after undergoing course of instruction in Field Sanitation at the XIII Corps School of Sanitation (62 Sanitary Section)	R.
"	[?]		Capt IRVINE R.A.M.C. having been granted leave of absence to the U.K. his work as M.O. to 11 E. Yorks is being performed by Capt A. WALES in addition to his other duties.	R.
"	8		Sunday Services. C.of.E. at 10 am Patients & Personnel under the Command of LIEUT COUPER. R.C.s at 10 am in the Church. Non C.of.E at 6.30 (Voluntary Service)	R.

WAR DIARY
~~INTELLIGENCE SUMMARY~~
(Erase heading not required) 1 Ambulance

Army Form C. 2118.

3

Place	Date July 1917	Hour	Summary of Events and Information	Remarks and references to Appendices
ELUIVRES	9	9	Made usual inspection. All antigas rubber goggles & ordinary type goggles withdrawn from unit today. Inspected all B112's of the unit and granted four good conduct strips to a number of men who had become eligible during the previous month.	
"	10		Usual inspection of camp. Inspected horse lines. Saw farrier corporals shoeing hock. Inspection of transport by the O.C. Train & Headquarters Company.	
"	11.		Usual inspection. Sgt. HOOK returned from Class of Instruction at N° 12 Veterinary Hospital NEUFCHATEL. He states that the course was a very good one and that they had been shown a lot of Sketch & Horse management.	
"	12		Usual inspection. The 11. E. Yorks moved into the line today. Capt WALES	

WAR DIARY or INTELLIGENCE SUMMARY

Army Form C. 2118.

Place	Date 1917	Hour	Summary of Events and Information	Remarks and references to Appendices
ECOIVRES	12 (cont)		Accompanied them as M.O. This necessitated a rearrangement of wards. Cap. McEWEN reported his return from leave of absence to the U.K. R.	
"	13		Made usual inspection. Went to CAMBLIGNEUL to see A.D.M.O on duty. R.	
"	14		Made usual inspection. P. McCOWAN granted a commission in the Infantry and under instructions from Divisional Headquarters left today for England with instructions to report. R.	
"	15		Sunday Services as follows:- 10. a.m. Patients & Personnel C of E. 10. a.m. R.C. 6.30 (Voluntary) Service of Non C of E. Received orders from A.D.M.O 31 Div to detail an officer for temporary duty with the 13 York & Lancs vice Capt ANDERSON who was leaving for ENGLAND on completion of contract	

WAR DIARY or INTELLIGENCE SUMMARY

Army Form C. 2118.

5

Place	Date	Hour	Summary of Events and Information	Remarks and references to Appendices
	1917			
	15 cont		Capt. BROWN whom I had selected for this duty, has developed Cellulitis of his arm due to a mosquito bite. I therefore detailed Lt. COUPER to be in addition to proceed if necessary. Informed A.D.M.S. by phone. R.	
ECOIVRES	16		Capt. BROWN unfit to proceed on to the 13 York & Lancs. So Lt. COUPER proceeded instead of him. Made usual inspection of whole place. Inspected straw huts & horses which being at present painted. R.	
"	17		Made usual inspection of lines. Capt. HALLAM granted special leave of absence to the U.K. for 18-31 on renewing his contract & left this afternoon. R.	
"	18		Routine work. Inspected lines & transport. Went to Aubigny to see new site of the XIII Corps Remount Station and to draw up plans for the camp that is to erected there. R.	

WAR DIARY or INTELLIGENCE SUMMARY.

Army Form C. 2118.

Place	Date	Hour	Summary of Events and Information	Remarks and references to Appendices
ELOUGES	July 1917 19		Routine work	
"	20		Capt M.B. KING at present attached to D.D.M.S. XIII Corps for instruction so D.a.D.M.S. granted leave of absence to the U.K from 20-30 July and left early this morning	
"	21.		Lieut L.V GATT who has been attached to the Corps Ammunition Sub park having become surplus to the Division owing to Capt BROWN R.A.M.C attached 169th Bde R.F.A being attached to Field Ambulances on the leaving of 169 Bde R.F.A was transferred to the 5th Division and struck off the strength of this unit accordingly	
"	22		Divine Services today as follows. C of E 10 am Pulunts + Personnel under the Command of Capt BROWN. R.C.s 10 am in the Church. Voluntary Service Non C of E 6.30 pm.	

WAR DIARY or INTELLIGENCE SUMMARY

Army Form C. 2118.

Place	Date 1917	Hour	Summary of Events and Information	Remarks and references to Appendices
ECOIVRES	July 23		Under instructions from A.D.M.S. 31st Division, the name of an officer who would be in readiness to proceed at short notice to another army was submitted. Capt. H. WALES being selected for this duty. Capt H. WALES reported his arrival from temporary duty with the 11. E. Yorks regiment on the return of Capt IRVINE. Name for leave of absence. A.D.M.S. 31st Div (acting D.D.M.S. XIII Corps.) came round and inspected the Corps Rest station. S. Sgt MOORE. R.E. foreman of works has been attached to this unit to supervise the work of removing huts from ACQ and re-erecting them at AUBIGNY. 1 Sgt + 15 O.R. from the 5th + 63 Divisions each have been attached as a working party and arrived today at 5 p.m. They are to proceed to ACQ tomorrow together with 2 HADDEN Cpl MOWBRAY and 15 O.R. of this unit.	

WAR DIARY
INTELLIGENCE SUMMARY.

Army Form C. 2118.

Place	Date	Hour	Summary of Events and Information	Remarks and references to Appendices
ECOIVRES	July 1917 24		Work started at ACQ today and one tent was taken down & marked ready to move. Orders (telephonic) received at 9.15 p.m. that Capt WALES was to be ready to proceed to Headquarters 5th Army tomorrow morning, destination to be notified later.	
"	25.		Capt WALES proceeded to PROVEN today with 5 other officers in his Motor Ambulance. Routine work in Camp. Inspection lines & transport. Owing to the scarcity of officers I have been obliged to take on one ward, which prevents me devoting time to supervising the general working &c.	
"	26.		Routine work & inspection. Owing to the way the men are wearing out their clothing in a large measure due to absolute carelessness on their part orders were issued on this subject and men will in future have to pay for clothing damaged thro carelessness	

WAR DIARY
or
INTELLIGENCE SUMMARY.

Army Form C. 2118.

Place	Date	Hour	Summary of Events and Information	Remarks and references to Appendices
ECOIVRES	July 1917 26		Work at ACD progressing more satisfactorily. One hut per diem being taken down. Applied for two lorries for tomorrow to take these huts to AUBIGNY.	
"	27		Lorries reported at 8 am & worked during day. It was found that one hut required about 6 lorries to move & that only one hut was moved today. S-Sgt MOORE removed to AUBIGNY to superintend the erection. Half the men to accompany him. Capt McEWEN in bed today with fever which gives additional work to all. Rev AUST Chaplain Corps attached temporarily to the unit & takes on ration duties.	
"	28		Capt McEWEN better today but still unfit for duty. Went on to AUBIGNY to see how work was progressing. One water cart for use at AUBIGNY of the 5 Div Arms Factory is out in today. Work progressing satisfactorily. Night march in preparation for all available men took place at 9.30 pm.	

WAR DIARY
or
INTELLIGENCE SUMMARY.
(Erase heading not required.)

Army Form C. 2118.

Place	Date JULY 1917	Hour	Summary of Events and Information	Remarks and references to Appendices
ECOIVRES	29		Sunday. Divine Services as follows. C of E. 10 am Patients + Personnel. L + A with A H A T. B.B. in Command. 98 patients attended. R.C. 10 am to the Church. Non C of E. Voluntary Service at 6.30 pm. Requested two lorries daily on Monday Tuesday + Wednesday to move remaining huts at ACQ.	
ECOIVRES	30.		Routine work. Inspection of transport + horses by Veterinary Officer. Went to AUBIGNY + ACQ to see how work getting on. Lorries arrived + moving huts. One hut framework erected.	
"	31.		Routine work. Nothing much to report. Gnr HARRISON 165 B R.F.A. patient in Post Card found under arrest under suspicion of trying by neglect wound in septic to ward this morning. reported to ADMS. Other evidences. Went to AUBIGNY. Work progressing.	Lieutenant Colonel Comm'g 94 d'Amb

Confidential   Volume IX

                    War Diary.

94th Field Ambulance   31st Division

                August 1917.

WAR DIARY or INTELLIGENCE SUMMARY

Army Form C. 2118.

Place	Date	Hour	Summary of Events and Information	Remarks and references to Appendices
ECOIVRES	August 1917 1st		Army Form [...] Staff [...] Completed for Gnr HARRISON 115th Bty RFA & forwarded to ADMS 31st Div. Went to ADMS re cases & dates of leave. [...] leave to V.K. for 3 C.B. Amb. Capt. M.B. KING M.C. & Capt HALLUM reported been relieved for leave & absence to D.R. Reported to ADMS. Went to AUBIGNY. [...] XIII Corps no answer. Went to MINGOVAL [...] found area reoccupied. Report to D.D.M.S. XIII Corps.	
ECOIVRES	2nd		LIEUT. COL. STEWART & self visited the Corps Rest Station which is being constructed at AUBIGNY. Took over command as LIEUT. COL. STEWART is going on leave from 3rd to 13th inst.	

WAR DIARY or INTELLIGENCE SUMMARY

Army Form C. 2118.

93rd Field Ambulance. 2

Place	Date August 1917	Hour	Summary of Events and Information	Remarks and references to Appendices
ECOIVRES	3rd		Made an inspection of whole of Rest Station.	
ECOIVRES	4th		CAPT. KING relieved LIEUT. COUPER who was acting as Medical Officer to the 13th YORKS & LANCS. LIEUT COUPER reported his return.	
ECOIVRES	5th		Church Service for personnel of ambulance held in one of the huts, the parade being taken by CAPT. HALLAM. Visited the new Corps Rest Station at AUBIGNY & went on to MINGOVAL & arranged to commence taking down the huts there tomorrow as they could be then occupied. Detailed party for the job.	
ECOIVRES	6th		Applied for 2 motor lorries to remove huts from MINGOVAL to AUBIGNY. These were granted. Made thorough inspection of Corps Rest Station.	

WAR DIARY or INTELLIGENCE SUMMARY

Army Form C. 2118.

94th Field Ambulance.

Place	Date August 1917	Hour	Summary of Events and Information	Remarks and references to Appendices
ECOIVRES	7th		Daily inspection of Rest Station. Visited ACS where removal of huts going on. Hut's on to MINGOVAL. One French hut almost completely erected to our large Rest Station & expect to have both erected from there by the 9th inst.	
ECOIVRES	8th		LIEUT REID A. R.A.M.C. reported his arrival & was taken on the strength having been attached to this Ambulance for duty.	
ECOIVRES	9th		French huts completely removed from MINGOVAL to AUBIGNY.	
ECOIVRES	10th		Attended Medical Board held at A.D.M.S. 31st Div. office.	
ECOIVRES	11th		Took summary of evidence for Field General Court Martial on No T/18929 Staff Sergeant Major COBLEY W.H. A.C.C. attached 94th Field Ambulance in charge when a Active Service Drunkenness. Visited AUBIGNY with D.A.D.M.S. XIII Corps & inspected an old	

WAR DIARY / INTELLIGENCE SUMMARY

Army Form C. 2118.

94th Field Ambulance

Place	Date	Hour	Summary of Events and Information	Remarks and references to Appendices
ECOIVRES	August 1917 11th		German Prisoners of War Camp which is being taken over as an adjunct to the New XIII Corps Rest Station. JMB	
ECOIVRES	12th		Church Service (C.of E.) for personnel patients — CAPT BROWN in command. Visited AUBIGNY & took over what was the XIII Corps Rest Station for Officers — putting in a holding party. JMB	
ECOIVRES	13th		With D.D.M.S. XIII Corps visited Corps Rest Station & Prisoners of War Camp at AUBIGNY. It is proposed to utilise the latter for Officers & personnel of the unit running the Rest Station. JMB	
ECOIVRES	14th		CAPT WALES returned from duty with 5th Army (61st C.C.S.) & proceeded to ENGLAND to report to War Office as he is resigning his commission on expiration of his year's contract. LIEUT REID detailed to join 61st C.C.S. as his relief.	

WAR DIARY
or
INTELLIGENCE SUMMARY
(Erase heading not required.)

94th Field Ambulance

Army Form C. 2118.

Place	Date August 1917	Hour	Summary of Events and Information	Remarks and references to Appendices
ECOYVRES	14th (cont)		LIEUT. COL. STEWART returned from 10 days leave of absence when I handed over command.	
"	14		Taken over this evening on return of leave to V.R. Went down to Aubigny to see how work was progressing.	
"	15		Proceeded after inspection of camp & wards to see D.D.M.S. XVII Corps & accompanied him to the new site at AUBIGNY & new officers Rest Station. D.D.M.S. very satisfied with progress of work. Went in afternoon to report to A.D.M.S. 51 Div.	
"	16		Made a thorough inspection of everything working & after lunch went to AUBIGNY.	
"	17		Routine work.	
"	18		Inspected Camp. Went to AUBIGNY and met the C.R.E. XVII Corps there and arranged with him	

WAR DIARY
or
INTELLIGENCE SUMMARY.

Army Form C. 2118.

Place	Date	Hour	Summary of Events and Information	Remarks and references to Appendices
ECOIVRES	August 1917 18	(contd)	about cementing the centres of the French huts there. Work on hour timer station. Work going on very well. Lorry drawing R-E. material today which was badly wanted.	
"	19		Church parades today as follows:- C of E. 10. am. Patients & personnel under Lt COUPER. R.Cs in Church. Non C of E (voluntary) 6-30.	
"	20		Routine work. Work at AUBIGNY progressing satisfactorily.	
"	21		Nothing to report.	
"	22		Proceeded to British Red Cross stores at HAM-EN-ARTOIS to make arrangement for furnishing the huts. Officer Q.M. Station at AUBIGNY. Saw the officer i/c and arranged details. Work at AUBIGNY progressing satisfactory and the huts are now nearly all ready for cementing.	

WAR DIARY or INTELLIGENCE SUMMARY

Army Form C. 2118.

Place	Date 1917	Hour	Summary of Events and Information	Remarks and references to Appendices
ECOIVRES	August 23		Made out requisition of Red Cross Stores. Went into D.A.H.Q. to AUBIGNY. Arranged for lorries to be here tomorrow to bring down Stores. Capt McEWEN will go up to Chirp?	
"	24		Very wet day. Work kept back considerably. Capt McEWEN got all the articles required and the work of finishing to commence tomorrow.	
"	25		Weather very broken. Work kept back in consequence. Arranged for lorries on Monday, Tuesday & Wednesday & Thursday next week to carry R.E. Stores & start getting down the Nissen Huts. Capt MOELLER USMC joined Sept 23 Aug	
"	26		Church Service. C.O.'s 10 am. Capt HALLAM in Command.	
"	27		Lorries drawing R.E. Material. Men employed on platforms and sheds at AUBIGNY. Officers wards opened. Lt COWPER transferred thence to take command. Troops of patients steadily accepting.	

WAR DIARY or INTELLIGENCE SUMMARY

Army Form C. 2118.

Place	Date	Hour	Summary of Events and Information	Remarks and references to Appendices
ECOIVRES	28		Nothing to report.	
"	29		Tonnie starts lining down Nissen huts specialising on hut started on various floor. Many not [illegible] tending only door work [illegible]	
"	30		Went to AUBIGNY all Nissen not done. Work going on satisfactorily.	
"	31		Inspected Rue [illegible]. Went to AUBIGNY, work going on very well down there. Nothing further to report.	

[signature]
Comd 94th 2nd [illegible]

Confidential 27   140/2438   Volume XXI
Sept 1917   Vol 19

War Diary.

94th Field Ambulance   31st Division

September 1917.

WAR DIARY or INTELLIGENCE SUMMARY

Army Form C. 2118.

Place	Date	Hour	Summary of Events and Information	Remarks and references to Appendices
	September 1917			
ECOIVRES	1		Routine work. Went to AUBIGNY and saw work there.	
"	2		Sunday. Divine services as follows:-	
			C of E. 10 am patients & personnel Capt Brown in [?]	
			R.C. 10 am Church	
			Non C of E. 6.30 pm voluntary	
	3		Inspected Camp. Made arrangements to send patients, who are now convalescent but still unfit to go to duty, to AUBIGNY for light work there. Court Martial on S. Sgt Major Cobley will take place tomorrow. All witnesses warned. Capt McEWEN to act as prosecutor.	
"	4		Strict orders issued with regard to saluting. Issued orders that this is to be read on parade by Lt JIBB at Headquarters & Capt McEWEN at AUBIGNY. Pte MIDDLETON who has absented himself whilst on leave to U.K. returned under escort, he was only absent 34 hours. Awarded 7 days F.P. No 2. Court Martial	

WAR DIARY or INTELLIGENCE SUMMARY

Army Form C. 2118.

Place	Date	Hour	Summary of Events and Information	Remarks and references to Appendices
ECOIVRES	September 1917	5	On Staff S.M. COBLEY postponed until the 7th inst. Sgt SATTERTHWAITE returned for duty at the Baths at MONT ST ELOY. Published orders re loss of Lavan etc. Standing orders read at AUBIGNY.	
"		6	Detailed witnesses for Court Martial. S.M. COBLEY warned. Issued orders with reference to D.D.M.S. XIII Corps memo re accidents with Pure Carbolic acid. Work at AUBIGNY progressing with Cemetery. Burying starting at once, material is not as plentiful as required.	
"		7	Court Martial held today. Had not concluded at the time the Court rose and was to be continued again on Sunday morning at 9.30 am. Capt L. COWPER R.A.M.C. will not be further required. Applied for allotment of leave for him and received warrant for him. Leave being granted for the 10th to 20th Octr he will be leaving on the 9th. Capt McEWEN will	

WAR DIARY or INTELLIGENCE SUMMARY

Army Form C. 2118.

3

Place	Date September 1917	Hour	Summary of Events and Information	Remarks and references to Appendices
ECOIVRES			perform his duty at the Officers Rest Station and Capt HALLAM when his work here will go to AUBIGNY to superintend the work there.	
"	8		Went to AUBIGNY and inspected there. All details correct. Published the orders our Accountant officer. Standing orders have been read at Headquarters by Q.M.S. MARSHALL.	
"	9		Court Martial ended. LT. COUPER reported his departure on leave of absence to U.K. Capt HALLAM proceeded to AUBIGNY. Divine Services as follows:— C of E 10 am parade of service Capt MOELLER in Command. R.C. 10 am in Church. Non Conf. 6.30 Voluntary.	
"	10		Routine work. 5 men left for 1st army Rest Camp. Inspected all the Rest Station and mess	

WAR DIARY or INTELLIGENCE SUMMARY.

Army Form C. 2118.

Place	Date 1917	Hour	Summary of Events and Information	Remarks and references to Appendices
ECOIVRES			definite orders re Poisons in Wards, a copy of the order to hang in each ward.	
"		11	Court Martial of P. HEANEY R.A.M.C. on a charge of accidentally injuring himself with an explosive took place at BUSNES today. I attended as Witness but as he pleaded guilty & gave a statement as to character Capt McEWEN attended him and performed my duties.	
"		12	Proceedings & sentence on S.S.M. COBLEY received, the sentence is that he is to forfeit 2 years in his present rank of Serjeant. Applied to ADMS that this W.O. be relieved of his duty here and a new W.O. appointed	
		13	Under instructions ADMS 31 Div the following moves took place. Capt HALLAM to 13. E. Yorks for temporary duty. Capt MOELLER to 11 E. Lancs for duty. Lt KNAPP U.S.M.C. reports his arrival for duty & is taken on	

WAR DIARY or INTELLIGENCE SUMMARY.

Army Form C. 2118.

Place	Date 1917	Hour	Summary of Events and Information	Remarks and references to Appendices
ECOIVRES		14	the Strength. Lt. REID on detached duty with 61 C.C.S. having proceeded to England on completion of contract in strength off the Strength of the Unit. Capt. M. B. DAWSON R.A.M.C.T. having reported his arrival is taken on the Strength.	
"		15	Routine work. Nothing to report.	
"		16	Divine services as under. C of E Patients and personnel 10 a.m. R.C.s in Church 10 a.m. Non C of E Voluntary service 6.30 p.m.	
		17	Court Martial on Pte HEANEY sentenced him to 14 days F.P. No 1. Pte CROWDER returned from XIII Corps School of Instruction.	

WAR DIARY or INTELLIGENCE SUMMARY.

Army Form C. 2118.

Place	Date	Hour	Summary of Events and Information	Remarks and references to Appendices
ECOIVRES	September 1917	18	Nothing to report.	
"		19	Went to AUBIGNY with the O.D.M.S. Routine work. Work at AUBIGNY progressing satisfactorily.	
"		20	Staff Sergeant Major COBLEY reverted to the rank of Sergeant at his own request. This leaves me one Sergeant surplus to Establishment Notified H.Q.M.S. of this fact.	
"		21	The undermentioned N.C.O's & men left today for 12 days at the 1st Army Rest Camp. Staff Sergeant Davy, Pte Robertson, Pte Martin & Pte Torry.	
"		23	Church services today as follows:— C of E 10.00 am were the Commanding Capt DAWSON. R.C. at 10 am in the Church. Non C of E at 6.30 pm Voluntary.	
"		24	Routine work. Nothing to report.	
"		25	Capt A.L. WALKER R.A.M.C. reports his arrival for 93 Field Amb and is taken on the strength from this date. 10 P.B. men arrived for	

WAR DIARY or INTELLIGENCE SUMMARY

Army Form C. 2118.

Place	Date September 1917	Hour	Summary of Events and Information	Remarks and references to Appendices
			Re bases to replace 10 A.S.C. Batmen Classified "A". Medical Board Consisting of self President & Capt Frew & Brown as members examined and classified the following as Category "A" S. Thomason G.H. S. Dabill, S. Franklaw, S. Kilmurry, S. Pearson, S. Thomas, S. Guffry, S. Holmes, S. Davidson & S. ————, under instructions of A.D.M.S. Hindquarters these were dispatched to report to the H.T. & S. Base Depot Havre. Sergeant Colley being surplus to establishment was detailed to proceed to the H.T. & S. Base Depot Havre & left today.	
ECOIVRES	29		T/13212 C.S.M. ALLAR of 6 Reserve Park arrived today on posting to S.S. 744 A.S.C. and is taken on the strength of the unit from this date.	
"	30		Under instructions of A.D.M.S. 31 Div. the Medical Board which met on the 25 assembled again this morning and examined & reported on the 10 P.B. men lately arrived. Services 10 a.m. C of E. Capt WALKER in Command R.Cs at 10 a.m. Non C of E voluntary at 6.30 pm	

Thwaite
L?o?R?a?n?e?
Comdg 94 D? Ch.

Confidential 97-11 140/2578 Volume XXII
Oct. 1917 Vol 20

War Diary

COMMITTEE FOR THE
MEDICAL HISTORY OF THE WAR
Date 17 JAN. 1918

94th Field Ambulance 31st Division

October. 1917.

WAR DIARY
or
INTELLIGENCE SUMMARY
(Erase heading not required)

Army Form C. 2118.

Instructions regarding War Diaries and Intelligence Summaries are contained in F. S. Regs., Part II. and the Staff Manual respectively. Title pages will be prepared in manuscript.

Place	Date	Hour	Summary of Events and Information	Remarks and references to Appendices
	October 1917			
ECOIVRES	1		Orders issued by D.D.M.S. XIII Corps closing the Rest Station from the 3rd until 11th October in order that the patients may be moved down to Aubigny. Moved to Aubigny today in order to superintend the arrival of patients. Work now progressing very rapidly towards completion.	
"	2		25 patients sent down today to AUBIGNY. C.E. XIII Corps came round inspecting the place. Nothing to report.	
"	3		Rest Station closed for the reception of patients from today except Eye cases and Chinese Coolies. C.E. XVII Corps was round today. 100 bedsteads, mattresses & pillows arrived by train from BOULOGNE and were unloaded and placed in wards. Work on the lighting of the camp started yesterday and is progressing satisfactorily. Engine House being extended & wires fixed.	

WAR DIARY or INTELLIGENCE SUMMARY.

Army Form C. 2118.

Place	Date October 1917	Hour	Summary of Events and Information	Remarks and references to Appendices
ECOIVRES		4	Half Medical Cars sent down today and Capt. BROWN was sent down in charge of them.	
			The work progressing satisfactorily but partly held up by the extremely wet weather.	
"		5	Remaining Medical Cars sent down.	
			C.S.M. ALLARD promotion to S.S.M. confirmed by Hd. quards today.	
"		6	Half Cars for the I.C.T. wounded sent today and Capt. DAWSON come down to be in charge of them	
"		7	Remaining I.C.T. Cars sent to AUBIGNY.	
AUBIGNY		8	All remaining Cars transferred today and Headquarters of the Ambulance moved today	
			Work on outbuildings going on but the weather continues extremely bad very large amount of rain with very high winds. The remainder of personnel from ECOIVRES come today Capt. McEWEN remaining behind at	

WAR DIARY or INTELLIGENCE SUMMARY

Army Form C. 2118.

Place	Date 1917	Hour	Summary of Events and Information	Remarks and references to Appendices
AUBIGNY	October	8	ECOIVRES to hand over places to Town Major.	
"		9	L. & Q' master D.H.A. JIBB granted leave on special grounds to U.K. for 8-18.	
			Sgt BUXTON R.A.M.C. proceeded on course of instruction in Gas duties to the Divisional Gas School	
"		10	Work now proceeding steadily again as weather has improved. All arrangements made for the cases arriving. There are. All sitting cases come down by Light railway to ECOIVRES where they are met by Cars from here belonging to 25.M.A.C. the number being telephoned daily by D.N.W.S. Lying Cases come direct to the Field Ambulance Cars. Discharges proceed to ECOIVRES by tram at 14.2 daily & go to Reinforcement Camp. Under instruction fr A.D.M.S. 31st Div LIEUT KNAPP U.S.M.R. proceeds to 12 East Yorks for temporary duty to replace Capt. MASON proceeding on leave	

WAR DIARY or INTELLIGENCE SUMMARY.

Army Form C. 2118.

Place	Date October 1917	Hour	Summary of Events and Information	Remarks and references to Appendices
AUBIGNY		11	Under instructions fm ADMS 51st Divn Capt WALKER proceeds to 13. East YORKS of temporary duty relieving Capt. HALLAM RAWIE who returned to Headquarters and proceeds to the Officers Rest Station in relief of Lt. COUPER. Rest Station reopened today for cases. Hitch occurred owing to the Cars being directed to the wrong place this has now been rectified	
"		12	Under telegraphic instructions fm the W. Office Lt. S. B. COUPER proceeds to ENGLAND and is struck off the Strength of the unit for this date.	
		13	Capt A.W. FREW granted Special 14 days leave to U.K. on renewing Contract and left yesterday. Capt WOODS 6 LONDON Field Amb & Capt PLEWS 4 London Field Ambulance arrived for temporary duty and are temporary taken on the Strength of the unit for this date and on above duties.	No 72/054469 Pte BROWN

WAR DIARY
or
INTELLIGENCE SUMMARY.
(Erase heading not required.)

Army Form C. 2118.

Instructions regarding War Diaries and Intelligence Summaries are contained in F. S. Regs., Part II. and the Staff Manual respectively. Title pages will be prepared in manuscript.

Place	Date October 1917	Hour	Summary of Events and Information	Remarks and references to Appendices
AUBIGNY			A.S.C. M.T. grants a commission in the R.F.C. left to day for ENGLAND & is struck off the strength and a reinforcement demanded.	
		14	Sunday. Divine Services. C. of E. 10 a.m. in Dining Hall (Cpl Dawson in charge). R.C's at 9 a.m. in Church. C. of E. voluntary service at 6.30.	
		16	Sgt CLATON Ptes HENDERSON & CRAWFORD left today for the 1st Army Rest Camp.	
		17	Capt. M.B. KING R.A.M.C. having been appointed by G.H.Q. as D.A.D.M.S. 57 Division left today for his new work and is taken off the strength of the unit from this date.	
		18	Work has been steadily carried on here. A library for patients and personnel has been opened and seems to promise well.	

WAR DIARY or INTELLIGENCE SUMMARY

Army Form C. 2118.

Place	Date	Hour	Summary of Events and Information	Remarks and references to Appendices
AUBIGNY	October 1917	19	The D.D.M.S. XIII Corps accompanied by the D.G. M.S. Armies inspected the Corps Rest Station & Officers Rest Station who was very pleased with everything and requested a plan of this place with a detail of the methods of running same. Lt. & Q'Master A.W. de JIBB returned from leave to U.K. today.	
"		20	Drew money today for payment of unit. Work proceeding satisfactory.	
"		21	Divine services as follows:— C of E. Communion service at 8 a.m. Parade services at 10 a.m. Capt Woods in Charge of parade. R.Cs in Church at 9 a.m. C of E Evening Service voluntary at 6 p.m.	
"		22	Orders received to be in readiness to move to our old line on relieve	

WAR DIARY or INTELLIGENCE SUMMARY

Army Form C. 2118.

Place	Date	Hour	Summary of Events and Information	Remarks and references to Appendices
AUBIGNY	October 1917			
	22		Further Winter scale of clothing issued to men. Sgt Staufuis A.S.C. proceeded home to U.K. Storm having fallen in waves. R.	
	23		Nothing to report. R.	
	24		L. KNAPP. U.S.M.C returned from leave, duty with 12 S. 7 N.B. & took over charge of C/236 B'y & A/235 B'y. R.F.A. duties. Kit inspection of unit orderlies. New bathing programme arranged whereby each patient receives bath & clean change weekly. R.	
	25		Capt WOODS R.A.M.C. P.R 6 London F.A. proceeded to 42 C.C.S. for permanent duty & was replaced here by Capt COLEMAN of the same Field Ambulance. R.	
	26		Fire piquet & instructions drawn up and issued to all. R.	
	27		Orders received re Brazier in Clover Building & the dangers of suffocation thereby. R.	

WAR DIARY
or
INTELLIGENCE SUMMARY.
(Erase heading not required)

Army Form C. 2118.

Place	Date	Hour	Summary of Events and Information	Remarks and references to Appendices
AUBIGNY	28		Divine Services as follow:- C of E Parade at 10 am Capt McEWEN in Charge. Voluntary at 6 pm R-C in Church at 9 am	
	29		Issued first Good Conduct badges to a number of men who had become eligible since last list compiled. Dr Eastwood posted to Canadian from E.U.R.	
	30		Lt KNAPP under instruction of others 31 to be promoted to 12 yr bonus for temporary duty. Capt DAWSON to perform eye duty in the means which is opposite the Battalion.	
	31.		The Corp Commander inspected the whole place. Officers Men statts & expressed himself very pleased with the place. Medical Board today examining all the R+ K of the units with a view to their classification as to A+B Categories. Capt FREW was detailed as	

WAR DIARY
or
INTELLIGENCE SUMMARY.
(Erase heading not required.)

Army Form C. 2118.

Place	Date	Hour	Summary of Events and Information	Remarks and references to Appendices
			Proceeded with Cpl BROWN + COLEMAN on motor Cycles A 15.6	
			" B 20	
			Cpl BROWN granted special leave to U.K. for 14 days from 1st £15 + kit listing.	
			[signature] Lt Col Rumm. Comdg 94th D'Arch.	

Confidential   140/2578   Volume XXIII

Nov. 1917   Vol 21

War Diary

COMMITTEE FOR THE
MEDICAL HISTORY OF THE WAR
Date   17 JAN. 1918

94th Field Ambulance 31st Division

November 1917

WAR DIARY or INTELLIGENCE SUMMARY.

Army Form C. 2118.

Place	Date	Hour	Summary of Events and Information	Remarks and references to Appendices
Aubigny	November 1917 1st		Medical Board of the following officers Cap FREW, Cap BROWN & Cap COLMAN examined and classified the R.A.M.C personnel of the unit. Cap M.B. DAWSON detailed to proceed daily to CAPELLE FERMONT to see sick of the 235 B & 236 B. R.F.A. Cap WALKER notified as having been struck off the strength of this unit from this date. [signature] Lt Col RAMC	
	2		One pair of Drawers withdrawn for personnel today in accordance with instructions from Div Headquarters. Inspection of all iron rations ordered. Work on Camp progressing satisfactorily. A.D.M.S. 47 Div came round Camp today and expressed great satisfaction at the work here.	

WAR DIARY or INTELLIGENCE SUMMARY.

Army Form C. 2118.

Place	Date 1917	Hour	Summary of Events and Information	Remarks and references to Appendices
Aubigny	November	3	No 62759 Pte Hicks. S. having been selected as candidate for a Commission in the Army was transferred to Base Establishment Etaples and taken off the strength of this unit. Work started on the M room huts facing B & C blocks. Engine of the lighting arrived and is being fitted up.	
"		4	Divine Services today as follows. C of E at 10 am Voluntary at 6.30. R.C. at 8.30. Capt DAWSON R.A.M.C proceeds to England under instructions from the War Office and is struck off the strength. Capt PLEVS 4 London F.A. having been relieved by Capt Tilterton name of the same unit proceeded on leave to the United Kingdom. One lieut ordinarie connecting	

WAR DIARY or INTELLIGENCE SUMMARY

Army Form C. 2118.

3.

Place	Date	Hour	Summary of Events and Information	Remarks and references to Appendices
Aubigny	November 1917 4		8 N.C.O's & 11 men arrived for duty fr 4 London Field Amb & are taken on the strength of the unit for rations etc.	
	5		Engine set up lighting completed and taken into use today. Issued orders re breakage of clinical thermometers.	
	6		No 60617 Pte Standhaft granted special leave of absence to U.K. from 6.11.17 to 20.11.17. Orders issued re the admission of patients under going field punishment or under arrest of any kind.	
	7		Opening of the Rest Station officially today. Conducted etc in divine service. DDMS XIII Corps ADMS & DADMS of 31st & 47th Div. C.R.E. Corps Troops & many others present.	P.
	8		Lieut A O BRADLEY R.A.M.C posted to unit as reinforcement and taken on the strength of the unit for the cluster.	P.

WAR DIARY or INTELLIGENCE SUMMARY

Army Form C. 2118.

November 1917

Place	Date	Hour	Summary of Events and Information	Remarks and references to Appendices
Autigny	9		Routine work nothing to report.	
"	10		Sunday services C of E. 10. a.m.	
			voluntary at 6 p.m.	
			R.C's at 8.30 a.m.	
			Received telegraphic instructions from a.D.M.S. 31 Div	
			Lieut BRADLEY proceeded to join the 48 Div and is struck off strength.	
			Capt Tillestin 4 London Field Ambulance also left for 48 Div and was replaced temporarily by Capt IRONSIDES.	
	11		Capt IRONSIDES relieved by Lt PIPER U.S.M.C. today - Returned to his unit.	
	12		Work proceeding well nothing unusual to report.	

WAR DIARY or INTELLIGENCE SUMMARY

Army Form C. 2118.

6

Place	Date	Hour	Summary of Events and Information	Remarks and references to Appendices
Aubigny	November 1917	17	Divisional orders re fires issued and precautions to be taken against fire.	
"		18	Sunday Services as follows: C. of E. 10 a.m. R.C. 8-30 a.m.	
"		19	Divisional orders regarding payments to be made to men in the mint and laid down scale of pay to be given to each rank and a minimum credit necessary.	
"		20	Leave reopens. Allotment 2 per diem until the 30th. Divisional orders re care of clothing.	
"		21	Nothing to report	
"		22	Nothing to report	

WAR DIARY or INTELLIGENCE SUMMARY

Army Form C. 2118.

Place	Date	Hour	Summary of Events and Information	Remarks and references to Appendices
Aubigny	November 1917 13		Routine work. Breaking of mission proceeding. [illegible] orders re kits of patients which are left in pack store.	
"	14		Inspection of [illegible] ration of unit. All [illegible] portion to be [illegible] over	
"	15		Capt FREW, Sgt HADDEN and SATTERTHWAITE proceed yesterday to BETHUNE for Course of instruction at 1st Army R.A.M.C school, for the 15-24 inclusive. Arrangements made for collecting tins of solder.	
"	16		Owing to men who are undergoing I-P [illegible] orders that all such cases should be reported at once so that when fit for discharge an escort can be arranged for.	

WAR DIARY
or
INTELLIGENCE SUMMARY

Army Form C. 2118.

Place	Date	Hour	Summary of Events and Information	Remarks and references to Appendices
Aubigny	1917 November 24		Lieut. W. Scott Piper U.S.M.C. left for duty with No 4 General Hospital under instructions of the D.D.M.S. XIII Corps. The undermentioned belonging to the 21st Division arrived for duty. Capt McPARRICK & 1 Lieut sub division 66 Field Amb. Lieut Gladden U.S.M.C. of 63 Field Amb. Lectures on matters strength & detailed towards for duty. Party of School arrived base.	P.
"	25		Capt COLMAN left yesterday to rejoin his unit, on the change of the Division out of Corps Area.	P.
"	26		Services as follows Coy E. Voluntary at 7 am Parade at 10 am Voluntary at 6 pm R.C. at 8.30 am Capt Hallam ...	P.

WAR DIARY or INTELLIGENCE SUMMARY

Army Form C. 2118.

Place	Date	Hour	Summary of Events and Information	Remarks and references to Appendices
Aubigny	1917 26		Two officers L. GEORGE & FORLONG U.S.M.C. posted as reinforcement today & taken on strength R.	
"	27		Demonstration to all officers & N.C.O.s on the use of the Thomas splint given by Capt. FREW. Afterwards all N.C.O.s put up splint under guidance 2 O[?]. S. Matheson & Hendren. Gas demonstration by Sgt Clayton to C. Sect. P.	
	28		Col Cree D.D.M.S. inspected today. A.D.M.S. 21 Division also was here. Orders received that the officers & personnel of the 21 Div. are to return to their units on the 30th. Afternoon. L. George & Sgt Clayton & Cpl Shaw left for 1st Army School P.	
	29		Received orders to send 5 O.R. to the 63 Field Amb.	

WAR DIARY
or
INTELLIGENCE SUMMARY

Army Form C. 2118.

Place	Date	Hour	Summary of Events and Information	Remarks and references to Appendices
	November 1917		...ordered Spr. Clark, Maddocks, Simcock, Harris & Morris to hold themselves in readiness to go.	
Aubigny	30		Five men proceeded to 63 F.A. & took off duty. Lieut. Gladden proceeded to report to ADMS 21 Div. Capt. M'Kitterick & Tent Sub Div 65 F.A. left.	

D. G. Rawe
Comd. 9th F. Amb.

Confidential Volume XXIV

Vol 22

War Diary

94th Field Ambulance 31st Division

December 1917.

WAR DIARY or INTELLIGENCE SUMMARY

Army Form C. 2118.

Place	Date	Hour	Summary of Events and Information	Remarks and references to Appendices
AUBIGNY	December 1917 1		Routine work. Sent off War Diary for November. Also War diary for August to Records. [illegible]	
"	2		Went up to Div H.Q to see Col D.A.D.O re [illegible] of Capt McEWEN. Arranged details. Learnt that the 56th Div were to relieve the 31st Div who were to leave 13 Corps.	
"	3		Routine work.	
"	4		Received A.D.M.S orders. I hand over to 2/1st London F.A on the 6th inst & be attached to 40 Brigade for move. To remain in present quarters by arrangement until we entrain probably on the 8th or 9th.	
"	5		Advance party of the 2/1st London arrived under Capt	

WAR DIARY
or
INTELLIGENCE SUMMARY
(Erase heading not required.)

Army Form C. 2118.

Place	Date December 1917 Hour	Summary of Events and Information	Remarks and references to Appendices
outpost	6	HARE showed his route. Main body to come tomorrow. Main body arrived, handed over to Col BREBNER. Cell correct. We are remaining until further notice in our billets.	
	7	Nothing to report.	
	8	Nothing to report.	
	9	Went to see A Dms as we were not being known. Arranged to send 3 officers + 140 OR to CAMBLIGNEUL at once. Arranged billets. Capt BROWN L' FURLONG + GEORGE with 140 OR left.	
	10	Route march.	

WAR DIARY or INTELLIGENCE SUMMARY

Army Form C. 2118.

Place	Date Dec 1917	Hour	Summary of Events and Information	Remarks and references to Appendices
Aubigny acq		11	Nothing to report.	
"		12	Moved whole unit to A.D.R. & got shelter. All satisfactory.	
"		13	Route march.	
"		14	Demonstration ("Thomas splint")	
"		15	Route march. granted leave to U.K. of 30 days. Handed over to Capt FREW [signature] Lt Col STEWART left this evening on leave to U.K.	
A.D.R.		16	Received R.A.M.C. operation orders No. 27. to take over line. Called on O.C. 2/3 LONDON F.A. to make arrangements regarding the move.	

WAR DIARY or INTELLIGENCE SUMMARY

Army Form C. 2118.

9th Field Ambulance

Place	Date	Hour	Summary of Events and Information	Remarks and references to Appendices
	Dec 1917			
ACQ	16		Unit Route march.	
"	17		Operation Orders No 27 cancelled. Demonstration Thomas Splint by Lieut George & myself.	
"	18		Received operation order No 28 to take over A.D.S. at Vancouver Rd. Conferred with O.C. No 4 Canadian Field Ambulance and detailed party.	
"	19		Completed Relief of A.D.S. Vancouver Rd. and reported same to A.D.M.S. Left Capt Brown in charge.	
"	20		Routine work. handed over to Capt McEwen.	
			Andrew Capt R.A.M.C. A.D.M.S.	
ACQ	21		Reported my arrival back from leave to U.K. Received operation orders No 29 from A.D.M.S. to take over by midday, the 22nd inst from O.C. 3/3 LONDON Field Ambulance the Main Dressing Station at ROCLINCOURT, the Advanced Dressing Station at TUNNEL DUMP, & Relay Post in TOMMY ALLEY	

WAR DIARY or INTELLIGENCE SUMMARY

Army Form C. 2118.

94th Field Ambulance

Place	Date Dec 1917	Hour	Summary of Events and Information	Remarks and references to Appendices
	21st contd		& Relay Post in TIRED ALLEY. Issued orders to CAPT FREW to proceed with 18 O.R. to ROCLINCOURT tonight & take over tomorrow morning the ADS & Relay Posts above mentioned. JMR	
ROCLINCOURT	22nd		Lt FURLONG R.R.T. WORCESTA. detailed for duty at ADS TUNNEL DUMP under CAPT FREW.	
ROCLINCOURT	23rd		Unit proceeded from ACS to ROCLINCOURT. Took over Main Dressing Station from O.C. 2/3 LONDON Field Ambulance. Relief completed for ADS & Relay Posts. Notified ADMS of completion of relief. Lt GEORGE R.M. WORCESTA. detailed for temporary duty with 18th W. YORKS. Copies of receipts of stores taken over from 2/3 LONDON Field Amb forwarded to ADMS. JMR. C.O. arrived ADS at 10 a.m. Complete inspection proceeding held. Proceeded to ADS. TUNNEL DUMP & ADS. CAMOUFLAGE ROAD & inspected these. JMR	

WAR DIARY or INTELLIGENCE SUMMARY

94th Field Ambulance

Place	Date	Hour	Summary of Events and Information	Remarks and references to Appendices
	1917			
ROCLINCOURT	24th		Inspected billets & paid the unit. JMcL	
ROCLINCOURT	25th		Xmas Day. All men that could be spared allowed off duty after midday. Special meals prepared for unit. JMcL	
ROCLINCOURT	26th		Inspected dumps. Temporary horse shed for A.S.C. completed. JMcL	
ROCLINCOURT	27th		Visited ADS. Tunnel Dump & Relay posts in connection with that ADS. Indented for timber for gas doors for these places. JMcL	
"	28th		Nothing to report. JMcL	
"	29th		Nothing to report. JMcL	
"	30th		Men at Relay posts changed over with men from Main Dressing Station. JMcL	
"	31st		Men at the two ADSs changed over with men from MDS. JMcL	

J McLaren
Capt RAMC
a/OC 94th Field Ambulance

Jan. 1918

120/784

No. 94. F.A.

3/

COMMITTEE FOR THE
MEDICAL HISTORY OF THE WAR

Date -8 APR 1918

WAR DIARY or **INTELLIGENCE SUMMARY**

Army Form C. 2118.

(Erase heading not required.)

94th Field Ambulance

Place	Date January 1918	Hour	Summary of Events and Information	Remarks and references to Appendices
ROCLINCOURT	1st		The men who were relieved yesterday from the A.D.S. & Relay Post were given special meals. JWE	
"	2nd		Lt FURLONG detailed for duty at A.D.S. VANCOUVER ROAD transferring him from A.D.S. TUNNEL DUMP. JWE	
"	3rd		Inspected the M.D.S. & horse lines thoroughly. Improvements being carried out. Received orders from A.D.M.S. to arrange guides for 1 officer & NCO of 56th Division to make a reconnaissance of the Medical Arrangements of the Left Brigade Sector tomorrow. This is the Sector which the A.D.S. VANCOUVER ROAD drains. JWE	
"	4th		Visited the A.D.S. V.R. with 1 officer & NCO from the 56th Division, also Relay Posts & Regimental Aid Posts of Left Sector, giving him a sketch of evacuation routes. JWE	
"	5th		Visited A.D.S. TUNNEL DUMP JWE	
"	6th		CAPT BROWN relieved Capt FREW at A.D.S. T. DUMP who returned to Head Quarters & proceeded to 18th W. YORKS as temporary M.O. relieving Lt GEORGE. JWE	

WAR DIARY or INTELLIGENCE SUMMARY

Army Form C. 2118.

94th Field Ambulance

Place	Date January 1918	Hour	Summary of Events and Information	Remarks and references to Appendices
ROCLINCOURT	7th		Nothing to note. JWE	
"	8th		New dispensary completed & inside of horse standings whitewashed. JWE	
"	9th		Inspected whole M.D.S. JWE	
"	10th		With the D.A.D.M.S. inspected the ground between ROCLINCOURT & THELUS on the ARRAS-LENS road for a position for new Advanced Dressing Station in case of a retiral, also the ground further back between the above mentioned road & the ARRAS-BETHUNE road. JWE	
"	11th		Lt. GEORGE detailed for temporary duty as M.O. to 18th W. YORKS in relief of CAPT. FREW who returned to Head quarters having been put under "close arrest" by O.C. of that unit. Under instructions from A.D.M.S. I went to the 18th W. YORKS with Capt. ARTHUR of 93rd Field Ambulance & took charge of Capt. FREW bringing him back to Head quarters here. CAPT FREW was suffering from 'gastritis' & was admitted to the officers' ward — CAPT ARTHUR be detailed in charge of him. The charge was being "Drunk whilst on duty". CAPT GRAHAM J RAMC T.F. reported arrival & was taken on the strength of this unit. JWE	

WAR DIARY or INTELLIGENCE SUMMARY

Army Form C. 2118.

94th Field Ambulance

Place	Date January 1918	Hour	Summary of Events and Information	Remarks and references to Appendices
RACLINCOURT	12th		CAPT FREW sent under escort of CAPT ARTHUR to Officers' Rest Station suffering from "gastritis" accompanied by a "confidential" memo to the O.C. XIII Corps Rest Station. JMcS	
"	13th		Church of England parade. D.D.M.S. Corps inspected Main Dressing Station & Advanced Dressing Station at TUNNEL DUMP inspecting the Relay Posts in TOMMY ALLEY. Received a memo from O.C. 18th W. YORKS saying that on the 11th inst. he had placed Capt. FREW R.A.M.C. temporary M.O. of this Battalion under close arrest for being "Drunk whilst on duty." Visited the Advanced Dressing Station at VANCOUVER ROAD. CAPT GRAHAM detailed for duty at that A.D.S. JMcS	
"	14th		New harness room for A.S.C. completed. Received confidential memo from A.D.M.S. to report action when CAPT FREW returned to his unit from the Officers' Rest Station so that Charge Sheet & Summary of Evidence could be prepared. JMcS	
"	15th		Canteen has been built & opened. Inspected whole Main Dressing Station. JMcS	

WAR DIARY or **INTELLIGENCE SUMMARY**

Army Form C. 2118.

94th Field Ambulance

Place	Date January 1918	Hour	Summary of Events and Information	Remarks and references to Appendices
ROCLINCOURT	16th		An officer from the 2/1 WEST YORKSHIRE Field Ambulance arrived to make a reconnaissance of the Medical arrangements. A guide was detailed to take him to the Advanced Dressing Station VANCOUVER ROAD, Lt. FURLONG took him round the Relay Posts & Regimental Aid Posts. Lt.Col STEWART returned from leave to the U.K.	
"	17		Returned from leave of absence last evening. Checked accounts & found all Correct. Went round the whole place and perused all orders etc issued since I left. D.H.Stewart Lt.Col Comm'd	
"	18		Reported at A.D.M.S. office. Board on Officer. Saw D.A.D.V.S. and arranged for the examination of the Veterinary Corps 31 Div. Sgt. STARLING reduced to permanent rank of Driver on account of inefficiency & sent to H.T. Depot Base.	

WAR DIARY or INTELLIGENCE SUMMARY

[Army Form C. 2118.]

Place	Date January 1918	Hour	Summary of Events and Information	Remarks and references to Appendices
ROCLINCOURT		19.	Examination of R.E. Patrol Section 31 Div.	
		20	Attend conference of Officers called by D.M.S. 1st Army at Army Headquarters with reference to the proposed reduction of Infantry Brigades and the reductions which could be made in the Medical units. L. George W.S.M.C. granted special leave of absence to Boulogne in order to attend an examination for a commission in the Regular Army. W.S. Leave granted from 20th to 25th. Completed examination of R.E. Patrol Section. Proceedings of Board signed and forwarded to the A.D.M.S. 31 Div.	

WAR DIARY
or
INTELLIGENCE SUMMARY

14 Field Amb.

Place	Date January 1918	Hour	Summary of Events and Information	Remarks and references to Appendices
Roclincourt	21		Proceeded this morning with D.A.D.M.S. 31 Div to A.D.S., Tunnel Dump and the Regimental aid posts & Relay posts attached. Found everything satisfactory. Recommended that the accommodation for personnel should be increased by banking the dugouts. Arranged that the clothing taken from men who were gassed should be noted and a list accompany the man in order that he may be able to get new ones in exchange. Examined half the men of the Relieving Corps 31 Div this afternoon.	
"	22		Concluded examination of Relieving Corps and forwarded proceedings of Board to A.D.M.S. Capt BROWN detailed as member of a board held at A.D.M.S. office on an officer	

WAR DIARY or INTELLIGENCE SUMMARY

Army Form C. 2118.

Place	Date	Hour	Summary of Events and Information	Remarks and references to Appendices
Roclincourt	January 1918 23		Went to Transport Lines 18 W. Yorks & saw Capt A.W. FREW and arranged with him for legal assistance at the Court Martial.	
"	24		Went round the left sector of the line & visited A.D.S Vancouver Road and aid posts. The work on new fore chambers proceeding well. The men's dug out requires more bunks. Gas curtains well fixed. Everything satisfactory. Relieved all aid posts & A.D.S. today. Method, the men work in 3 reliefs each relief having a Sgt & Corporal & 24 men. A new relief from Headquarters proceeds to A.D.S. A.T.D at 7am. On relief the personnel of T.D proceeds to V-R & relieve the personnel there who return to	

WAR DIARY
or
INTELLIGENCE SUMMARY

(Erase heading not required.)

Army, Form. C. 2118.

Instructions regarding War Diaries and Intelligence Summaries are contained in F. S. Regs., Part II. and the Staff Manual respectively. Title Pages will be prepared in manuscript.

Place	Date January 1918	Hour	Summary of Events and Information	Remarks and references to Appendices
Roclincourt			Headquarters. Before leaving each man hands in one pair of socks and daily afterwards clean socks are sent up of the bearers to replace dirty ones which are sent down, by this means all the bearers have a clean dry pair of socks daily. Cap. McEwen relieves Lt Furlong at V.R.a.D.S. today.	
"	25.		Indents for material of the erection of a separate hut for dental surgeon and also for the provision of beds in No 1 & 2 wards. No present dressing hut has been replaced by a marquise and the hut turned into ward for lying cases.	
"	26		Have had to put some of the personnel in tents owing to the wetness of the dugouts occupied by them, No sign of the three Nissen huts which I asked for fittings arriving	

WAR DIARY
or
INTELLIGENCE SUMMARY
(Erase heading not required.)

Army Form C. 2118.

4 Field Ambulance

9

Place	Date	Hour	Summary of Events and Information	Remarks and references to Appendices
Rochinat	January 1918 27		D.D.M.S XIII Corps inspected M.D.S. and appeared pleased. S.	
"	28		Lt. GEORGE returned from leave to Boulogne age camp. Inspected T.D aid posts & A.D.S. everything satisfactory. Lt. FURLONG relieved Lt. KNAPP who returned to Headquarters. Examining f/p B M.T. S.A.P.N Corps (Caterpillar Section).	
"	29		Nothing to report.	
"	30		Completed examination of Caterpillar Section & did f/p MT personnel at 99 H. Arty Brigade. Went round T.D & aid posts with the O.C. 1/1 W. Riding Field Ambulance.	
"	31		Finished Boards proceeding sent to A.Dms. Relief of aid posts as before. Lt. GEORGE relieved Capt. GRAHAM who relieved Lt. FURLONG at T.D.

Feb. 1918.

No. 94.7.a.

COMMITTEE FOR THE
MEDICAL HISTORY OF THE WAR

Date -8 APR. 1918

WAR DIARY or INTELLIGENCE SUMMARY

Army Form C. 2118.

Vol 24

Place	Date February 1918	Hour	Summary of Events and Information	Remarks and references to Appendices
ROCLINCOURT	1		Capt A.W. FREW's trial today at Div Arty Headquarters. Capt BROWN R.A.M.C. to attend as witness. Issued orders re economy of service clothing. Pte COLE sent to Forward Transportation Depot SAVY under instructions fr A.D.M.S. & struck off strength. Lt. KNAPP on sick list. Sent in War Diary for January to A.D.M.S.	
	2		Lt. KNAPP transferred to 30. C.C.S. today suffering from trench Nephritis.	
	3		Sunday - Divine Services for troops at 10.30. Revd R. HAYWARD C.F. reports his arrival on posting to unit - taken on strength.	

WAR DIARY or INTELLIGENCE SUMMARY

Army Form C. 2118.

Place	Date	Hour	Summary of Events and Information	Remarks and references to Appendices
ROCLINCOURT	February 1918 4		Went up to A.D.S. Vancouver Road and the R.A.P.s & relay posts in HUDSON Trench. Everything satisfactory. Went to see A.D.M.S. re Lt. BARLOW with a view to getting this officer leave. Saw the C.R.A. on same subject. Strained & gave certificate to Lt. BARLOW that he was free (as far as I could say) from Syphilis.	
"	5		Sent R. ROBINSON to OC 31 D.A.C. for massage work. Capt A.W. FREW returned from 18. WEST YORKS on release after promulgation of Court Martial in which he was charged (a) Drunkenness (b) Conduct prejudicial to good order & military Discipline in that he on the 11th January was unfit to carry out his duty owing to the effects of alcohol. The Court found him not guilty on the first Charge & guilty on the Second Charge	

WAR DIARY or INTELLIGENCE SUMMARY

Army Form C. 2118.

94 Field Amb.

Place	Date	Hour	Summary of Events and Information	Remarks and references to Appendices
	February 1916			
			& "reprimanded" him. Saw A.D.M.S. & requested that he would for Capt FREW transferred to another unit preferably at the Base as he was over 42 years of age - had served with a Division for over 2½ years. P.	
ROCLINCOURT	6		Went up to Tunnel Dump A.D.S. and the R.A.P. & relay posts. All satisfactory. Everything at the A.D.S. was in good order. Capt GRAHAM returns to HQ. P.	
	7		Relief 2 Bearers today. 26 bearers for HQ to T.D. & 26 bearers for T.D. to V.R. the latter on relief returning to HQ. Capt McEWEN on relief by Capt BROWN at V.R. proceeded to T.D. and Capt GRAHAM returned to Headquarters. Capt ALEXANDER Lt. M.O. 18 WEST YORKS on the battalion	

WAR DIARY or INTELLIGENCE SUMMARY

Army Form C. 2118.

(Erase heading not required.)

Place	Date February 19	Hour	Summary of Events and Information	Remarks and references to Appendices
ROCLINCOURT		7	being taken up is posted to my unit as reinforcement & taken on the strength. R.	
"		8	Board held today on remaining members of A.V.C. 35 Division & Classification was made. Proceedings forwarded to A.D.M.S. for disposal. R.	
"		9	Lecture at 1st Army Headquarters by A.D.M.S. Sanitary G.H.Q. detailed Capt FREW & Lt FURLONG to go there. Went up to T.D with D.D.M.S. XIII Corps inspected them then went across to WILLERVAL & Div Artillery H'Q' and then returned. D. O[illegible] [illegible] [illegible] with [illegible]. Lt. & Q. Mr A.H.A JIBB [illegible] leave of absence to U.K. from 10th to 24th and left Headquarters today orders received that Capt FREW was to proceed to 93 F.A. for duty R.	

WAR DIARY or INTELLIGENCE SUMMARY

94 Field Ambulance

Place	Date 1918	Hour	Summary of Events and Information	Remarks and references to Appendices
ROCLINCOURT	February	10	Went up to T.D today & proceeded up Centre road to ARLEUX LOOP Trench. Our new R.A.P. then down trench & across to V.R. everything in a satisfactory condition. Tommy Tunnels very good. Reports sent to A.D.M.S. Went to see D.D.M.S. and H.Q. XIII Corps as he wants to see me with reference to the CLAYTON championship. Capt FREW reported his departure to 93rd F.A. 4 Reinforcements arrived today all Class B men and in my opinion unsuitable for F.A. work. R.	
		11	Lt KNAPP reported by O.C. 30 C.C.S as having been evacuated to base is struck off the strength of this unit from this date. R.	
		12	Went up to A.D.S. V.R. with Capt FARMER O.C. 74 Sanitary Sect. who was making an inspection. Left him with M.O. and inspected relay posts & also tested the evacuation stretcher carries &	

WAR DIARY or INTELLIGENCE SUMMARY

Army Form C. 2118.

Place	Date	Hour	Summary of Events and Information	Remarks and references to Appendices
ROCLINCOURT			found it worked excellently. A patient could be carried by two men from the R.A.P. to the A.D.S. by in half the time 4 men could previously carry him. Reported A.D.M.S. Issued instructions that all Aid posts are to be equipped with Thomas Splints & suspension bars to the scale laid down by D.M.S. 1st Army. Viz. 2 in each R.A.P. & A.D.S. R	
"		13	nothing to report. R	
"		14.	Relief of bearers today. 26 bearers from H.Q. to T.D. 26 bearers from T.D. to V.R. and the bearers from V.R. to Strong Point also completed satisfactorily. Capt. McEWEN having been relieved by Lt. GEORGE returned to Headquarters & Lt. FURLONG relieved Lt. GEORGE at V.R.	
"		15	Seven recruits arrived of 62 Div today all class B men but better than the previous lot. R	

WAR DIARY or INTELLIGENCE SUMMARY

Army Form C. 2118.

Place	Date	Hour	Summary of Events and Information	Remarks and references to Appendices
ROCLINCOURT	February 1918 16		6 further reinforcements for 62 Division arrived. Everything checked. No blankets sent to WDMS.	
"	17		Sunday services	
"	18		Checked equipment in store. Found all correct. ~~Reinforcements for 62 Division leaving~~ Issued orders re Censorship. DADMS came round here with Lt Col FAICHNIE.	
"	19		Went up to A.D.S. T.D. and thence up ARLEUX Road to ORCHARD DUGOUT which I consider very suitable for new A.D.S. Conference in afternoon at ADMS office. Questions re equipment of Ambulances, ADS work etc discussed	
"	20		Conference at DDMS office	

WAR DIARY or INTELLIGENCE SUMMARY

Army Form C. 2118.

Place	Date	Hour	Summary of Events and Information	Remarks and references to Appendices
ROCLINCOURT	21		Went up with D.A.D.W.s & V.R. Inspection everything satisfactory. New Room for Bt. Commandants House at ROCLINCOURT almost completed. Site selected for proposed A.D.S. of Heavy Artillery on side of tram road. P.H. helmets all taken in today. Relief of teams 26 teams for HQ to T.D. 26 of T.D. to V.R. and 26 for V.R. to HQ. Lt. Capt. BROWN relieves Lt. GEORGE at T.D. and Capt. GRAHAM proceeds to V.R. all relief satisfactorily carried out.	
"	22		Issued new time table today to take effect forthwith. Capt. ROCHE R.A.M.C. transferred from 93 Field Ambulance is taken on the strength, this officer is now proceeding on leave to U.K. He was formerly M.O. to 1/6 West Yorks.	

WAR DIARY or INTELLIGENCE SUMMARY

Army Form C. 2118.

(Erase heading not required.)

Place	Date	Hour	Summary of Events and Information	Remarks and references to Appendices
ROULINCOURT		23	Checked all extra stores at H.Q. all correct.	
"		24	Sunday Service. Went up to ARLEUX road with Sgt. MAJOR to see new site of A.D.S. Arranged details as to proposed alteration. Went to A.D.S. T.O. Capt. BROWN in bed, will relieve him tomorrow morning if possible. Lt. PEORGE detached for duty with No 2 Lancer & left H.Q.	
"		25	Court of enquiry held respecting death of No. 75/0,77,183 Pte AARON who died at 30 C.C.S. as the result of an accident while driving Ford Ambulance on duty on the 20.2.18. Death resulted on 22.2.18 from extensive rupture of liver.	
"		26	Capt ALEXANDER proceeded to V.R. in relief of Lt. FURLONG who was ordered to proceed to T.D. & relieve Capt BROWN	

WAR DIARY or INTELLIGENCE SUMMARY

Army Form C. 2118.

10

Place	Date	Hour	Summary of Events and Information	Remarks and references to Appendices
	26		WO returned to HQ., Rev. HAYWARD proceeded to ST OMER for a choice of temporary took of duty. Capt M?EWEN proceeded to BAILLEUL AUX CORNAILLES to arrange details of relief Rec. work of OC. 2/1 W. Riding F.A. Lt. & Q.M. A.H.A. JIBB returned fr. leave to U.K. (granted one day extension by W.O)	
	27		Issued orders re relief by the 2/1 W. Riding F.A. Copy of order attached. Arranged with O.C. 2/1 W. Riding F.A. as to details. Capt M?EWEN + 26 men proceeded as advance party to BAILLEUL AUX CORNAILLES. One Officer + 26 O.R. 2/1 W. Riding F.A. arrived here & accommodated for the night	See Field amb order No 19.

WAR DIARY or INTELLIGENCE SUMMARY

Army Form C. 2118.

(Erase heading not required.)

Place	Date	Hour	Summary of Events and Information	Remarks and references to Appendices
ROCLINCOURT	28		Officers & bearers at T.D. returned to H.Q. this evening handing over A.D.S. & relay posts to 2/c W. Riding F.A. All equipment handed over, receipt obtained. Field ambulance equipment brought down counting, check. One Officer + 26 O.R. for 2/c W. Riding F.A. & one M.O. ambulance orderly handed over to taken over V.R. tomorrow. Handing completed.	

Dun Stewart.
D. L. L. Rowan
Comd 9 & 7 Amb.

COPY No. SECRET.

94th FIELD AMBULANCE ORD.R No.19. by Lieut-Col. HUGH
STEWART, D.S.O., M.C., R.A.M.C., Commanding 94th Field Ambulance.

Ref. Map 36 B. 1:40000.   27.2.18.

1. The 31st Division is to be relieved in the line by the 52nd Division
   and will move into VILLERS CHATEL for training. Reliefs to be completed
   by March 4th.

2. THE Ambulance will be relieved by the 2/2nd West Riding F.A. as
   follows:-
   Feb. 28. Right Brigade Sector.
   Mar. 1. Left Brigade Sector.
   Mar. 2. Main Dressing Station.

3. DETAIL. The Officer i/c A.D.S., T.D., will prepare a list of Trench
   Stores to be handed over in triplicate - one copy will be given to the
   Officer i/c party incoming Unit - the other two copies duly completed and
   signed will be handed into this Office. The 2/2nd West Riding F.A. will
   send a party consisting of 1 Officer and 26 Other Ranks to A.D.S., T.D.,
   on the morning of the 28th. Lieut. FURLONG will then head over the
   forward posts and afterwards the A.D.S. on completion of relief he will
   march his party to Headquarters, leaving Q.M.S. MARSHALL and 1 Other Rank
   in charge of the Field Ambulance equipment. Arrangements have been made
   that a special truck will run on the train to T.D. bringing up the
   equipment of the 2/2nd West Riding F.A. and will bring back the
   equipment of the 2/2nd. Q.M.S. MARSHALL will be responsible that all
   Ambulance equipment is brought down. The A.D.S. and Relay Posts will be
   handed over in a clean condition and a certificate to this effect
   obtained.

   B. W.R. The Officer i/c V.R. will prepare similar lists as the Officer
   i/c T.D. and dispose of them in a similar manner. The 2/2nd East Riding
   F.A. will send 2 Officers and 26 Other Ranks to take over the A.D.S. and
   posts on the morning of the 1st March. On completion of relief the
   Field Ambulance party will return to Headquarters. Sgt. HAGARTY and 1
   Other Rank will remain behind and bring down the Field Ambulance
   equipment and be responsible that all is brought down. The Ambulance
   equipment is the equipment of the 2/2nd West Riding F.A. will bring back
   the Field Ambulance equipment.

   C. MAIN DRESSING STATION. The Main Dressing Station will be handed
   over on the 2nd March to the 2/2nd West Riding F.A. The Field Ambulance
   will remain in their present Billets the night of the 2nd March and will
   move to ECOIVRES by train on the 3rd and to BAILLEUL-AUX-CORNAILLES by
   train on the 4th. Times will be notified later.

4. Capt. McEWEN and 26 Other Ranks will proceed in charge of the Transport which will
   move by road on the 3rd and 4th March. Time of march will be notified
   later.

5. Capt. ALEXANDER will proceed in charge of the Transport which will
   move by road on the 3rd and 4th March. Time of march will be notified
   later.

6. The Quartermaster will be responsible that all stores etc. are
   correctly handed over to the incoming Unit and receipts obtained.

7. ACKNOWLEDGE.

                                           [signature]
                                           Lt.Col. R.A.M.C.
                                           Commanding 94th Field Ambulance.

Copies to:- 1. O/c A.D.S., T.D.
            2. O/c A.D.S., V.R.
            3. Capt. McEWEN.
            4. Capt. ALEXANDER.
            5. Lt. & Q.M. JIBB.
            6. OFFICE.
            7 & 8. WAR DIARY.

Mar. 1918

140/2902

92nd Field Ambulance

COMMITTEE FOR THE
MEDICAL HISTO
Date -6 JUN.1918

WAR DIARY or INTELLIGENCE SUMMARY

Army Form C. 2118.

Place	Date	Hour	Summary of Events and Information	Remarks and references to Appendices
ROCLINCOURT	March 1918 1		A.D.S. and relay post Vancouver Road handed over to party of 2/2 W. Riding Field Ambulance. Cap GRAHAM and party returned to Headquarters. Advance party of 2/2 W. Riding Field Ambulance. Bullecourt Reserve.	
"	2		Handed over Main Dressing Station to 2/2 W. Riding Field Ambulance. All preparations made for move. Train arranged. Cap ALEXANDER to take the transport. Saw Cap McEWEN about billets everything satisfactory.	
Mt S.T ELOI	3		Moved to OTTAWA Camp today.	
BAILLEUL AUX CORNAILLES	4		Personnel dismounted moved under orders of Cap BROWN to RATINQUES by rail and thence by road. Transport moved under orders of Cap ALEXANDER. On arrival unit moved into	

WAR DIARY
or
INTELLIGENCE SUMMARY

Army Form C. 2118.

2/4 Field Ambulance

Place	Date	Hour	Summary of Events and Information	Remarks and references to Appendices
BAILLEUL AUX CORNAILLES		4	prepared billets. Sent notification to A.D.M.S. 31 Div. Forwarded banking over certificates. Capt ALEXANDER ordered to 31 Div Machine Gun Battalion reported his departure and is struck off the strength from today.	
"		5	Devoted day to cleaning up wagons & men preparatory to D.M.S. 1st Army inspection. G.	
"		6	Inspection by D.M.S. 1st Army. Inspection of men. March past. Transport. The D.M.S. congratulated unit on their smart turn out. Drew up programme of training for remainder of week. G.	
"		7	Training begun. Physical drill. Squad & Company drill and lecture by Capt GRAHAM on "Haemorrhage". L Furlong	

WAR DIARY or INTELLIGENCE SUMMARY

Army Form C. 2118.

1/4 Field Ambulance

Place	Date	Hour	Summary of Events and Information	Remarks and references to Appendices
	March 1918			
BAILLEUL AUX CORNAILLES	7		With Sgt Sutton went to 1st Army School of Instruction today	
	8		Route march today. Lecture on application of THOMAS Splint followed by practical work by Cpl BROWN.	
"	9		Squad & Company drill after C.O's parade. No training in afternoon. Capt. BROWN leave to U.K. 10-24	
"	10		Church parade service 9.30. Kit inspection	
	11		C.O's parade. Physical drill. Squad & Company drill. "B" Section equipment checked & wagons loaded.	
	12		C.O's parade. Saluting order drill. Early dismiss. Route march & Football match.	
	13		C.O's parade. Squad drill. Lecture by Capt McEWEN on Dentistry	

WAR DIARY or INTELLIGENCE SUMMARY

Army Form C. 2118.

Place	Date	Hour	Summary of Events and Information	Remarks and references to Appendices
BAILLEUL AUX CORNAILLE	MARCH 1918 14		C.O's parade. "C" Section equipment checked & loaded. Practical instruction & application of Thomas Splints. Squad drill & stretcher drill with respirations. Officers Class. Arrangement details of sections.	
"	15		C.O's parade. Physical drill. Squad & Coy drill. Stretcher roller drill. Lecture 1st Aid Capt ROWE. Officers Class. Conference at D.M.S. Offices. Capts McEWEN & GRAHAM made a reconnaissance of ground for Field day with 92 Brigade.	
"	16		Field day 92 I.B. Detailed orders issued. Capt McEWEN acting as O.C. formed A.D.S. Capt GRAHAM with bearers. Work were carried out very intelligently.	
"	17		Church parade 9-30.	

WAR DIARY
or
INTELLIGENCE SUMMARY
(Erase heading not required.)

Army Form C. 2118.

5.

Place	Date MARCH 1918	Hour	Summary of Events and Information	Remarks and references to Appendices
BAILLEUL AUX CORNAILLES		18	L̶ Furlong returned fr 1st Army School yesterday. Lt. GEORGE posted to 11. E. James arr think off Strength. Training resumed. Previous order drill practices.	
"		19	Lt. Furlong posted permanently to 10. E. Yks & taken off Strength this leaves us 3 officers short. Lecture by T + Q Master A.H.A. JIBB on "Economy" + "Salvage".	
"		20	Received orders that unit to return to the line on the 25th & to g. to ANZIN.	
"		21	G.O.C. 31 Div inspected unit on parade & said "Good Bye" on handing over Command of the Division. Order to move to line cancelled. Received warning order 4 "B" to be prepared to Entrain for 3rd Army Area at 8 am tomorrow. this received at 12 midnight. Issued all necessary orders. Cpt. ROCHE to take transport. Lt. JIBB to bring on Motors after lorry loaded.	

WAR DIARY or INTELLIGENCE SUMMARY

Army Form C. 2118.

Place	Date	Hour	Summary of Events and Information	Remarks and references to Appendices
BAILLEULMONT	MARCH 19/18 22		Paraded unit at 7 a.m. & marched to entraining point. Entraining completed at 10.30, proceeded via ST. POL, FREVENT & DOULLENS to detraining point & marched there. The enemy have delivered a strong attack against 3rd & 5th Armies and the Division has moved up in support. The Queen's Bays relieve 95th F. Amb. & 93rd B. with 95 F.a. moved up shortly into line. Field Ambulance were warned to move into action with 93 B. & when on point of starting received orders for a. suc'd to stand fast. Went to A. Dons. office for orders but learned [?] letter & no information on the subject, the operation. Capt. McEWEN. GRAHAM promoted Major.	
	23		Remained waiting for orders all day. Capt. P. MAJOR GRAHAM & Capt. ROCHE proceeded to relieve 95 F.a. who have had two officers killed while 93	

WAR DIARY or INTELLIGENCE SUMMARY

Army Form C. 2118.

(Erase heading not required.)

Place	Date 1918	Hour	Summary of Events and Information	Remarks and references to Appendices
BAILLEULMONT	March		Have had two wounded. Nothing known as to nature of operations.	
"	24		Still under orders. Saw D.A.D.M.S. 31st Div., situation still obscure. In the afternoon heard we were likely to take over VI Corps Post Station and at 11 p.m. orders received f. a. d. m. s. to take over early next day. P.	
GOUY en ARTOIS	25		Proceeded here at 7.30 a.m. and took over VI Corps Post Station. Many sick remaining which moved to evacuation to 6 Stationary Hospital FREVENT by train from AVESNES LE COMTE. Also took over officers post station at BARLY. D.D.M.S. Corps came round and told me to get the billets cleaned and closed up. Made all arrangements for same. P.	

WAR DIARY or INTELLIGENCE SUMMARY

Army Form C. 2118.

Place	Date	Hour	Summary of Events and Information	Remarks and references to Appendices
GOUY-en-ARTOIS	26		Officers Rest Station Closed. Some Staff handed over to B.R.C. The remaining stores are being checked and stored. Evacuated most of the cases unable to walk as the situation appears to be rather precarious.	
"	27		Situation better, most cases being cleared. [illegible] round & satisfied	
"	28		Routine work.	
"	29		Routine work	
"	30		A. Dms 32 Div Came round in order to see arrangements with view to their taking over. Explained everything. Orders received later to the effect	

WAR DIARY or INTELLIGENCE SUMMARY

Army Form C. 2118.

Place	Date	Hour	Summary of Events and Information	Remarks and references to Appendices
GOUY-EN-ARTOIS	MARCH 1918 31.		Checking and handing over. Advance party sent to IVERGNY under Major McEwan. Capt BROWN left last night for 165 B. R.F.A. temp. duty. Advance party of 90 Field Amb arrived. There has been much rain during the last three days which has apparently held up the Germans in their advance. Took all papers + orders ready for march tomorrow. We are now under the orders of the 93 Brigade for tomorrow. Lt Colonel Commd 94 F Amb	

140/2902.

94th Field Ambulance

COMMITTEE FOR THE
MEDICAL HISTORY OF THE WAR
Date -6 JUN. 1918

WAR DIARY or INTELLIGENCE SUMMARY

(Erase heading not required.)

94 Field Amb

Army Form C. 2118.

19

VR 261

Place	Date	Hour	Summary of Events and Information	Remarks and references to Appendices
IVERGNY	1		Unit marched from GOUY-EN-ARTOIS to IVERGNY & went into billets overnight	Graham Major RAMC
HOUVELIN	2		Unit embussed at Beaudricourt & proceeded to Billets at HOUVELIN with 93rd Brigade. Brigade being under three hours notice to move.	
"	3rd to 7th		This time was taken up with kit & equipment inspections & men bathed & given clean clothes.	
	7th		Major Graham proceeded to ANZIN with working party of 25 men.	
	8th		Nothing to Report.	
TINCQUES	9th		Unit marched to TINCQUES & went into billets	
	10th		Unit embussed at 6pm. Arrived at MERRIS 7am on 11th April.	
MERRIS	11th		Major Graham & party from ANZIN rejoined.	
STRAZEELE	12th		Two officers & 19 O.R. proceeded to M.D.S. OUTTERSTEENE. One Officer & 69 O.R. reported for duty with 93rd F. Amb. Remainder of unit formed MDS at STRAZEELE. Party from MDS. OUTTESTEENE rejoined. Lieut. Col. Hugh Stewart DSO M.C. RAMC Commg. the unit & Lieut & Q.M. A.H.A. JIBB were killed & Major T. McEWEN M.C. RAMC(SR) seriously wounded by a shell bursting outside the M.D.S. Major Graham handed over to Lieut Col POLLARD DSO RAMC Comg. 93rd F. Amb. & proceeded with the unit to establish an M.D.S at BORRÉ.	
BORRÉ	13th		General Routine of MDS carried on. Lieut Col HUGH STEWART DSO MC RAMC buried in churchyard at Borré.	
LA KREULE	14th		On the division being withdrawn from the line the MDS at Borré was evacuated & unit proceeded to LA KREULE. Under instructions from A.D.M.S 31 Div Major C.L.T Arthur RAMC took over Temp. Command of the unit	Graham Major RAMC

WAR DIARY or INTELLIGENCE SUMMARY

(Erase heading not required.)

Army Form C. 2118.

Instructions regarding War Diaries and Intelligence Summaries are contained in F. S. Regs., Part II. and the Staff Manual respectively. Title Pages will be prepared in manuscript.

Place	Date	Hour	Summary of Events and Information	Remarks and references to Appendices
LA KREULE	April 15		Col. A.W. BEWLEY CMG. AMS. visited the unit & said Goodbye on the occasion of his leaving the Division. Major Rawe	
"	16		Under instruction of ADMS 31 Div. M.I. Room was opened at HONDEGHEM. Lieut SEAPORT MARCASA proceeded in charge.	
"	17		M.I. Room enlarged. Lieut MARTIN RAMC sent up in charge. On Composite Brigade going into Rearm Defences M.D.S was opened at LA KREULE (Sheet 27 V.16.B.7.6.). Capt. J.G. LEE RAMC reported arrival for temp. duty with unit.	
"	18		Nothing to report.	
LES CINQ RUES	19		Capt LEE returned to duty with 15 W. Yorks. M.D.S at LA KREULE handed over to 89th F. Amb. Unit marched to LES CINQ RUES & took over M.D.S from 3 Aust. F. Amb. at (V.19.C.2.6 Sheet 27) A.D.S formed by 98th & 75th F. Amb. at LA MOTTE D.30.d.1.7. Evacuation carried out by F. Amb. cars from A.D.S & M.D.S thence to No. 15 CCS by M.A.C. Major E.C. LONG DSO. RAMC. arrived to take over command of the unit.	
"	20			
LES CINQ RUES	21st to 26th		Nothing of importance to report. The unit is still running Main Dressing Station.	
LES CINQ RUES	27th		The main Dressing Station was handed over to 89th Field Ambulance 29th Division, and the unit marched by road to LA KREULE (Sheet 27 V.16.b.5.5) and was accommodated in huts on old C.C.S. site	

WAR DIARY or INTELLIGENCE SUMMARY

Army Form C. 2118.

(Erase heading not required.)

Place	Date	Hour	Summary of Events and Information	Remarks and references to Appendices
LA KREULE	27th		Major GRAHAM J. and Lieut. MARTIN W. proceeded with 14 O.R, one motor ambulance and one horsed ambulance wagon to establish a collecting post to deal with the sick from 93rd Inf. Bde at C18 d.0.3 Sheet 36 A.	
LA KREULE	28th		Nothing to report beyond normal routine, all cases from Major Graham's post being evacuated to 95th Field Ambulance, who have established a field hospital at V 4 c 2 6.	
LA KREULE	29th		Conference of A.D.M.S. and O.C. field ambulances held at Div. HQ. to consider evacuation of equipment of field ambulances and also scheme of defence of HAZEBROUCK and disposition of medical services to deal with the situations arising therefrom.	
LA KREULE	30th		Major Long proceeded to reconnoitre routes of evacuation and site for A.D.S. in connection with above scheme.	

Signed.
Major Rome
O.C. 94th Field Ambce.

Confidential   2   Volume xxix

Vol 27

140/283

War Diary

94th Field Ambulance

May, 1918.

~~May 1918~~

COMMITTEE FOR THE
MEDICAL HISTORY OF THE WAR
Date 9 JUL 1918

WAR DIARY
or
INTELLIGENCE SUMMARY
(Erase heading not required.)

Army Form C. 2118.

Place	Date	Hour	Summary of Events and Information	Remarks and references to Appendices
LA KREULE	1.5.18		The ambulance is stationed at LA KREULE Sheet 27 V/16 b.5.5. with a detached post, under Major GRAHAM J. to evacuate sick from 93rd Inf. Bde. map ref Sheet 36a. C.18.d.0.3.	
LA KREULE	2.5.18 to 8.5.18		Nothing to report.	
LA KREULE	9.5.18		The ambulance relieved 1st Australian Field Ambulance in the forward area. Major GRAHAM and party returned from detached duty. Headquarters of unit remained at LA KREULE. A.D.S. formed at CAESTRE. Sheet 27 W.2.b.8.75. Personnel Major GRAHAM J, Lieut MARTIN W.B. and 28 O.R. with 2 ambulance cars and 1 water cart. The ADS is situated in a chateau with long cellar. Car loading post at FLÊTRE W.6.0.6.7. One car parked here which was car bringing patients to ADS, another returns to take its place. Evacuation from ADS by motor ambulances of 95th Field Ambulance to main dressing station at V.4.c.2.5. run by 95th Field Ambulance.	

WAR DIARY or INTELLIGENCE SUMMARY

(Erase heading not required.)

Army Form C. 2118.

Place	Date	Hour	Summary of Events and Information	Remarks and references to Appendices
LA KREULE	9.5.18		Forward area evacuation placed in charge of Major ROCHE O. who is situated at W.6.6.9.1. with two Bearer Squads and carry from his H.Q. to car loading post. Reserve Battalion R.A.P. and Relay Post established at X.1.d.5.2. Personnel 1 Sgt. and two Bearer Squads who carry across a track from his H.Q. to motoring post. Support Battalion R.A.P. and Relay Post at X.30.0.3. Personnel 1 Cpl. and two Bearer Squads who bring patients on wheeled stretchers along road to next post. Left Line Battalion R.A.P. at X.3.d.5.7. 1 Runner and 1 Bearer Squad attached who use wheeled stretcher along road to next post. The road between Reserve and Support R.A.P. is under direct observation from METEREN. Right Line R.A.P. at X.14.c.7.3. 1 Runner and two Squads attached who bring patients at night on wheeled stretcher to Relay post at X.7.d.5.7.	

WAR DIARY or INTELLIGENCE SUMMARY

Army Form C. 2118.

(Erase heading not required.)

Place	Date	Hour	Summary of Events and Information	Remarks and references to Appendices
LA KREULE	9.5.18		Personnel at Relay Post 1 N.C.O. and 1 stretcher squad who carry from hut along a track to Reserve Battalion R.A.P. at X.1.d.2.5. Evacuation takes place from Regtl & left Sectors back onto swinging hut. She road from Regtl Line R.A.P. to cross roads at X.13.b.6.1 lies under direct observation from METEREN and can only be used in daylight in very dull or misty days.	
LA KREULE	10.5.18		Nothing to report.	
LA KREULE	11.5.18		Road between Reserve and Support R.A.P.s been shelled by military police who could not allow traffic onward. Support R.A.P. altered to X.2.c.5.7. cases carried by hand along a track from hut running about 300 yards north of the road to X.1.d.4.3. This track also is continued forward to Left Line R.A.P. Walking wounded signs placed along track to guide patients.	

WAR DIARY or INTELLIGENCE SUMMARY

Army Form C. 2118.

Place	Date	Hour	Summary of Events and Information	Remarks and references to Appendices
LA KREULE	12-5-18		Anti-gas defences of A.D.S. at CAESTRE inspected by R.E. officer who arranged to put them in a state of repair	
LA KREULE	13-5-18		Evacuation from Battalion R.A.P. at X.7.d.7.9. is now being carried out by wheeled Stretchers in daylight & Cars at night along road via R.32.c.3.5. and LE ROUKLOSHILLE to Car Loading Post. In the event of CAESTRE - FLETRE road being unusable owing to shell holes or enemy fire, evacuation of cars concentrated to be via THIEUSHOUK.	
LA KREULE	14-5-18		Nothing to report	
LA KREULE	15-5-18		Relay Post on right sector at X.7.d.3.7. taken over by R.F.A. as an O.P. A new Relay Post established at W.12.d.3.9. and cases from right R.A.P. brought on wheeled stretchers at night along road via COURTE CROIX. Cars at night use main FLETRE -METEREN Road as far as X.7.d.3.7. and thence to cross roads at X.13.b.6.1.	
LA KREULE	16-5-18		Nothing to report	
LA KREULE	17-5-18		Right line R.A.P. changed to X.14.a.5.1. evacuation as before	
LA KREULE	18-5-18		Lieut. MARTIN, W.E. evacuated sick to 95th Field amb.	

WAR DIARY or INTELLIGENCE SUMMARY

Army Form C. 2118.

(Erase heading not required.)

Place	Date	Hour	Summary of Events and Information	Remarks and references to Appendices
LA KREULE	9.5.18 to 22.5.18		Nothing to report.	A.L.
LA KREULE	23.5.18		One bearer officer and 5 squads from 27th Fld Amb 9th Div arrived to relieve one half of party in forward area who on being relieved returned to Headquarters.	A.L.
LA KREULE	24.5.18		Party at A.D.S. relieved by 27th Fld. Amb. and returned to Headquarters. The unit left LA KREULE and proceeded to rest billets at QUIESTÈDE, transport by road, dismounted personnel by motor busses.	A.L.
QUIESTÈDE	25.5.18		Remainder of forward area party having been relieved by 27th Fld. Amb. arrived at Headquarters in busses. The unit has taken over the billets occupied by the South African Field Ambulance, and is dealing with the SBR of 93rd Brigade Group. Light cases are being evacuated to D.R.S. run by 93rd Fld. Amb. at LUMBRES, remaining cases to 2 & 15 C.C.S. or to special centres.	A.L.
QUIESTÈDE	26.5.18		Nothing to report.	A.L.
QUIESTÈDE	27.5.18		Programme of training while in reserve area begun including physical drill, squad & company drill, SBR drill, lectures on first aid, Thomas splint, Route marches etc.	

Place	Date	Hour	Summary of Events and Information	Remarks and references to Appendices
QUIESTÈDE	28.5.18 to 30.5.18		Programme of training continued	
QUIESTÈDE	31.5.18		A practice parade of 93rd Brigade Group was held by G.O.C. 93rd Inf. Bde. in preparation for inspection to be held by Divisional Commander on June 3rd for the purpose of presenting rewards & decorations awarded to officers & other ranks of 93rd Bde. Group during the recent fighting.	

Rhames
Lt-Col. R----
O.C. 94th Fd. Ambce.

June 1918

140/3046.

94.F.A.

COMMITTEE FOR THE
MEDICAL HISTORY OF THE WAR
Date   7 AUG 1918

WAR DIARY or INTELLIGENCE SUMMARY

Army Form C. 2118.

94 Fd Amb
Vol 28

Place	Date	Hour	Summary of Events and Information	Remarks and references to Appendices
QUIESTEDE	1.6.18		The ambulance is in rest billets at QUIESTEDE evacuating sick of 93rd Inf. Bde. Admissions Wounded nil Sick Officers 2 Major C.F. MILSON A.S.C. SSO 31 Div. Asthma to CCS on same date. O.R nil. Lieut W.E. MARTIN RAMC having been evacuated to Base on 22.5.18 is Struck off the Strength from that date.	
QUIESTEDE	2.6.18		Admissions Officers nil. O.R. Sick 3 Wounded nil. Evacuated same date.	
QUIESTEDE	3.6.18		The transport of 93rd Brigade Group was inspected in the morning by G.O.C. 31st Div. who expressed his satisfaction at the appearance of the horses, harness & vehicles. Dismounted personnel in review order inspected by the 2nd Army Commander in the afternoon, for the purpose of presenting rewards & decorations awarded on the recent fighting. The following from 94th Fed Ambulance were presented Major C Roche. Bar to Military Cross. Sgt T Booth. Military Medal	

WAR DIARY or INTELLIGENCE SUMMARY

Army Form C. 2118.

(Erase heading not required.)

Place	Date	Hour	Summary of Events and Information	Remarks and references to Appendices
QUIESTEDE	3.6.18		Admissions Officers. Sick nil. Wounded nil. OR Sick 4 Wounded nil.	Ch
QUIESTEDE	4.6.18		Major J. GRAHAM and Capt. R.M. McMINN left the unit to proceed on 14 days leave to United Kingdom. Admissions Officers nil OR Sick 4 Wounded nil.	Ch
QUIESTEDE	5.6.18		Re-inoculation of personnel commenced. Admissions Officers Sick Major WHITE R.C. 13th Y & L Regt. Wounded nil. OR Sick 3 Wounded nil Evacuated Same date.	Ch
QUIESTEDE	6.6.18		Inoculation of personnel continued. Admissions Officers nil OR Sick 2 Wounded nil. Evacuated Same date. M.O. i/c 15th W. Yorks Regt. reports occurrence of a considerable number of cases of Influenza among that battalion & 93rd L.T.M.B. 7 of these sent to D.R.S. run by 93rd Fld Amb. Remainder isolated regimentally in marquee & treated by M.O. i/c 15th W. Yorks Regt.	Ch

WAR DIARY or INTELLIGENCE SUMMARY.

Army Form C. 2118.

Place	Date	Hour	Summary of Events and Information	Remarks and references to Appendices
QUIESTEDE	7.6.18		Capt G.M. MILLER M.C. proceeded for temporary duty as M.O./c 38th Labour Group.	
			M.O./c 15th W. Yorks Regt reports number of cases of Influenza diminishing.	
			In accordance with orders from A.D.M.S. arrangements made for "delousing" all cases diagnosed Trench Fever. Inhaling tent fitted to act as bathing tent & supply of clean underclothing indented for. Instructions issued that all such cases are to be bathed, hair cut & in necessary pubic & axillary hair shaved & are treated with paraffin. Clean underclothing to be supplied & patient warmed in pyjamas. All patients clothing to be disinfected in Thresh disinfector at WARDRECQUES. Inoculation of personnel continued. Admissions Sick nil. Wounded nil. A.P.	
			Temp Lieut & Q.M. J.G. FRASER reported his arrival & is taken on the strength from this date. A.P.	

WAR DIARY or INTELLIGENCE SUMMARY.

Army Form C. 2118.

(Erase heading not required.)

Place	Date	Hour	Summary of Events and Information	Remarks and references to Appendices
QUIESTEDE	8.6.18		In accordance with orders from A.D.M.S. three horsed ambulances & three G.S. wagons detailed to follow 94th Inf. Bde. on the line of march to LUMBRES area, as two battalions of the Brigade are heavily infected with malaria, & it was anticipated that many men will fall out. Major ROCHE proceeded in charge of the party. Admissions Officers nil O.R. Sick 7 Wounded nil Evacuated 5 to CCS. Remaining 2	At
QUIESTEDE	9.6.18		Tents erected to accommodate slight cases as D.R.S. is now full. Accommodation provided 42 beds. Admissions Officers nil O.R. Sick 1 Wounded nil	At
QUIESTEDE	10.6.18		Admissions Officers Sick 1 (Major W.H.D GIFFIN. A.S.C. 19th Aux Horse Coy.) Wounded nil. O.R. Sick 4 Wounded nil Evacuations Officers 1. O.R. 2 to CCS	At
QUIESTEDE	11.6.18		Admissions Officers Sick one Wounded nil. O.R. Sick 2 Wounded nil Evacuations to CCS. Officers Sick one. O.R. Sick one.	At

WAR DIARY or INTELLIGENCE SUMMARY.

(Erase heading not required.)

Army Form C. 2118.

Place	Date	Hour	Summary of Events and Information	Remarks and references to Appendices
QUIESTEDE	12.6.18		Admissions. Officers Sick nil Wounded nil OR Sick 8 Wounded nil. Evacuations to C.C.S. Officers nil OR Sick 6 Wounded nil. Prevailing disease Influenza (4) OR	
QUIESTEDE	13.6.18		Admissions Officers Sick nil Wounded nil OR Sick 8 Wounded nil. Evacuations to C.C.S. 4 Prevailing Disease Influenza (4) OR	
QUIESTEDE	14.6.18		Admissions Officers. Sick one Wounded nil OR Sick 6 Wounded nil. Evacuations to C.C.S. Officers Sick one Wounded nil OR Sick 3 Wounded nil Prevailing Disease Influenza (4) 5 OR. reinforcements arrived	
QUIESTEDE	15.6.18		Admissions. Officers nil OR Sick 4 Wounded nil. Evacuations Officers nil OR Sick 4 Wounded nil. Received orders to proceed by march route with 93rd Inf. Bde. to area South of HONDEGHEM. Y. Camped at V.1.C.5.2 (Sheet 27) Capt. J.A RYLE with B Section personnel left behind	

WAR DIARY or INTELLIGENCE SUMMARY.

Army Form C. 2118.

(Erase heading not required.)

Place	Date	Hour	Summary of Events and Information	Remarks and references to Appendices
QUIESTEDE	15.6.18		to look after a large number of influenza cases which Regimental MOs were treating in billets and who were unfit for duty. 1 G.S. wagon, 1 limbered wagon, 1 water cart & 1 Daimler ambulance car left behind with rear party.	
HONDEGHEM	16.6.18		Admissions (Rear Party) Officers Sick 7 Wounded nil O.R. Sick 157 Wounded nil. Prevailing disease influenza (140). Evacuations nil. Cases of influenza occurring with main body evacuated to billets with rear party.	
HONDEGHEM	17.6.18		Capt Q.M. MILLER returned from temp. duty with 38th Labour Group. Admissions. Officers Sick 1 Wounded nil O.R. Sick 11. Wounded nil. Evacuations Officers Sick 2. Wounded nil. O.R. Sick 7 Wounded nil. Prevailing disease Influenza (9). Received orders from 93rd Inf. Bde to proceed by march route to SERCUS area Sheet 36 a. C 17 c 8 6	

WAR DIARY or INTELLIGENCE SUMMARY

Army Form C. 2118.

Place	Date	Hour	Summary of Events and Information	Remarks and references to Appendices
SERCUS	18.6.18		Admissions Officers nil OR Sick 33 Wounded nil	
			Evacuations Officers Sick 1 Wounded nil	
			Evacuations O.R. 10 Sick Wounded nil	
			Prevailing disease Influenza (32)	
SERCUS	19.6.18		Admissions Officers nil OR Sick 1 Wounded nil	
			Evacuations Officers nil OR Sick 5 Wounded nil	
			Discharges to duty Officers nil OR 60	
SERCUS	20.6.18		Admissions Officers Sick 1 Wounded nil OR Sick 7 Wounded nil. Evacuations Officers Sick 2 Wounded nil OR Sick 10 Wounded nil Discharges to duty OR 25. Received orders that 31st Div. was to relieve 29th Div. in the line and 94th Fd Ambulance to be responsible for evacuating forward and main Dressing Station to be run by 93rd Field Ambulance at La Cinque Rues. The following dispositions were made to relieve the	

WAR DIARY or INTELLIGENCE SUMMARY.

(Erase heading not required.)

Army Form C. 2118.

Place	Date	Hour	Summary of Events and Information	Remarks and references to Appendices
SERCUS	20.6.18		84th Field Ambulance in the forward area.	
			Left Bde. Sector	
			Left line R.A.P. at E.8.a.7.4. 1 bearer squad attached.	
			Relay post at E.8.c.5.6. 2 bearer squads & 1 car.	
			Right line R.A.P. E.14.d.5.3. 1 bearer squad attached.	
			Relay post E.19.b.8.8. 1 car & 2 bearer squads.	
			Cars can come up to R.A.P. in daylight, and the roads are in good condition.	
			Reserve Bn. at D.6.d.8.8. 1 squad attached.	
			Evacuation from these posts is by car or wheeled stretcher along road via SPEARMINT CORNER E.13.c.3.4. and D.18.c.7.2. to A.D.S. No.1 at D.18.a.5.3.	
			Personnel of A.D.S. Capts RYLE & MILLER with one tent subdivision & one car. The Dressing Station is situated in a farm, with two sandbag shelters on the opposite side of the road partly protected by walls of a house	

WAR DIARY or INTELLIGENCE SUMMARY.

Army Form C. 2118.

(Erase heading not required.)

Place	Date	Hour	Summary of Events and Information	Remarks and references to Appendices
SERCUS	20/6/18		Evacuation from here is to main Dressing Station of 93rd Field Ambulance at the CINQ RUES by car. ADS No 2 is situated in TEXAS FARM D.9.a.1.8. Personnel: Major ROCHE and one Tent Subdivision. This is intended for dealing with over flow cases from the forward ADS in case of many casualties occurring, or as alternative site to fall back on in event of the front line being driven back. 1 car is posted here. Dressing rooms are equipped both in the house itself & in dug outs in the field behind it. Major J. GRAHAM returned from 14 days leave in UK. Capt J. RYLE and B Section returned from QUIESTEDE.	
WALLON CAPPEL	21/6/18		Admissions: Officers Sick 2 wounded 1. OR Sick 19. wounded nil. Evacuations: Officers Sick 1 wounded 1. OR Sick 32 wounded nil. Discharges to duty Officers 4. OR 42.	

WAR DIARY or INTELLIGENCE SUMMARY.

Army Form C. 2118.

(Erase heading not required.)

Place	Date	Hour	Summary of Events and Information	Remarks and references to Appendices
WALLON CAPELLE	21.6.18		Headquarters and transport marched at 8 am to WALLON CAPELLE area and took over side from 84th Fd Amb at U 24 c 2.0 (Sheet 27) Received orders that 92nd Inf Bde was to take over the line from 84th Inf Bd on night of 21st/22nd. R.A.Ps are to be as follows, on the Right Brigade Sector. Right line RAP FETTLE FARM D 24 a 3.2 1 Squad attached Left line RAP E 30 a 9.1 1 Squad attached. Reserve Bn at LE GRAND HAZARD. Evacuation from Right RAP straight to ADS Evacuation from Left RAP through Rt Rly Evacuation from reserve Bn changed to ADS no 2.	
WALLON CAPELLE	22.6.18		Admissions nil Evacuations nil	
WALLON CAPELLE	23.6.18		Admissions nil Evacuations nil	

WAR DIARY or INTELLIGENCE SUMMARY.

Army Form C. 2118.

(Erase heading not required.)

Place	Date	Hour	Summary of Events and Information	Remarks and references to Appendices
WALLON CAPELLE	24/6/18		Admissions nil, evacuations nil. A small number of cases of influenza are occurring in the unit which are being treated in billets without being admitted as patients.	R.L.
WALLON CAPELLE	25/6/18		Major POORE, Lieut HIGGINS and 2 Sergeants of the U.S.M.C. arrived for 4 days instruction in field ambulance work. Admissions nil, evacuations nil.	R.L.
WALLON CAPELLE	26/6/18		A small operation for the improvement of the line to take place on night of 26th/27th conducted by 2 Coys. of 15th W Yorks Regt in region of ANKLE FARM E.7.a.7.a. R.A.P. advanced to COBLEY COTTAGE E.21.a.9.3. 3 squads of bearers attached to R.A.P. and one squad to form relay post at E.20.d.4.9. 3 extra long cars brought up to assist in evacuating. Capt J.M. BROWN to A.D.S. no 1. Admissions nil, evacuations nil.	R.L.

WAR DIARY or INTELLIGENCE SUMMARY.

Army Form C. 2118.

Place	Date	Hour	Summary of Events and Information	Remarks and references to Appendices
WALLON CAPELLE	27.6.18		Operations commenced 12.30 am under artillery barrage lasting till 1 am. At 1.30 am first car load of sitting cases arrived and cars continued to arrive at intervals during remainder of night. One car load of stretcher cases diverted to ADS no 2, remainder being treated at ADS no 1. Evacuation arrangements worked smoothly. Cars being sent to pick up as far as N end of B ride (E.20.d.7.9) on LA MOTTE - VIEUX BERQUIN Road. There was little hostile shelling. Number of cases dealt with about 70.	
WALLON CAPELLE	28.6.18		An operation is being undertaken today by 31st & 5th Divs to advance the line eastwards towards the VIEUX BERQUIN Road. 92nd & 93rd Inf Bdes to carry out the attack on 31st Div sector with 94th Bde in support. Dispositions of Medical Services. Forward RAPs advanced in AVAL WOOD to the following	

WAR DIARY
or
INTELLIGENCE SUMMARY.
(Erase heading not required.)

Army Form C. 2118.

Place	Date	Hour	Summary of Events and Information	Remarks and references to Appendices
~~WOOLWICH~~ GAPELLE	28.6.13		10th E. YORKS Regt. to E 28 a 0.2. 4 Squads of Reme bearers attached	
			11th E. YORKS & 11th E. LANCS combined RAP at E 27 a 0.2. 8 Squads attached with Wheeled Stretchers	
			There is a light railway running through the wood & trollys are used to evacuate from RAPs.	
			15th W. YORKS Regt. RAP to E 21 a 9.3. 4 Squads attached with Wheeled Stretchers	
			Other RAPs as before.	
			Relay posts of 4 Squads each at North end of A.A. & C Rides. Car posts formed at ends of B & C rides. Other car posts & relays as before.	
			Walking Wounded tracks marked out from various posts on the line to ADS no 1.	
			Bearer Subdivisions of 93rd & 95th Field Ambulances brought up & distributed in forward area under	

WAR DIARY or INTELLIGENCE SUMMARY.

(Erase heading not required.)

Army Form C. 2118.

Place	Date	Hour	Summary of Events and Information	Remarks and references to Appendices
WALLON CAPELLE			Capts. Miller & Ryle were in charge of right & left Actors respectively. 12 motor ambulances provided for Stretcher cases & 6 horsed ambulance wagons & 2 motor lorries to pick up walking wounded at D.16.b.8.6. & convey them to MDS. Zero hour 6 am. Walking wounded began to arrive at ADS at 6.50 & Stretcher cases at 7.20. About 700 cases passed through the ADS during 24 hours midnight 27/28th to midnight 28/29th including about 250 Stretcher cases. When ADS no 1 became congested Stretcher cases were diverted to ADS no 2. All walking wounded were passed through ADS no 1. About 60 German prisoners were also employed as Stretcher bearers during part of the operations when large numbers of cases required evacuation.	

WAR DIARY or INTELLIGENCE SUMMARY.

Army Form C. 2118.

(Erase heading not required.)

Place	Date	Hour	Summary of Events and Information	Remarks and references to Appendices
WALLON CAPELLE	28.6.18		Arrangements for evacuation worked smoothly & there was no undue delay in getting patients back. The casualties from the attack were all cleared from forward area by 2 p.m. although fresh cases kept arriving in a continuous stream up till midnight.	
WALLON CAPELLE	29.6.18		A number of wounded who had been lying out in cornfields near front line & had been overlooked were recovered & evacuated, including several wounded German prisoners. The front line was quiet, with few fresh casualties.	
WALLON CAPELLE	30.6.18		Admissions Officers nil, OR nil. Evacuations Off nil, OR nil. From midnight 29/6/18 to 9 a.m. 30/6/18 about 110 wounded were received and evacuated. These casualties occurred in an inter-battalion relief which was caught in an enemy barrage. About 60 sick from 94th Inf. Bde. were evacuated by horsed ambulance during the evening.	

WAR DIARY or INTELLIGENCE SUMMARY

Army Form C. 2118.

Place	Date	Hour	Summary of Events and Information	Remarks and references to Appendices
WALLON CAPPEL	30.6.18		All bearers from 93rd Fd Amb returned to their unit 29/6/18	
			Bearers of 95th Field Amb returned to their unit in motor lorries & horsed ambulances on 30/6/18	
			Dispositions of 94th Fd Amb personnel in forward area is now as follows:-	
			Left Sector RAP at E8.a.6.4. 1 Squad Car Post & 2 men at RP RAP at D6.d.9.9 1 Squad & runner RAP at E14.d.6.3 1 Squad Relay Post at E.19.b.88. 1 Squad and Car	
			Right Sector RAP at E.20.a.9.1. 1 Squad RAP at E.27.a.5.1. 2 Squads RAP at E.28.a.1.9. 1 Squad Relay Post at E.20.b.5.0 2 Squads & Car.	
			Total admissions, evacuations & discharges for month of June	
			Admissions Officers Sick 17 Wd 1 OR Sick 279 Wd nil	
			Evacuations Officers Sick 13 Wd 1 OR Sick 110 Wd nil	
			Discharges Officers Sick 4 Wd nil OR Sick 136 Wd nil	
			Schorey(?) Lt-Col. Round(?) OC 94th Fd Ambce.	

July 1918.

114 q/3131

No. 94 7. a.

24

WAR DIARY
or
INTELLIGENCE SUMMARY.
(Erase heading not required.)

Army Form C. 2118.

94 Fd Amb
Vol 29

Place	Date	Hour	Summary of Events and Information	Remarks and references to Appendices
WALLON CAPELLE	1.7.18		The ambulance is still in the same situation as in June evacuating the forward area, with headquarters near WALLON CAPELLE.	
			The dispositions in the forward area are now as follows:	
			Left Bde Sector	
			Left RAP E 8 c 7.3 1 Squad attached	
			Right RAP E 14 d 5.3 1 Squad attached	
			Reserve Bn. RAP D 6 d 8.9 1 Squad attached	
			Left Relay & Car Post E 8 c 5.6	
			Right Relay & Car Post E 19 b 8.8	
			Right Bde Sector	
			Left RAP E 28 a 0.2 2 Squads attached	
			Right RAP K 4 a 0.0 2 Squads attached	
			Relay Posts K 3 a 4.7 2 Squads	
			E 20 a 9.1 1 Squad	
			Reserve Bn. RAP E 19 d 1.1	

WAR DIARY or INTELLIGENCE SUMMARY.

Army Form C. 2118.

(Erase heading not required.)

Place	Date	Hour	Summary of Events and Information	Remarks and references to Appendices
WALLON CAPELLE	1.7.18		Evacuation from Right R.A.P. is by hand carry to relay post, where two bearers at Right change with 4 stretcher cases. Trucks are pushed along our line as far as north end of "B" ride E.20.a.7.0 & thence by hand carry to car post at E.20.a.9.1. Evacuation from Left R.A.P. is by truck as far as E.20.a.7.0 & thence as before. Two bearers at Right at this R.A.P. A.D.S. nos 1 & 2 unchanged. Admissions nil. Evacuations nil.	C.P.
WALLON CAPELLE	2.7.18		As the result of a conference between the A.D.M.S. & O.C. Field Ambulances on the recent operations the following suggestions were made. (1) That as wheeled stretchers had proved so useful the number ought to be increased to 30 per division. (2) That none bearers in future operations should be located nearer to the A.D.S.	

WAR DIARY
or
INTELLIGENCE SUMMARY.
(Erase heading not required.)

Army Form C. 2118.

Place	Date	Hour	Summary of Events and Information	Remarks and references to Appendices
WALLON CAPELLE	2.7.18		(3) That motor lorries would be useful for bringing sitting cases from Relay posts to ADS and also for clearing from ADS to MDS.	
			(4) That MAC Cars should be available to clear from the ADS in cases of emergency.	
			(5) That a reserve of 200 Stretchers should be kept at MDS.	
			(6) That more accommodation should be provided at the ADS including two large dug-outs.	
			Admissions nil. Evacuations nil.	Rh
WALLON CAPELLE	3.7.18		Admissions nil. Evacuations nil.	Rh
do.	4.7.18		The emergency dressing dug-out at TEXAS FARM having been condemned by the RE is unsafe is being rebuilt with elephant shelters and sandbags.	
			Admissions nil. Evacuations nil.	Rh
			2 officers & 5 OR. U.S. army reported for course of instruction at ADS	

WAR DIARY or INTELLIGENCE SUMMARY.

Army Form C. 2118.

(Erase heading not required.)

Place	Date	Hour	Summary of Events and Information	Remarks and references to Appendices
WALLON CAPELLE	5.7.18		3 Officers & 5 O.R. of U.S. Army Medical Corps arrived for a course of instruction at the A.D.S. Admissions nil. Evacuations nil.	
do.	6.7.18		3 Officers & 5 O.R. of U.S. Army reported for course of instruction at A.D.S. Construction of two dug-outs at A.D.S. no. 1 commenced. These are to be made of elephant shelters & sand bags & to hold 12 stretcher cases each. Construction is being supervised by O.C. 223 Field Coy. R.E. 30403 S.M. Crossley A. R.A.M.C. reported his arrival. Admissions nil. Evacuations nil.	
WALLON CAPELLE	7.7.18		Lt.Col. LANG D.S.O. R.A.M.C. proceeded today on leave to the United Kingdom. 3 Officers & 5 O.R. of U.S. Army arrived at Hqrs from A.D.S. Nothing special to report. Admissions nil. Evacuations nil.	
do.	8.7.18		Visited ADS I & ADS II. Ordinary routine work. Admissions nil. Evacuations nil.	
do.	9.7.18		Visited ADS I & ADS II & forward posts. Satisfactory progress being made with the dug-outs at both A.D.S. Additional dug-out in process of construction at Right RAP on R Sector. 3 Officers & 5 O.R. of U.S. Army departed from Hqrs on completion of course. Visit by A.D.M.S. Admissions nil. Evacuations nil.	

WAR DIARY or INTELLIGENCE SUMMARY.

Army Form C. 2118.

Place	Date	Hour	Summary of Events and Information	Remarks and references to Appendices
Walton Capelle	10.7.18		Visited No 1 & No 2 A.D.S. 1st Lieut. Haveland Carr M.O.R.C. U.S.A reported his arrival from 40th Division & taken on the Strength. Admissions nil. Evacuations nil.	
	11.7.18		Visited No 1 & No 2 A.D.S. Major Roche returned to Headquarters with injury to Rt. arm caused by his horse rearing & falling on him while he was on duty visiting the R.A.Ps. Admissions nil. Evacuations nil.	
	12.7.18		Visited No 1 & No 2 A.D.S. Major Roche evacuated by No 93rd F. Amb to No 2 Australian C.C.S. Instructions received for Capt Miller to proceed for duty with 30th Division. He is accordingly struck off the strength of the Unit. Captain George Rainford R.A.M.C reported his arrival from 30th Division & taken on the Strength. Admissions nil. Evacuations nil.	
	13.7.18		Visited No 1 & No 2 A.D.S. Visit from A.D.M.S to Headquarters. Admissions nil. Evacuations nil.	
	14.7.18		Visited No 1 & No 2 A.D.S. Under instructions from A.D.M.S. 31st Div. a working party of one Sergeant and twenty four men reported their arrival at A.D.S. last night from 95th F.A. to assist in construction of the dugouts. Admissions nil. Evacuations nil.	

WAR DIARY or INTELLIGENCE SUMMARY.

Army Form C. 2118.

Instructions regarding War Diaries and Intelligence Summaries are contained in F. S. Regs., Part II. and the Staff Manual respectively. Title pages will be prepared in manuscript.

(Erase heading not required.)

Place	Date	Hour	Summary of Events and Information	Remarks and references to Appendices
Wallon Capelle	15/7/18		Visited A.D.S. No 1 & No 2. Capt. G.M. Brown R.A.M.C. evacuated to C.C.S with ? Appendicitis. Usual routine work. Admissions nil. Evacuations nil.	
	16/7/18		Visited A.D.S No 1 & No 2. Usual routine work. Admissions nil. Evacuations nil.	
	17/7/18		Visited A.D.S No 1 & No 2. Notification received that Capt. G. M. Brown R.A.M.C. evacuated to base. Lieut F. L. Rigby R.A.M.C. reported for temporary duty from 95th Field Ambulance. Admissions nil. Evacuations nil.	
	18/7/18		Visited both A.D.S & forward area to make arrangements for forthcoming 93rd Bde Operations. Visit by A.D.M.S. to Headquarters. Admissions nil. Evacuations nil. 60849 Pte WRIGHT T. R.A.M.C. 94th Fd Amb was killed in action.	
	19/7/18		Further orders having been received from 93rd Inf. Bde that operations would commence at 7 am 19/7/18 instead of 20/7/18 proceeded at once to A.D.S No 1 about 12.30 am & made necessary arrangements. The intention of the operation was to advance our line on the Rt. Brigade sector (93rd Bde) to the line of the Plate Becque – the left Brigade (94th) conforming slightly also. Operation commenced at 7am without artillery preparation.	

WAR DIARY or INTELLIGENCE SUMMARY.

Army Form C. 2118.

(Erase heading not required.)

Place	Date	Hour	Summary of Events and Information	Remarks and references to Appendices
Wallon Capelle	19.7.18		Dispositions of medical services - Rt. Brigade Sector - Rt. R.A.P. (15 West York R) at K4a00 3 squads R.A.M.C. Bearers attached with 3 wheeled stretchers Left R.A.P. (18th D.L.I) at E28a02 3 Squads R.A.M.C Bearers attached. Relay Post at K3a47 with 1 N.C.O + 3 squads. " " " E27a02 " " " Rigid Car Post at E20a91 with 1 N.C.O + 1 squad Ambre " " " E19.8.8 " 1 N.C.O + 2 squads. Left Brigade Sector as before. Forward area under charge of Capt Ryles. Capt Rainford + Lieut Rigby at A.D.S No 1 Lieut Carr at A.D.S No 2 The working party of 24 men + 1 N.C.O. from 95th 7 Amb. at A.D.S 1 acted as bearers during the operation Wounded cases began to arrive at A.D.S. 1 about 8.50 a.m 91 Casualties in all + 1 German were passed thro' A.D.S from 7 a.m till 7 pm practically all being evacuated by 2.30 pm.	

WAR DIARY
or
INTELLIGENCE SUMMARY.
(Erase heading not required.)

Army Form C. 2118.

Place	Date	Hour	Summary of Events and Information	Remarks and references to Appendices
Watton Capelle	19.7.18		Four large cars cleared the forward area — a small car being also used in the left sector. These cars were mainly loaded at top end of B pide & the route of evacuation being largely via La Motte owing to other roads being shelled. Walking Wounded mainly used the route X track — F Nle Farm — A.D.S. owing to shelling of roads. Four large cars evacuated from ADS to MDS — two cars being borrowed from 93rd F.A. The Horse Ambulances of 94th F.A. were also employed to evac. walking cases from A.D.S. to M.D.S. The arrangements for evacuation moved smoothly & there was no delay or congestion at any of the posts or A.D.S.	
	20.7.18		During the night 19th–20th six squads of R.A.M.C. bearers were attached to the right & left R.A.P on the Rt. Sector respectively under the R.M.Os to assist in clearing, with authority from ADMS, cases forward of these posts which could not be brought in in daylight or had been overlooked. Only 27 casualties passed thro' ADS from 7 pm to 7 am. The Road from E 13 b 08 to E 20 c 76 is in bad state from Shell holes & there has been considerable shelling in vicinity of Rt Car post.	

WAR DIARY or INTELLIGENCE SUMMARY.

Army Form C. 2118.

Instructions regarding War Diaries and Intelligence Summaries are contained in F. S. Regs., Part II. and the Staff Manual respectively. Title pages will be prepared in manuscript.

(Erase heading not required.)

Place	Date	Hour	Summary of Events and Information	Remarks and references to Appendices
Wallon Capelle	20.7.18		Visit to Hqrs. from ADMS. Admissions nil. Evacuations nil.	
Wallon Capelle	21.7.18		Capt Ryle brought back to Hqrs. Lieut Carr sent forward to A.D.S.1 to return each morning to ADS 2 in order to see sick &c. Car at Rt. Car post withdrawn to centre car post. One squad with wheel stretcher retained at Glim Farm in dugout there. One car brought back into reserve at ADS from forward area. Admissions nil. Evacuations nil.	
Wallon Capelle	22.7.18		Visited A.D.S. No 1 & No 2. also centre & right car posts. Admissions nil. Evacuations nil.	
Wallon Capelle	23.7.18		Capt. Ryle returned to ADS No 1. Under instructions from ADMS. Lieut. F.L. Rigby R.A.M.C. returned to 95th F. Amb. & 1st Lieut H. Carr M.O.R.C. U.S.A. was sent on temporary duty to the 18th D.L.1 to relieve 1st Lieut R.R. McHenry M.O.R.C. U.S.A. proceeding on leave. Lt Col. E.C. Laing D.S.O. R.A.M.C. today returned from leave to U.K. Admissions nil. Evacuations nil.	

WAR DIARY or INTELLIGENCE SUMMARY.

Army Form C. 2118.

Place	Date	Hour	Summary of Events and Information	Remarks and references to Appendices
WALLON CAPELLE	24.7.18		An alternative route from Right Bde. Sector reconnoitred for evacuation of cases in event of B ride being shelled. This route runs from south end of B ride along track no 2 and thence by River track to the Saw Mill on LA MOTTE – VIEUX BERQUIN road, where cases can be transferred to cars, or if necessary along X track to FETTLE FARM & thence by car to ADS no 1. Admissions nil. Evacuations nil.	R.L.
WALLON CAPELLE	25.7.18		Lieut. & Qm. J. G. FRASER proceeded to Boulogne to embark for U.K. on 14 days leave. Admissions nil. Evacuations nil.	R.L.
WALLON CAPELLE	26.7.18		Lieut. H. CARR M.O.R.C. proceeded for duty to ADS 2. Satisfactory progress is being made with dug-outs for Patients at both A.D.Ss. A small dug-out is being constructed at left car part for car drivers & orderly in case of shelling. Admissions nil. Evacuations nil.	R.L.

WAR DIARY or INTELLIGENCE SUMMARY.

Army Form C. 2118.

Place	Date	Hour	Summary of Events and Information	Remarks and references to Appendices
WALLON CAPELLE	27.7.18		Capt. G Rainford proceeded for Temp. duty with 18th Bn West Yorks Regt. in place of Capt. J.G. Lee. Sick. Admissions nil. evacuations nil.	R.L.
WALLON CAPELLE	28.7.18		Lieut. H. CARR. M.O.R.C. U.S.A. proceeded for temp. duty with 18th D.L.I. in place of Lieut R.R. Mac Henry M.C. Granted 14 days leave to U.K. Capt. W.H. SMITH M.O.R.C. reported for temporary duty from 93rd Fd. amb. and proceeded to A.D.S. 1 for duty. Admissions nil. evacuations nil.	A.L.
WALLON CAPELLE	29.7.18		Considerable hostile activity displayed during the night of 29th/30th July. 4 W2 wounded passed through A.D.S. No. 1. 2 O.R. 94th Fd. amb (Ptes Bowden & Weins) wounded by splinters from a bomb dropped by enemy aeroplane near the Relay Post at S end of B ride. Admissions nil. evacuations nil	R.L.

WAR DIARY or INTELLIGENCE SUMMARY

Army Form C. 2118.

Place	Date	Hour	Summary of Events and Information	Remarks and references to Appendices
WALLON CAPELLE	30.7.18		Admissions nil Evacuations nil	

WALLON CAPELLE	31.7.18		The XI Corps Commander under authority delegated by the F.M. C. in C. has awarded the Military Medal to the undermentioned for gallantry & devotion to duty in the operations of June 28th 1918.
			
			 60666 Pte. Spurr T.H. Ramd. 94th Fld amb.
			 M2/120179 Pte. New L. ASC MT att 94th Fld amb
			 Authority. XI Corps Routine Order 426 of 28/7/18
			
			 Total Admissions during month of July nil
			  " Evacuations " " " " nil
			  " Discharges to duty " " " " nil
			
			 Rhang
			 Lt-Col. Ramd
			 OC 94th Fld Ambce	

Aug. 1918.

140/3259

94th F. Amb.

COMMITTEE FOR THE
MEDICAL HISTORY OF THE WAR
Date 9 NOV 1918

WAR DIARY or INTELLIGENCE SUMMARY.

94 Fd Amb
Vol 30
Army Form C. 2118.

Place	Date	Hour	Summary of Events and Information	Remarks and references to Appendices
WALLON CAPELLE	1.8.18		The ambulance is in the same position as in July 5.8 evacuating the forward area. Dispositions of personnel in forward area unchanged. The Right Bde. Sector is now being held by 92nd & 93rd Inf. Bdes. and the Left Bde Sector by 94th Inf. Bde. and 121st Inf. Bde. from 40th Div. A R.A.P. for the Reserve Bn. in Right Sector is being constructed at E 25 d 9.4. Route of evacuation from here is by River Track to main road at Sawmills & thence to Rt. Car. past. Admissions. Officers nil. O.R. nil. Evacuations Officers nil O.R. nil.	
WALLON CAPELLE	2.8.18		Nothing to report. Admissions nil evacuations nil	
WALLON CAPELLE	3.8.18		The undermentioned officers from 136th Fd. Amb. 40th Div. reported their arrival for a fortnights course of instruction in Fd. Amb. work. 1st Lt. W.H. STONER M.O.R.C. 1st Lt. W.F. WIGGINS. U.S.A. Admissions nil evacuations nil	

WAR DIARY or INTELLIGENCE SUMMARY.

Army Form C. 2118.

(Erase heading not required.)

Place	Date	Hour	Summary of Events and Information	Remarks and references to Appendices
WALLON CAPELLE	4.8.18		CAPT W. H. SMITH. M.O.R.C. U.S.A. who had been sent from 93rd Fld. amb. for temporary duty at A.D.S. 1 was evacuated to M.D.S. 1st Lt. W. H. STONER to A.D.S. 1. Admissions nil evacuations nil	R.L.
WALLON CAPELLE	5.8.18		All R.A.Ps in the front line and two Reserve Bn. R.A.Ps have been completed to scale laid down by A.D.M.S. for Trench Stores, to be handed out to relieving Bns. Lt. W.F. WIGGINS to A.D.S. 1. Admissions nil. evacuations nil.	R.L.
WALLON CAPELLE	6.8.18		Major C. ROCHE M.C. returned to Headquarters from XV Corps Officers Rest at Hardelot Plage. Admissions nil. evacuations nil.	R.L.
WALLON CAPELLE	7.8.18		Major J. GRAHAM proceeded to A.D.S. no 2 " C. ROCHE " " no 1. Capt. J. RYLE returned to Headquarters on relief. The Divisional Commander and the A.D.M.S. visited A.D.S. no. 1. Admissions nil evacuations nil.	R.L.

WAR DIARY or INTELLIGENCE SUMMARY.

Army Form C. 2118.

(Erase heading not required.)

Place	Date	Hour	Summary of Events and Information	Remarks and references to Appendices
WALLON CAPELLE	8.8.18		Nothing to report. Admissions nil evacuations nil	
WALLON CAPELLE	9.8.18		About 110 gassed cases passed through ADS no 1 during the night 9/10th, including cases of both phosgene & mustard gas poisoning. 103 of these were from 15th W. Yorks. Regt. Admissions nil evacuations nil	
WALLON CAPELLE	10/8/18		Capt. R.M. McMINN is posted to 12th KOYLI for permanent duty & is struck off the strength from this date. Admissions nil Evacuations nil	
WALLON CAPELLE	11/8/18		Capt. G RAINFORD returned from temporary duty with 15th W. Yorks. Regt. Admissions nil Evacuations nil	
WALLON CAPELLE	12/8/18		1st Lieut W.H STONER proceeded to 93rd Field Amb for temporary duty. 1st Lieut A.D. TYREE MORC USA returned from 93rd F.A. to take temporary duty at ADS no 1	

WAR DIARY or INTELLIGENCE SUMMARY.

Army Form C. 2118.

Place	Date	Hour	Summary of Events and Information	Remarks and references to Appendices
WALLON CAPELLE	12/8/18		About 40 wounded passed through ADS No 1 during the night 12/13th. One of the two dug-outs for Stretcher cases at ADS No 1 is now completed & ready for use. Admissions nil. Evacuations nil.	
WALLON CAPELLE	13.8.18		Received orders from ADMS to take over a Medical Post at D.28.b.8.4. from 61st Div. for 49 S. Bty R.G.A. & 21 Heavy Battery R.G.A. Visited the Post & arranged to send 1 squad from ADS no 2 to relieve squad from 2/2 South Midland Fd amb 14/8/18. Evacuation by hand carry to car Post of 61st Div. at J.4.b.5.3. & thence to ADS of 61st Div.	R.L.
WALLON CAPELLE	14.8.18		Capt. RAINFORD. G. detached to see the Sick of 31st Bn. M.G.C. during the absence on leave of Lieut. of Capt. ALEXANDER. Admissions nil. Evacuations nil.	R.L. R.L.

WAR DIARY
or
INTELLIGENCE SUMMARY.
(Erase heading not required.)

Army Form C. 2118.

Instructions regarding War Diaries and Intelligence Summaries are contained in F. S. Regs., Part II. and the Staff Manual respectively. Title pages will be prepared in manuscript.

Place	Date	Hour	Summary of Events and Information	Remarks and references to Appendices
WALLON CAPELLE	15.8.18		Nothing to report. Admissions nil. Evacuations nil	A↓
WALLON CAPELLE	16.8.18		About 130 gassed cases were received & passed thro' ADS no 1 during the morning, an extra large car being sent up to assist in evacuation. All cases were cleared by 9 p.m. Admissions nil. Evacuations nil	A↓
WALLON CAPELLE	17.8.18		1 OR reinforcement (C of E) taken on strength from Base Depot 14/8/18. Admissions nil. Evacuations nil	A↓
WALLON CAPELLE	18.8.18		The following alterations in dispositions in forward area have been made. Left Bn RAP has been moved to a cellar at E10 c 7.5. Two squads attached with 2 wheeled stretchers. Left Car Post to SANITAS CORNER E9 c.8.0. 2 men as loading party. Dug-out for this party is being constructed. Remaining dispositions are as before. Admissions nil. Evacuations nil.	A↓

WAR DIARY
or
INTELLIGENCE SUMMARY.

(Erase heading not required.)

Army Form C. 2118.

Place	Date	Hour	Summary of Events and Information	Remarks and references to Appendices
WALLON CAPELLE	19.8.18		Received information that an attack was to be carried out by 12th Norfolk Regt. on left of 94th Inf. Bde. front in conjunction with 29th Div. on their left, with a view to straightening their line between OUTTERSTEENE and VIEUX BERQUIN. The attack to be carried out by 2 Coys of 12th Norfolk Regt. Zero hour 5 pm. 3 Squads of bearers with wheeled stretchers attached to R.A.P. 3 large cars were used to evacuate from a point on the road at E.16.a.3.5. back to A.D.S. 4 large cars used to evacuate back to M.D.S. Total casualties dealt with. Officers 4. O.R. 82. P.O.W. 13. Comprising Stretcher cases 43. Sitting cases 56. The R.A.P. was cleared of cases by 3 a.m.	A.b.
WALLON CAPELLE	20.8.18		1st Lieut. H. CARR M.R.C. U.S.A. proceeded to report for duty to O.C. 11th East Yorks, vice Capt. O.C. IRVINE who is proceeding to 2nd Army Officers Hostel for 7 days. Admissions nil. Evacuations nil.	A.b.
WALLON CAPELLE	21.8.18		Nothing to report. Admissions nil. Evacuations nil.	A.b.

WAR DIARY
or
INTELLIGENCE SUMMARY.

Army Form C. 2118.

Instructions regarding War Diaries and Intelligence Summaries are contained in F. S. Regs., Part II. and the Staff Manual respectively. Title pages will be prepared in manuscript.

(Erase heading not required.)

Place	Date	Hour	Summary of Events and Information	Remarks and references to Appendices
WALLON CAPELLE	22.8.18		Advance party of 135th Fld. Amb. 40th Div. arrived to take over posts in the forward area. Half of each post was relieved by 135th Fld. Amb. Remainder of 93rd Fld. Amb. proceeded to TEXAS FARM on relief. Admissions kil. Evacuations nil.	
WALLON CAPELLE	23.8.18		Remainder of forward area and ADS not relieved by 135th Field Ambulance. Two men relieved being sent to TEXAS FARM for accommodation for the night. Capt. RYLE proceeded with an advance party to take over Main Dressing Station from South African Field Ambulance, 9th Div. at V.H.0.2.5.	
HONDEGHEM	24.8.18		Headquarters and Transport and party from TEXAS FARM proceeded on relief to Main Dressing Station. The Dressing Station is established on an old C.C.S. site, and includes Nissen Huts for Dressing Room, Wards, Orderly Room etc. with Tunnel Marquees & operating tents for Stores, inoculating & dental room etc.	

WAR DIARY or INTELLIGENCE SUMMARY

Army Form C. 2118.

Place	Date	Hour	Summary of Events and Information	Remarks and references to Appendices
HONDEGHEM	24.8.18		A Bath House has been erected but so far has not been fitted out with baths. Arrangements have been made for delousing of patients clothing by dry heat in a "Russian Pit" and also in a "Disinfestator" as designed by 15th Field Ambulance. Evacuation from the M.D.S. is undertaken by 14 M.A.C. Cases of diarrhoea are treated and Smears sent to Advanced Army Dysentery Centre at 136th Field Ambulance for examination & report as to the presence of dysentery bacilli. Admissions. Officers nil. O.R. Sick 4 wd. nil. Transfers from S.A. Fd. Amb. O.R. Sick 14 wd. 1. Evacuations. Officers nil. O.R. Sick 3 wd. nil.	
HONDEGHEM	25.8.18		Admissions. Officers Sick 1 wd 2. O.R. Sick 33 wd. 24. Evacuations Officers Sick 1 wd 2 O.R. Sick 12. wd. 20 Deaths 1. (Bullet wd. chest, penetrating abdomen) Prevailing Disease, Diarrhoea (14) P.t.	

WAR DIARY or INTELLIGENCE SUMMARY.

Army Form C. 2118.

(Erase heading not required.)

Place	Date	Hour	Summary of Events and Information	Remarks and references to Appendices
HONDEGHEM	25.8.18		Capt. G. RAINFORD proceeded to XV Corps Skin Centre for 3 days course of instruction	Ph
HONDEGHEM	26.8.18		A team from 94th Fld Amb consisting of 1 NCO mounted, 1 Horse Ambulance Wagon & 1 water cart was awarded 2nd prize at 31st Div. Horse Show. Admissions. Officers Sick 2 wd. 2 OR Sick 31. wd 95 (86 Shell gas wd) Evacuations. Officers Sick 2 wd. 2 OR Sick 15. wd. 91 Prevailing Diseases Diarrhoea 4 Scabies 4	Ph
HONDEGHEM	27.8.18		Admissions Officers Sick 1 wd 1 OR Sick 43 wd 25 Evacuations Officers Sick 1 wd 1 OR Sick 36 wd 28 Prevailing disease Influenza (7)	Ph
HONDEGHEM	28.8.18		Admissions. Officers Sick 3 wd 1 OR Sick 51 wd. 18 Evacuations Officers Sick 3 wd 1 OR Sick 38 wd 14 Prevailing disease Diarrhoea 22 Capt G. RAINFORD returned from Course of instruction at XV Corps Skin Centre.	Ph

WAR DIARY or INTELLIGENCE SUMMARY

Army Form C. 2118.

Place	Date	Hour	Summary of Events and Information	Remarks and references to Appendices
HONDEGHEM	29.8.18		~~Capt Rainford~~ Admissions. Officers Sick nil wd. 1. O.R. Sick 34. wd. 6. Evacuations. Officers. Sick nil. wd. 1. O.R. Sick 24. wd. 6. Prevailing disease Diarrhoea (12)	A
HONDEGHEM	30.8.18		1st Lieut. H. CARR M.O.R.C. returned from temporary duty with 11th East Yorks Regt. Admissions. Officers Sick 1. wd nil. O.R. Sick 34. wd 2. Evacuations. Officers Sick 1. wd nil. O.R. Sick 35. wd. 1. Prevailing disease N.Y.D. pyrexia (4)	A
HONDEGHEM	31.8.18		Orders were received that medical units were to move into positions further forward in consequence of change in the military situation. The A.D.S. at CAESTRE run by 93rd Fd. Amb. moved to vicinity of METEREN and the A.D.S. at CAESTRE was taken over by 93rd Fd. amb. as a main dressing station. 94th Fd. amb. remains in its present site and functions as Divisional Rest Station.	

WAR DIARY or INTELLIGENCE SUMMARY.

Army Form C. 2118.

Place	Date	Hour	Summary of Events and Information	Remarks and references to Appendices
HONDEGHEM	31-8-18		5 Small Hospital Marquees taken over from 93rd Fld. Amb, and accommodation provided for 100 patients. Admissions. Officers nil. O.R. Sick 22. wd. 4. Evacuations. Officers nil. O.R. Sick 24. wd. 4. Total admissions for the month of August. Officers Sick 8. wd. 7. O.R. 255. wd. 174. Total evacuations for the month of August. Officers Sick 8. wd. 7. O.R. Sick 187 wd. 164. Total discharges to duty. Officers nil O.R. Sick 45. wd. 9. Shang, Lieut. Col. RAMC O.C. 94th Fld. Amb.	

Sept. 1918

'19
149/3327

94th F.A. Amb.

WAR DIARY or INTELLIGENCE SUMMARY

Army Form C. 2118.

94 3rd Aust
Vol 31

Place	Date	Hour	Summary of Events and Information	Remarks and references to Appendices
HONDEGHEM	1.9.18		The ambulance is still functioning as Divisional Rest Station. Location Sheet 27 VH 10 a 5. Admissions: Officers Sick 1 wd. nil. OR Sick 48 wd. nil. Evacuations: Officers Sick 1 wd. nil OR Sick 24 wd. nil Prevailing disease Diarrhoea (19)	Rt
HONDEGHEM	2.9.18		Orders were received that the Site was to be handed over to 1st Australian C.C.S, which advance party arrived during the morning. A fresh site for the D.R.S. was selected at P 35 d 2.2. the present Site of 92nd Inf. Bde. Hq. There are 5 small nissen huts already in position. 6 small hospital marquees were erected in readiness to receive patients tomorrow. - picked from present Site, and were equipped as wards. Admissions: Officers nil. OR Sick 38 wd. nil Evacuations Officers nil OR Sick 13 wd. nil Prevailing disease diarrhoea (20)	Rt
HONDEGHEM	3.9.18		All patients were transferred to new Site and remainder of personnel, transport and equipment moved to the new location during the day. Capt. G. RAINFORD started for temp. duty as OC 56th San Sect.	

WAR DIARY or INTELLIGENCE SUMMARY.

Army Form C. 2118.

(Erase heading not required.)

Place	Date	Hour	Summary of Events and Information	Remarks and references to Appendices
HONDEGHEM	3.9.18		Admissions. Officers nil. O.R. Sick 22 wd nil. Evacuations Officers nil O.R Sick 23 wd nil Prevailing disease Scabies (6) 3 OR Rand reinforcements arrived	At
ST. SYLVESTRE CAPPEL	4.9.18		Admissions Officers nil. O.R. Sick 3 wd nil Evacuations Officers nil OR Sick 5 wd nil Prevailing disease Hordeolum (3). 3 OR ASC reinforcements arrived	
ST. SYLVESTRE CAPPEL	5.9.18		Major J. GRAHAM, Lieut H. CARR, and one Section proceeded to establish a main Dressing Station at BAILLEUL STATION where a Collecting Post of 89th Fd. Amb. 29th Div. was established. The remainder of the unit remained in present site. Admissions. Officers nil. OR Sick 2 wd nil. Evacuations Officers nil. OR Sick 3 wd nil Discharged to duty OR Sick 18. Prevailing disease Diarrhoea. (2)	At
BAILLEUL	6.9.18		The remainder of the unit having closed down the Divisional Rest Station moved to FONTAINE HOUCK. Admissions Officers Sick nil wd 5 OR Sick 3 wd 95	

WAR DIARY or INTELLIGENCE SUMMARY.

Army Form C. 2118.

(Erase heading not required.)

Place	Date	Hour	Summary of Events and Information	Remarks and references to Appendices
BAILLEUL	6.9.18		Evacuations. Officers Sick nil wd 4. OR Sick 12, wd 93. Desch. to duty. Officers Sick nil wd 1. OR Sick 11 wd nil. Deaths 2 OR (GSW abdomen, GSW leg R)	A.L.
BAILLEUL	7.9.18		Orders were received to evacuate the M.D.S. in BAILLEUL as the town is suspected of being mined. Marquees were erected in a field in the vicinity of METEREN (X15.a.1.1) and M.D.S. opened there. Admissions Officers Sick nil wd 9. OR Sick 15 wd 222. Evacuations Officers Sick nil wd 8. OR Sick 25 wd 213. To duty OR Sick 6 wd 4. Deaths 1 Officer Major R. GRESLEY M.C. 119 Bde. A.F.A. Prevailing disease Diarrhoea (3)	A.L.
METEREN	8.9.18		Admissions Officers Sick nil wd 4. OR Sick nil wd 103. Evacuations Officers Sick nil wd 4. OR Sick nil wd 103.	

WAR DIARY
or
INTELLIGENCE SUMMARY.

Army Form C. 2118.

Instructions regarding War Diaries and Intelligence Summaries are contained in F. S. Regs., Part II. and the Staff Manual respectively. Title pages will be prepared in manuscript.

(Erase heading not required.)

Place	Date	Hour	Summary of Events and Information	Remarks and references to Appendices
METEREN	9.9.18		Capt. G. RAINFORD and T.E. FLITCROFT reported their return from temporary duty with 56th San. Sec. and 31st Div. Train respectively. 2 O.R. having been evacuated sick are struck off the strength. 5 O.R. reinforcements reported their arrival & are taken on the strength. Admissions. Officers Sick 1 wd 5. O.R. Sick nil. wd 77 Evacuations. Officers Sick 1. wd 5. O.R. Sick nil. wd 74. Deaths. 3 O.R. (Wounds in action) Prevailing disease dysentery (chronic) & malaria. Major V.J. SCULLY D.S.O. C.F.	R.L.
METEREN	10.9.18		The Main Dressing Station was visited by the Consulting Surgeon 2nd Army Col. MAYNARD SMITH. Admissions. Officers Sick nil wd 2. O.R. Sick nil, wd. 13 Evacuations. Officers Sick nil. wd 2 O.R. Sick nil. wd. 12 Deaths. 1 O.R (wounds) Major J.J. BILL 32 S. Btg. R.G.A. evacuated wounded	R.L.
METEREN	11.9.18		In accordance with orders from A.D.M.S. 31st Div. Major C. ROACHE, Capt. G. RAINFORD and one Section with transport proceeded to QUIESTEDE to take	

WAR DIARY
or
INTELLIGENCE SUMMARY.
(Erase heading not required.)

Army Form C. 2118.

Instructions regarding War Diaries and Intelligence Summaries are contained in F. S. Regs., Part II. and the Staff Manual respectively. Title pages will be prepared in manuscript.

Place	Date	Hour	Summary of Events and Information	Remarks and references to Appendices
METEREN	11.9.18		over the XV Corps Skin Depot from 28th Fld. Amb. About 200 patients taken over, principally cases of Scabies and I.C.T. Routine treatment of Scabies carried out as follows. On admission the patient has his hair cut short & is taken to the Bath House where his clothing is taken away to the disinfector. He is then rubbed all over with Soft Soap and soaks in a hot bath for 15 minutes, after which he is scrubbed all over with a hard nail brush to open up all burrows & vesicles. He then dries himself and is rubbed all over with Sulphur ointment, Special attention being paid to the axillae, wrists, genitals, thighs etc. He is clothed in pyjamas & sent to a ward. The inunction with Sulphur is repeated on the second & third days & examined for any unruptured vesicles which require further treatment. On the fourth day he again has a bath is dressed in his clothing which has been disinfected and discharged to duty.	

WAR DIARY or INTELLIGENCE SUMMARY.

Army Form C. 2118.

Place	Date	Hour	Summary of Events and Information	Remarks and references to Appendices
METEREN	11.9.18		Admissions. Officers nil. OR Sick 2 wd 5. Evacuations. Officers nil. OR Sick 2 wd. 4. Deaths. 1 OR (wounds in action)	
METEREN	12.9.18		Admissions. Officers Sick 1 wd 1. OR Sick nil wd 19. Evacuations. Officers Sick 1 wd 1. OR Sick nil wd 18. 1 OR disch to duty (wd.)	
METEREN	13.9.18		Admissions. Officers nil. OR Sick nil wd. 20. Evacuations. Officers nil. OR Sick nil wd 19. Deaths. 1 OR (G.SW legs.)	
METEREN	14.9.18		Admissions. Officers nil. OR Sick 2 wd 12. Evacuations. Officers nil. OR Sick 2 wd. 10. Deaths. OR 2 (wounds)	
METEREN	16.9.18		Admissions. Officers nil. OR Sick 3 wd 4. Evacuations. Officers nil. OR Sick 3 wd. 4. 6 Armstrong huts were received from ADMS and erected as dressing rooms for Stretcher cases, sick & walking wounded. The marquees at present in use as dressing rooms being converted into waiting and evacuating rooms.	

WAR DIARY
or
INTELLIGENCE SUMMARY.
(Erase heading not required.)

Army Form C. 2118.

Place	Date	Hour	Summary of Events and Information	Remarks and references to Appendices
METEREN	16.9.18		Admissions. Officers Sick nil wd. 2. OR Sick 2. wd. 46.	
			Evacuations. Officers Sick nil wd 2. OR Sick 2. wd. 45.	
			Deaths. OR 1 (wounds)	
METEREN	17.9.18		Admissions. Officers nil. OR Sick 5. wd. 24.	
			Evacuations. Officers nil. OR Sick 5. wd. 24.	
METEREN	18.9.18		Admissions. Officers Sick 1. wd. nil. OR Sick 15 wd. 10.	
			Evacuations. Officers Sick 1, wd nil. OR Sick 15. wd. 10.	
			Prevailing disease. Dysentery (Clinical) 3.	
			1st Lieut. H. CARR MRC USA reported his departure for duty as MO i/c 13th York & Lancs Regt.	
			Capt. J.S. ALEXANDER RAMC reported for temporary duty at M.D.S. from 31st Bn. M.G.C.	
METEREN	19.9.18		Admissions. Officers, Sick 1. wd. 3. OR Sick 18 wd. 70.	
			Evacuations. Officers Sick 1, wd. 3. OR Sick 18. wd 68	
			Return to duty OR 2 (wd)	
			Prevailing disease N.Y.D. (pyrexia) 4	

WAR DIARY
or
INTELLIGENCE SUMMARY.
(Erase heading not required.)

Army Form C. 2118.

Place	Date	Hour	Summary of Events and Information	Remarks and references to Appendices
METEREN	19.9.18		The main dressing station was visited by the D.M.S. 2nd Army, accompanied by the Consulting Surgeon 2nd Army and the Editor of the British Medical Journal.	Ap
METEREN	20.9.18		Admissions. Officers Sick nil wd nil. OR Sick 13 wd 27. Evacuations Officers nil. OR Sick 17 wd 27. Prevailing disease N.Y.D. pyrexia 4. 6 OR 94th Fd Amb having been evacuated sick on 13.9.18 an enquiry of the sample accordingly.	Ap
METEREN	21.9.18		Admissions. Officers nil. OR Sick 22 wd 19. Evacuations Officers nil. OR Sick 23 wd 19. Prevailing disease N.Y.D. pyrexia 5.	Ap
METEREN	22.9.18		Admissions. Officers Sick 2 wd nil. OR Sick 32 wd 22. Evacuations Officers Sick 2 wd nil OR Sick 30 wd 22. Deaths 1 OR (G.S.W. Back). Prevailing disease N.Y.D. pyrexia 7.	Ap

WAR DIARY or INTELLIGENCE SUMMARY

Army Form C. 2118.

Place	Date	Hour	Summary of Events and Information	Remarks and references to Appendices
METEREN	23.9.18		Admissions. Officers nil. OR Sick 23 wd 7	
			Evacuations. Officers nil. OR Sick 20 wd 7	
			Prevailing disease N.Y.D. Pyrexia 5	
METEREN	24.9.18		Admissions. Officers Sick 2 wd 1. OR Sick 30 wd 13	
			Evacuations. Officers Sick 2 wd 1. OR Sick 29 wd 3	
			Prevailing disease Chronic Dysentery 6	
METEREN	25.9.18		Admissions. Officers nil. OR Sick 22 wd 12	
			Evacuations. Officers nil. OR Sick 21 wd 12	
			Prevailing disease N.Y.D. Pyrexia 3	
METEREN	26.9.18		Admissions. Officers nil. OR Sick 26 wd 13	
			Evacuations. Officers nil. OR Sick 21 wd 11	
			Prevailing disease Dysentery (Chronic) 7	
METEREN	27.9.18		Admissions. Officers Sick 1 wd nil. OR Sick 37 wd 21	
			Evacuations. Officers Sick 1 wd nil. OR Sick 35 wd 8	
			Deaths. 3 OR (G.S. wounds)	
			Prevailing disease N.Y.D. Pyrexia 4	
			Major C. ROACHE M.C. 9th Fd. Amb. evacuated sick to N.Z. Stat. Hp.	

WAR DIARY
or
INTELLIGENCE SUMMARY.

(Erase heading not required.)

Army Form C. 2118.

Place	Date	Hour	Summary of Events and Information	Remarks and references to Appendices
METEREN	15.4.18		Corps Rest Depot moved from QUIESTEDE to LES CINQ RUES (Sh. 27. V 19 c 1.7) under arrangements made by D.D.M.S. XV Corps. The Main Dressing Station closed down at present site at 7 pm and was opened at S 30 c 1.9. (the previous A.D.S.) by 93rd Fd. Amb. in consequence of the alteration in the military situation. 94th Fd. Amb. received orders to be in readiness to move forward & establish a Main Dressing Station at or near S. 30. c when the situation permits. Capt. J.S. ALEXANDER proceeded to new M.D.S. for temporary duty with 93rd Fd. Amb. Capt. T.E. FLITCROFT proceeded to D.R.S. at BORRE for temporary duty with 93rd Fd. Amb. Admissions. Officers Sick 2 wd. 0. O.R. Sick 33 wd. 18 Evacuations. Officers Sick 2 wd 0. O.R. Sick 36. wd. 17. Prevailing Disease. M.T.D. Influenza 5.	

WAR DIARY or INTELLIGENCE SUMMARY

Army Form C. 2118.

Place	Date	Hour	Summary of Events and Information	Remarks and references to Appendices
METEREN	29.9.18		26 OR detailed for duty as bearers with 75th Fld Amb & 3 horsed ambulance wagons. Admissions. Officers Sick 1. Wd 3. OR Sick 17. Wd 62. Evacuations Officers Sick 1. Wd 3. OR Sick 21. Wd 62. Prevailing disease NYD pyrexia 2.	
METEREN	30.9.18		Admissions. Officers nil. OR Sick 11 Wd 2. Evacuations. Officers nil. OR Sick 12. Wd 2. Prevailing disease NYD pyrexia 2. The following Officers attached their arrival having taken on the strength accordingly. CAPT. O. A GEE and CAPT. A.B.R SWORN Royal 1st Lieut. T.A PITTS. M.R.O. USA Total Admissions during Sept. Officers Sick 13 Wd 38. OR Sick 449 Wd 934. Total Evacuations during September Officers Sick 13 Wd 36. OR Sick 419 Wd 914. Prevailing Diseases. Diarrhoea & Dysentery 62. NYD pyrexia 39. Round Lt-Col. Round OC 94th Fld. Amb.	

Oct. 1918.

140/3401.

94º 7. 9.

WAR DIARY or INTELLIGENCE SUMMARY

94th Fld Amb
Army Form C. 2118.
Vol 32

Place	Date	Hour	Summary of Events and Information	Remarks and references to Appendices
METEREN	1.10.18		Orders were received from ADMS to proceed to S.30.c.9.1 to take over Main Dressing Station from the bearers of 93rd Fld. Amb. there. Major J. GRAHAM proceeded in charge of the parties. Headquarters & Transport lines remaining at METEREN. The Site consists of an old artillery headquarters which had been damaged by shell fire. The huts have been repaired by 95th Fd. Amb. & used as ADS. Marquees were erected for sick, gassed & walking wounded reception rooms, & Armstrong huts for dressing rooms etc. Admissions: Officers nil OR Sick 12 wd. nil. Evacuations: Officers nil OR Sick 12 wd. nil.	
GOUGH LINES	2.10.18		Admissions. Officers Sick nil wd 1. OR Sick 22 wd 15. Evacuations. Officers Sick nil wd 1. OR Sick 22 wd 15. Prevailing disease NYD Pyrexia (4)	

WAR DIARY or INTELLIGENCE SUMMARY.

Army Form C. 2118.

(Erase heading not required.)

Place	Date	Hour	Summary of Events and Information	Remarks and references to Appendices
GOUGH LINES	3.10.18		Admissions. Officers nil OR Sick 57 wnd 9 Evacuations. Officers nil OR Sick 50 wnd 9 Prevailing disease NYD Pyrexia (4)	
GOUGH LINES	4.10.18		The Main Dressing Station was inspected by the D.M.S. 2nd Army, accompanied by the D.D.M.S. XV Corps. Major O. ROWE MC having been evacuated to the Base is struck off the Strength from this date. Admissions. Officers Sick 4 wnd nil OR Sick 34 wnd 7 Evacuations. Officers Sick 4 wnd nil OR Sick 34 wnd 7 Prevailing disease ICT (9)	
GOUGH LINES	5.10.18		Major OAK LYNE 64th Bde A.F.A. evacuated sick Capt. W. BAINE RAMC reported his arrival & was taken on the strength. Admissions. Officers Sick 3 wnd nil OR Sick 39 wnd 4 Evacuations. Officers Sick 3 wnd nil OR Sick 39 wnd 4 Prevailing disease Scabies 7	

WAR DIARY or INTELLIGENCE SUMMARY.

Army Form C. 2118.

(Erase heading not required.)

Place	Date	Hour	Summary of Events and Information	Remarks and references to Appendices
GOUGH LINES	6.10.18		Admissions. Officers Sick 1 wd. nil. O.R. Sick 36 wd 4. Evacuations. Officers Sick 1 wd nil. O.R. Sick 36 wd 4. including Major GARDINER. A.J. 64th Bde. A.F.A. Sick. Prevailing disease Dysentery (Clinical) 6	
GOUGH LINES	7.10.18		Admissions. Officers Sick nil, wd. 1. O.R. Sick 26 wd 6. Evacuations. Officers Sick nil wd 1. O.R. Sick 33 wd 6. including Lt. Col. NUTT A.V. 15th W. Yorks Regt. wounded. Prevailing disease. N.Y.D. pyrexia 7	
GOUGH LINES	8.10.18		Admissions. Officers Sick 1 wd nil. O.R. Sick 30 wd 20. Evacuations Officers Sick 1 wd nil. O.R. Sick 30 wd 20. Prevailing disease. N.Y.D. Influenza 5	
GOUGH LINES	9.10.18		Capt. G. RAINFORD, Lieut. QM J.G. FRASER and remainder of personnel from XV Corps Skin Centre reported their return on closing down of Skin Centre. Admissions. Officers Sick nil wd. nil. O.R. Sick 27 wd nil. Evacuations. Officers Sick nil, wd. nil. O.R. Sick 27 wd nil. Prevailing Disease. Influenza 6	

WAR DIARY or INTELLIGENCE SUMMARY.

Army Form C. 2118.

Place	Date	Hour	Summary of Events and Information	Remarks and references to Appendices
GOUGH LINES	10.10.18		Admissions. Officers Sick nil wd. 1. O.R. Sick 31 wd 2. Evacuations. Officers Sick nil, wd. 1. O.R. Sick 31 wd 2. Prevailing disease N.Y.D. Pyrexia 5.	
GOUGH LINES	11.10.18		Capt T.E. FLITCROFT R.A.M.C. having reported his departure for the United Kingdom on completion of contract is struck off the strength from this date. Capt W. BAINE reported his departure for temporary duty as M.O. to 15th West Yorks Regt. Admissions. Officers nil. O.R. Sick 34 wd 2. Evacuations. Officers nil. O.R. Sick 34 wd 2. Prevailing disease. Diarrhoea 13.	
GOUGH LINES	12.10.18		Admissions Officers Sick 1 wd. nil. O.R. Sick 37 wd 4. Evacuations. Officers Sick 1 wd nil O.R. Sick 37 wd 4. Prevailing disease Influenza. 11.	
GOUGH LINES	13.10.18		1st Lieut. T.A. PITTS reported his departure for temporary duty with 13th York & Lancs Regt.	

WAR DIARY or INTELLIGENCE SUMMARY

Army Form C. 2118.

Place	Date	Hour	Summary of Events and Information	Remarks and references to Appendices
GOUGH LINES	3/10/18		Capt. J.M. MOYES having been transferred from 95th Fld Amb. is taken on the Strength from this date, but remains with 95th Field Ambulance for temporary duty. Admissions Officers nil OR Sick 24 wd 4 Evacuations Officers nil OR Sick 24 wd 4 Prevailing disease NYD Influenza 9	
GOUGH LINES	4/10/18		Admissions Officers nil OR Sick 29 wd 4 Evacuations Officers nil OR Sick 29 wd 4 Prevailing disease NYD pyrexia 10	
GOUGH LINES	5/10/18		Admissions Officers Sick 3 wd nil OR Sick 86 wd 6 Evacuations Officers Sick 3 wd nil OR Sick 86 wd 6 Prevailing disease Influenza 11	
COURTE OREVE Fm	6/10/18		In consequence of the retirement of the enemy the main dressing station was moved up to the site of the advanced dressing station at	

… **WAR DIARY** or **INTELLIGENCE SUMMARY**

Army Form C. 2118.

Instructions regarding War Diaries and Intelligence Summaries are contained in F. S. Regs., Part II. and the Staff Manual respectively. Title pages will be prepared in manuscript.

(Erase heading not required.)

Place	Date	Hour	Summary of Events and Information	Remarks and references to Appendices
COURTE DREVE FARM	16.10.18		COURTE DREVE FARM Sheet 27 T.24.a. Major GRAHAM proceeded in command of the party. Headquarters & transport lines remaining on same site. Admissions Officers Sick 2 wd nil, OR Sick 20 wd 7. Evacuations Officers Sick 2 wd nil, OR Sick 20 wd 4. Deaths 1 OR (98M Kg) Prevailing disease N.Y.D. pyrexia 5.	Ph
COURTE DREVE FARM	17.10.18		Admissions Officers Sick 1 wd nil, OR Sick 44 wd nil. Evacuations Officers Sick 1 wd nil, OR Sick 44 wd nil. Prevailing disease N.Y.D. pyrexia 11.	Ph
QUESNOY	18.10.18		In consequence of the continued enemy retirement the Main Dressing Station was again moved to the site of the advanced dressing station in QUESNOY being accommodated in some German huts. Headquarters & transport lines also moved. Admissions Officers Sick 1 wd nil, OR Sick 31 wd nil. Evacuations Officers Sick 1 wd nil, OR Sick 31 wd nil. Prevailing disease N.Y.D. pyrexia 13.	Ph

WAR DIARY or INTELLIGENCE SUMMARY

Army Form C. 2118.

(Erase heading not required.)

Place	Date	Hour	Summary of Events and Information	Remarks and references to Appendices
MOUVEAUX	19.10.18		The main dressing Station including Headquarters and transport moved to F 14 d 3 3 (Sh. 36) taking over a Jesuit House of retreat which had been used by the enemy as a hospital. The building is large and in every way fitted for use as a hospital providing accommodation for about 400 patients. Arrangements were made to retain patients as the journey to the nearest C.C.S. was very long and the wards congested owing to the bridges over the LYS having been demolished. Admissions. Officers Sick nil, wd 2. OR Sick 18 and 17. Evacuations Officers Sick nil, wd 2. OR Sick 17, wd 17. Prevailing disease. Influenza. 3.	
MOUVEAUX	20.10.18		The main dressing Station was visited by D.M.S. 2nd Army, who arranged to send an advance party next day from No 2 Canadian C.C.S.	

WAR DIARY or INTELLIGENCE SUMMARY.

Army Form C. 2118.

Instructions regarding War Diaries and Intelligence Summaries are contained in F. S. Regs., Part II. and the Staff Manual respectively. Title pages will be prepared in manuscript.

(Erase heading not required.)

Place	Date	Hour	Summary of Events and Information	Remarks and references to Appendices
MOUVEAUX	20.10.18		to take over the Site as an advanced operating centre for the treatment of urgent cases pending the arrival of a complete C.C.S., and the establishment of railway communication.	
			Admissions. Officers Sick nil wd 1. O.R. Sick 30. wd 6.	
			Evacuations Officers Sick nil wd 1. O.R. Sick 4. wd 2.	
			Prevailing disease N.Y.D. pyrexia & Ch	
LANNOY	21.10.18		the ambulance proceeded by road to establish a Main Dressing Station at Q.19.b.22. (Sh. 37) near LANNOY, the late Site having been taken over by No 2 Can. C.C.S. as an advanced operating centre.	
			The M.D.S. is established in a chateau, the dressing rooms and wards for Sick with administrative offices being in the main building & personnel accommodated in the stable loft.	
			Arrangements made to detain slightly Sick cases	

WAR DIARY or INTELLIGENCE SUMMARY.

Army Form C. 2118.

(Erase heading not required.)

Place	Date	Hour	Summary of Events and Information	Remarks and references to Appendices
LANNOY	21.10.18		Serious sick cases & slightly wounded evacuated to CCS's at REMY SIDING and seriously wounded to the advanced operating centre at MOUVAUX. Admissions. Officers nil. OR Sick 29. wd 6. Evacuations. Officers nil. OR Sick nil. wd 8. Prevailing disease N.Y.D. pyrexia 7.	
LANNOY	22.10.18		Evacuation of Serious Sick & Slightly wounded cases is now to Nos 8 & 17 CCS near ARMENTIERES. 6 OR reinforcements having been transferred from RAMC Base Depot on 16.10.18 and 9 OR on 19.10.18 are taken on the strength accordingly, two being subsequently transferred to 95th Fd. Amb. as surplus to establishment. Admissions. Officers nil. OR Sick 23. wd 1. Evacuations. Officers nil. OR Sick 31. wd 1. Prevailing disease N.Y.D. Influenza 5.	

WAR DIARY or INTELLIGENCE SUMMARY.

Army Form C. 2118.

Place	Date	Hour	Summary of Events and Information	Remarks and references to Appendices
LANNOY	23.6.18		Admissions Officers nil. OR Sick 15. wd 8.	
			Evacuations Officers nil. OR Sick 21. wd 8.	
			Prevailing disease N.Y.D. pyrexia 5.	A.h
LANNOY	24.10.18		Capt. W. Bain reported his return from temporary duty as MO i/c 15th West Yorks Regt.	
			Admissions Officers Sick nil wd 1. OR Sick 27 wd 7.	
			Evacuations Officers Sick nil wd 1. OR Sick 7 wd 7.	
			Prevailing disease N.Y.D. pyrexia 6.	R.h
LANNOY	25.6.18		1st Lieut R.R. McHenry M.R.C. USA. marched Sick	
			Capt. W. Bain proceeded to assume duty in his place as MO i/c 18th D.L.I.	
			Capt A.B.R. Sworn reported his departure for duty as MO i/c 31st Div Train	
			Admissions Officers nil. OR Sick 38. wd 12.	
			Evacuations Officers nil. OR Sick 23. wd 7.	
			Prevailing Disease N.Y.D. Influenza 19.	
			Discharged to duty 10.	R.h

WAR DIARY or INTELLIGENCE SUMMARY.

(Erase heading not required.)

Army Form C. 2118.

Place	Date	Hour	Summary of Events and Information	Remarks and references to Appendices
LANNOY	26/10/18		Admissions. Officers Sick 1. wd. nil. OR Sick 81. wd. nil.	
			Evacuations. Officers Sick 1. wd. nil. OR Sick 52. wd. 1	
			Prevailing disease. Influenza 43.	Rh.
CUERNE	27/10/18		The main Dressing Station at LANNOY was handed over to 136th Field Ambce. 40th Div. and the unit proceeded by march route to H.14.d.3.6. Sh. 29. and was accommodated in billets in the old mill.	
~~CUERNE~~			Admissions. Officers Sick 3. wd. nil. OR Sick 39. wd. 4.	
			Evacuations. Officers Sick 3 wd. nil. OR Sick 94. wd. 5.	
			Transferred to 136 Fld. Amb. OR. Sick 12.	
			Prevailing disease N.Y.D. pyrexia 12.	Rh.
HARLEBEKE	28/10/18		The ambulance proceeded by march route to HARLEBEKE H.11.d.5.8. and took over the main Dressing Station of 9th Div. from 27th Fld. Amb. The Dressing Station is situated in a school, the school rooms providing good dressing rooms	

WAR DIARY or INTELLIGENCE SUMMARY.

Army Form C. 2118.

(Erase heading not required.)

Place	Date	Hour	Summary of Events and Information	Remarks and references to Appendices
HARLEBEKE	28.10.18		for stretcher & walking wounded, sick & gassed cases. Evacuation is by no 4 M.A.C. Walking wounded & sick by motor lorries to WINKEL ST. ELOI where there is an entraining station on the light railway which carries them to 36 & 44 CCS at PASSCHENDAELE. Serious wounds of head, chest & abdomen, and fractured femurs to Adv. operating centre at MOORSELE. Other stretcher cases, both sick & wounded to 3rd Aust. & 64 CCS. at LEDEGHEM by M.A.C. cars. Admissions nil. Evacuations nil. 10 OR sick discharged to duty.	A.L.
HARLEBEKE	29.10.18		All evacuations are now to 3rd Aust. & 64 CCS. the entraining station having closed down. Admissions, Officers sick 2 wd 2. O.R. sick 49 wd 58. Evacuations, Officers sick 2 wd 2. O.R. sick 49 wd 55. Prevailing disease. Influenza 18.	A.L.

WAR DIARY or INTELLIGENCE SUMMARY.

Army Form C. 2118.

Place	Date	Hour	Summary of Events and Information	Remarks and references to Appendices
HARLEBEKE	30.10.18		Capt. O.A. GEE having reported his departure for duty with 28th Fld. Amb. 9th Div. is struck off his strength from this date.	
			Admissions. Officers sick 4 wd 2. O.R. sick 115. wd 92	
			Evacuations. Officers sick 4 wd 2. O.R. sick 111 wd 91 including a/Maj. J.K.M. HAMILTON. a/Bde. Maj. 92nd Inf. Bde. (sick)	
			Deaths. 1 O.R. (G.S.W.)	
			Prevailing disease. Influenza 49.	
HARLEBEKE	31.10.18		Major J.M. MOYES reported his return from temporary duty with 95th Fld. Amb.	
			Arrangements were made to deal with casualties from an attack carried out by 94th Inf. Bde. Four lorries were attached for walking wounded two working between A.D.S. at VICHTE STATION and M.D.S. and two between M.D.S. and light railway entraining station at HULSTE where a field ambulance	

WAR DIARY
or
INTELLIGENCE SUMMARY.
(Erase heading not required.)

Army Form C. 2118.

Place	Date	Hour	Summary of Events and Information	Remarks and references to Appendices
MARLEBEKE	3.10.18		of the 9th Div. had established a Walking Wounded Collecting Post.	
			Extra ambulance cars from No 4 M.A.C. were attached for stretcher cases.	
			Zero hour 05.25 hours. Wounded commenced to arrive about 0900 hours. Arrangements for evacuation were satisfactory & there was no congestion. The majority of the casualties being cleared from MDS by 01.00 hours. The battle casualties evacuated from the attack were Officers 12. OR 248 including P.o.W. Offs 2. OR 68.	
			Admissions. Officers Sick 3 wd. nil. OR Sick 72. wd 57.	
			Evacuations. Officers Sick 3 wd. nil. OR Sick 70. wd 55	
			Prevailing Disease. Influenza. 50.	
			Total admissions & evacuations during the month of October are as under	

WAR DIARY or INTELLIGENCE SUMMARY.

Army Form C. 2118.

Place	Date	Hour	Summary of Events and Information	Remarks and references to Appendices
HARLEBEKE	31.10.18		Total Admissions. Officers Sick 30 wd. 11. OR. Sick 1130, wd. 362	
			" Evacuations. Officers Sick 30. wd. 11. OR. Sick 1088 wd. 348	
			" Deaths. 3 OR (GS Wounds)	
			Prevailing Diseases In Phunga. 191.	
			NYD In Phunga. 109.	
			NYD pyrexia 38	
			Chong Lt. Col. R.A.M.C. OC 94th Fld. Amb.	

Nov. 1918

140/3481

No. 94 ?. a.

COMMITTEE FOR THE
MEDICAL HISTORY OF THE WAR
Date 6 MAR 1919

WAR DIARY or INTELLIGENCE SUMMARY.

(Erase heading not required.)

Army Form C. 2118.

94 Fd Amb

Vol 33

Place	Date	Hour	Summary of Events and Information	Remarks and references to Appendices
HAARLEBEKE	1.11.18		The Unit is still functioning as Main Dressing Station in the same site. Admissions. Officers Sick 3. wd. 12. OR Sick 43 wd. 237 Evacuations. Officers Sick 3 wd. 12 OR Sick 45 wd. 243 Deaths. 1 OR. G.S.W. Face. Prevailing disease H.T.O. Pyrexia 18. (NB. These casualties were sustained in connection with the operations mentioned in War Diary for 31.10.18.)	P.L.
HAARLEBEKE	2.11.18		Admissions. Officers Sick 3. wd 4. OR Sick 61 wd. 84 Evacuations. Officers Sick 3 wd 4 OR Sick 62 wd. 80 Deaths 3 OR G.S Wounds. The majority of these casualties occurred as the result of an enemy air raid on the town. Prevailing disease. Influenza. 25 The Division having been withdrawn from the line the ambulance ceased to function as a Main Dressing Station.	P.L.
RONCQ	3.11.18		The Ambulance proceeded by march route from HAARLEBEKE to RONCQ, moving under orders from HQ 93rd Inf Bde and accompanying the 93rd Bde Group.	

WAR DIARY or INTELLIGENCE SUMMARY.

Army Form C. 2118.

(Erase heading not required.)

Place	Date	Hour	Summary of Events and Information	Remarks and references to Appendices
RONCQ	3-11-18		The personnel are accommodated in a convent, the lower storey of which is being used to accommodate slight cases of sickness in the Bde. Group. Serious cases are being evacuated to C.C.S. and mild influenza cases to 95th Fld. Amb. which has established a Divisional Rest Station at RECKEM. Admissions. Officers Sick 4 wd. 1. OR Sick 64. wd. 6. Evacuations. Officers Sick 4 wd. O. OR Sick 64 wd. 6. Major W.T. LAW. D.A.A.G. 31st Div. acc. injury rtd. to duty. Prevailing disease. NYD pyrexia. 24.	
RONCQ	4-11-18		Admissions. Officers nil. OR Sick 14 wd nil. Evacuations. Officers nil. OR Sick 2 wd nil. Prevailing disease. Influenza. 5.	
RONCQ	5-11-18		Admissions. Officers Sick 2 wd nil. OR Sick 14 wd nil. Evacuations. Officers Sick 2 wd nil. OR Sick 20 wd nil. Prevailing disease. Influenza 12.	
RONCQ	6-11-18		Admissions. Officers nil. OR Sick 8 wd nil. Evacuations. Officers nil. OR Sick 12 wd nil. Prevailing disease. Influenza 5.	

WAR DIARY or INTELLIGENCE SUMMARY

Army Form C. 2118.

Place	Date	Hour	Summary of Events and Information	Remarks and references to Appendices
RONCQ	7.11.18		Admissions. Officers Sick 4 wd nil OR Sick 12 wd nil. Evacuations. Officers Sick 4 wd nil OR Sick 12 wd nil. Marching Major J.M. FETHERSTONHAUGH 175th Bde RFA (Sick) Prevailing disease Influenza 8	Rt
SWEVEGHEM	8.11.18		The ambulance proceeded by march route from RONCQ to SWEVEGHEM and established a Main Dressing Station in the School taking over the site from 105th Fld. Amb. 35th Div. Evacuation by No 2 M.A.C. to MOORSELE Group of C.C. Stns. & advanced operating centre at COURTRAI. Admissions. Officers nil OR Sick 6 wd nil. Evacuations. Officers nil OR Sick 5 wd nil. Prevailing disease Influenza 3	Rt
SWEVEGHEM	9.11.18		Admissions. Officers Sick 2 wd nil OR Sick 9 wd 1. Evacuations. Officers Sick 2 wd nil OR Sick 9 wd 1. Marching Major E.C. GRAHAM 20th Railway Coy RE (Sick) Prevailing disease Influenza 4	Rt

WAR DIARY or INTELLIGENCE SUMMARY.

Army Form C. 2118.

(Erase heading not required.)

Place	Date	Hour	Summary of Events and Information	Remarks and references to Appendices
RUGGE	10.11.18		orders were received to move forward the main Dressing Station to keep in touch with the advancing troops who have crossed the river ESCAUT. Main dressing station established in the school at RUGGE, the whole of the unit moving there by march route. Owing to the bridge having been blown up & with when it was not considered advisable to move the M.D.S. across the river as the pontoon bridge is not yet strong enough to take many cars. 3 Horsed ambulances lent to 93rd Fd. Amb. to evacuate forward area. Admissions Officers R.P 1 and nil OR SK 13 and 3. Evacuations Officers R.P 1 and nil OR SK 17 and 2. Prevailing disease Influenza 5. O.R	
RENAIX	11.11.18		Orders were received to move all the unit across the ESCAUT. The Ambulance proceeded by march route to RENAIX and was accommodated in a large factory at X.16.c.3.2.	

WAR DIARY or INTELLIGENCE SUMMARY.

Army Form C. 2118.

(Erase heading not required.)

Place	Date	Hour	Summary of Events and Information	Remarks and references to Appendices
RENAIX	11.11.18		During the day information was received that an Armistice had been signed & hostilities ceased at 1100 hours. Admissions. Officers nil OR Sick 28 and nil. Evacuations Officers nil OR Sick 26 and nil. Prevailing disease Influenza. 6.	
RENAIX	12.11.18		Orders were received to relieve 93rd Fd. Amb. in the evacuation of forward area. Car Collecting Posts established as under. To 92nd Inf. Bde. U 11 a 8.9 i/c Lt. PEACOCK (attached by 95th Fd. Amb.) To 95th Inf. Bde. S 16 d.4.3 i/c Corpl. RYLE. Personnel attached last 1 NCO 7 other men. Admissions. Officers Sick 0 and 1. OR Sick 14 and 0. Evacuations. Officers Sick 0 and 1. OR Sick 9 and 0. Prevailing disease Influenza. 6.	

WAR DIARY
or
INTELLIGENCE SUMMARY.

Army Form C. 2118.

(Erase heading not required.)

Place	Date	Hour	Summary of Events and Information	Remarks and references to Appendices
RENAIX	13.11.18		Capt. T. J. LLOYD R.A.M.C. having reported his arrival for duty is taken on the strength accordingly. In accordance with orders from A.D.M.S. Our posts with 92nd & 93rd Inf. Bdes. were withdrawn & returned to Headquarters. Admissions. Officers Sick 1 wd. nil. O.R. Sick 2 wd. nil. Evacuations. Officers Sick 1 wd. nil. O.R. Sick 13 wd. nil.	
HEESTERT	14.11.18		The ambulance proceeded by march route, accompanying 93rd Inf. Bde. & billeted for the night at HEESTERT. Admissions nil. Evacuations nil.	P.L.
BISSEGHEM	15.11.18		The ambulance proceeded with the 93rd Inf. Bde. to BISSEGHEM & billeted there for the night. 1 N.C.O. & 10 men proceeded for temporary duty to XIX Corps dump at COURTRAI, relieving detachment of 140th Fd. Amb. 1 nursing orderly to No 10 Squadron R.A.F. at MENIN for temporary duty. Admissions. Officers nil. O.R. Sick 8 wd. nil. Evacuations. Officers nil. O.R. Sick 8 wd. nil. Prevailing disease Influenza 2.	P.L.

WAR DIARY or INTELLIGENCE SUMMARY

Army Form C. 2118.

Place	Date	Hour	Summary of Events and Information	Remarks and references to Appendices
WEVELGHEM	16.11.18		The ambulance accompanied the 93rd Inf. Bde. by march route to WEVELGHEM, & billetted in the School. Admissions. Officers sick 1. wd. nil OR sick 5. wd. nil. Evacuations. Officers sick 1 wd. nil OR sick 5 wd. nil. Prevailing disease Influenza 2.	
WEVELGHEM	17.11.18		Major J.M. MOYES reported his departure for temporary duty with XIX Corps Headquarters as D.A.D.M.S. Admissions. Officers nil. OR sick 4 wd. nil. Evacuations. Officers nil. OR sick 4 wd. nil. No prevailing disease.	
WEVELGHEM	18.11.18		1st Lieut. C.H. HEACOCK M.O.R.C. U.S.A. having reported his arrival from 89th Fd. Amb. for duty is taken on the strength accordingly. The ambulance proceeded by march route (dismounted personnel only) to MARCKE where a parade of the 3 divisional field ambulances was held by A.D.C. 31st Div. for the purpose of presenting ribands of decorations awarded during recent operations. The following from 94th Fd. Amb. received the M.M. Ptes. H.G. BUTCHER & L. NEW, A.S.C. M.T.	

WAR DIARY or INTELLIGENCE SUMMARY.

(Erase heading not required.)

Army Form C. 2118.

Place	Date	Hour	Summary of Events and Information	Remarks and references to Appendices
WEVELGHEM	18.11.18		Admissions nil. Evacuations nil	
WEVELGHEM	19.11.18		An association football match was played between 94th & 95th Fd. Amb. at RECKEM in connection with the selection of a team to represent the R.A.M.C. in the Divisional Football Competition. 95th Fd. Amb. won by 3 goals to nil. Admissions. Officers nil. OR Sick 4 wd. nil Evacuations Officers nil OR Sick 4 wd. nil Prevailing disease I.C.T. 2	
WEVELGHEM	20.11.18		Admissions. Officers nil. OR Sick 5 wd. nil. Evacuations Officers nil OR Sick 3 wd. nil. Prevailing disease Diarrhoea 2. The 94th Fd. Amb. Stn was visited by the D.D.M.S. XIX Corps.	
WEVELGHEM	21.11.18		Admissions. Officers nil. OR Sick 13 wd. nil. Evacuations Officers nil OR Sick 13 wd. nil. Prevailing disease Influenza 3	

WAR DIARY or INTELLIGENCE SUMMARY.

Army Form C. 2118.

(Erase heading not required.)

Place	Date	Hour	Summary of Events and Information	Remarks and references to Appendices
WEVELGHEM	22.11.18		DMS 2nd Army inspected representative parties from 93rd, 94th & 95th Field Ambulances at MARCKE on the occasion of the 31st Division leaving 2nd Army. T. Lieut. J. M. McCORMACK RAMC having reported his arrival for duty is taken on the strength accordingly. Admissions. Officers nil. OR Sick 3 wnd nil. Evacuations. Officers nil. OR Sick 3 wnd nil.	
MENIN	23.11.18		Orders were received that 31st Div. would proceed by march route to ST. OMER area. 94th Fd. Ambulance accompanied 93rd Inf. Bde to MENIN, and billetted in X Corps reception camp for the night. 2 motor ambulances from No 4 MAC and 1 motor lorry were attached for the move. Admissions. Officers nil. OR Sick 8 wnd nil. Evacuations. Officers nil. OR Sick 8 wnd nil. Prevailing disease. Pleurisy 2.	

WAR DIARY or INTELLIGENCE SUMMARY.

Army Form C. 2118.

Place	Date	Hour	Summary of Events and Information	Remarks and references to Appendices
VLAMARTINGE	24.11.18		The 94th Fld. Amb. proceeded to VLAMARTINGE, and billetted for the night in the Chateau. Sick evacuated to No 39 Stationary Hosp. LILLE. Admissions. Officers sick 2 wnd nil. OR sick 15 wnd nil. Evacuations. Officers sick 2 wnd nil. OR sick 15 wnd nil. Prevailing disease Influenza 4.	Ah
STEENVOORDE	25.11.18		The 94th Fld. Amb. proceeded to STEENVOORDE, and billetted in an empty house for the night. Admissions. Officers nil. OR sick 3 wnd nil. Evacuations. Officers nil. OR sick 3 wnd nil. Evacuations to St. OMER Group, 9 CCS & Stat. Hos. Prevailing disease NYD pyrexia 2.	Ah
BLENDECQUES	26.11.18		The 94th Fld. Amb. proceeded to final destination at BLENDECQUES & was accommodated in an empty house. Admissions. Officers nil. OR sick 4 wnd nil. Evacuations. Officers nil. OR sick 4 wnd nil. Prevailing disease NYD pyrexia 3.	Ah

WAR DIARY or INTELLIGENCE SUMMARY.

Army Form C. 2118.

(Erase heading not required.)

Place	Date	Hour	Summary of Events and Information	Remarks and references to Appendices
BLENDECQUES	27.11.18		The 2 M.A.C. Cars & motor lorry attached returned to their respective units. D.R.S. opened at ST OMER by 93rd Fld Amb for slight cases.	
BLENDECQUES	28.11.18		Admissions Officers nil OR Sick 1 wd nil Evacuations Officers nil OR nil	
BLENDECQUES	29.11.18		Admissions Officers nil OR Sick 8 wd nil Evacuations Officers nil OR Sick 10 wd nil Prevailing disease I.O.T. 3	
BLENDECQUES	30.11.18		Admissions Officers nil OR nil Evacuations Officers nil OR nil	

Total admissions during the month of November
Officers Sick 25 wd 18. OR Sick 389 wd 381

Total evacuations during the month of November
Officers Sick 24 wd 17 OR Sick 379 wd 332
Total discharges to duty Officers Sick 1 wd 1. OR Sick 73 wd 5.
Total Deaths 4. OR (wounds) Prevailing disease Influenza 90
Signed Lt-Col. Rome OC 94th Fld Amb.

Dec. 1918

140/3481

9 ab F.A.

COMMITTEE FOR THE
MEDICAL HISTORY OF THE WAR
Date   6 MAR 1919

9/2 94 Fd Amb

WAR DIARY or INTELLIGENCE SUMMARY.
Army Form C. 2118.
(Erase heading not required.)

V8 34

Place	Date	Hour	Summary of Events and Information	Remarks and references to Appendices
BLENDECQUES	1-12-18		The 94th Field Ambulance is still located in BLENDECQUES evacuating from 93rd inf Bde and 31st Div Artillery. In connection with the Educational scheme classes are being held in the following subjects:- French, Hygiene & Physiology, Book keeping, Mathematics & Shorthand, Rugby & Association football, Cross Country running, Boxing & tug of war, are all being indulged in. A [illegible] [illegible] [illegible] ... Admissions Officers nil OR Sick 7 wd nil Evacuations Officers nil OR Sick 7 wd nil Remaining Officers [ ] Sick [ ] wd [ ]	
BLENDECQUES			No 1 T/Lt J Lloyd reported for duty from 3rd DAC. Admissions Officers Sick 1 wd nil OR Sick 3 wd nil Evacuations Officers Sick 1 wd nil OR Sick 3 wd nil Remaining Sick NYD Lynn & [illegible]	

WAR DIARY
or
INTELLIGENCE SUMMARY.

Army Form C. 2118.

(Erase heading not required.)

Instructions regarding War Diaries and Intelligence Summaries are contained in F. S. Regs., Part II. and the Staff Manual respectively. Title pages will be prepared in manuscript.

Place	Date	Hour	Summary of Events and Information	Remarks and references to Appendices
BLENDECQUES	3-12-18		Admissions Officers nil OR SICK 10 and nil	
			Evacuations Officers nil OR SICK 10 and nil	
			Prevailing disease [illegible]	
BLENDECQUES	4-12-18		Admissions Officers nil OR SICK 3 and nil	
			Evacuations Officers nil OR SICK 3 and nil	
			Prevailing disease	
BLENDECQUES	5-12-18		Admissions Officers nil OR SICK 8 and nil	
			Evacuations Officers nil OR SICK 8 and nil	
			Prevailing disease	
BLENDECQUES	6-12-18		Admissions Officers nil OR SICK 13 and nil	
			Evacuations Officers nil OR SICK 13 and nil	
			Prevailing disease	
BLENDECQUES	7-12-18		Major J.M. MOYES attached from [illegible] XIX Corps	
			Lieut. C.H. HEADICK [illegible]	
			Admissions Officers nil OR SICK 11 and nil	
			Evacuations Officers nil OR SICK 11	
			Prevailing disease	

A5834 Wt. W4973/M687 750,000 8/16 D. D. & L. Ltd. Forms/C.2118/13.

WAR DIARY or INTELLIGENCE SUMMARY

Army Form C. 2118.

Place	Date	Hour	Summary of Events and Information	Remarks and references to Appendices
BLENDECQUES	8.12.18		Lieut. J.M. M°CORMICK attached for duty to M.O.T. XIX Corps Troops.	
			Admissions. Officers Sick 3 wd nil. OR Sick 6 wd nil	
			Evacuations. Officers Sick 3 wd nil. OR Sick 6 wd nil	
			Prevailing disease Influenza 3.	
BLENDECQUES	9.12.18		Admissions Officers nil OR Sick 6 wd nil	
			Evacuations Officers nil OR Sick 6 wd nil	
			Prevailing disease Influenza 2	
BLENDECQUES	10.12.18		2 OR ASC HT having reported sick admitted on ration strength from this date.	
			Admissions. Officers Sick 1 wd nil. OR Sick 2 wd nil	
			Evacuations Officers Sick 1 wd nil. OR Sick 2 wd nil	
BLENDECQUES	11.12.18		Admissions Officers nil. OR Sick 5 wd nil.	
			Evacuations Officers nil. OR Sick 5 wd nil.	
			Prevailing disease Influenza 4.	

WAR DIARY
or
INTELLIGENCE SUMMARY.
(Erase heading not required.)

Army Form C. 2118.

Instructions regarding War Diaries and Intelligence Summaries are contained in F. S. Regs., Part II. and the Staff Manual respectively. Title pages will be prepared in manuscript.

Place	Date	Hour	Summary of Events and Information	Remarks and references to Appendices
BLENDECQUES	12-12-18		2 O.R. sent to XIX Demobilisation Camp for which he (coal miners?). Capt. J.A. RYLE and 3 O.R. with one long ambulance car proceeded to LA KREULE (Sh. 27 V.10.a.5.3) to establish a medical post at XIX Corps Demobilisation Depot Camp. 4 O.R. proceeded to R.O.D. MALHOVE for course of instruction in engineering. Admissions Officers nil, O.R. Sick 5, nil nil. Evacuations Officers nil, O.R. Sick 5, nil nil. Prevailing diseases Influenza 4, P.U.O.	
BLENDECQUES	13-12-18		7 O.R. proceeded to XIX Corps Demobilisation Camp, release as coal miners. 1 N.C.O. & 14 men attached Corps Demobilisation supplies proceeded for temporary duty to 4th Divisional Area. Admissions Officers nil, O.R. Sick 4, nil nil. Evacuations Officers nil, O.R. Sick 4, nil nil. Prevailing diseases Influenza.	

WAR DIARY or INTELLIGENCE SUMMARY

Army Form C. 2118.

(Erase heading not required.)

Place	Date	Hour	Summary of Events and Information	Remarks and references to Appendices
BLENDECQUES	14.12.18		1 OR proceeded to XIX Corps Staging Camp for demobilization as a coal miner.	
			3 OR proceeded to 31st Div MT Coy for canning instruction	
			25 OR proceeded to New Zealand Stationary Hospital for temporary duty	
			Admissions Officers nil OR sick 9 inj nil	
			Evacuations Officers nil OR sick 7 inj nil	
			Remaining diseases influenza 3	
BLENDECQUES	15.12.18		Admissions Officers nil OR sick 5 inj nil	
			Evacuations Officers nil OR sick 5 inj nil	
BLENDECQUES	16.12.18		1 OR proceeded to No 15 RE Workshop for Army of Occupation	
			Admissions Officers sick 1 inj nil OR sick 9 inj nil	
			Evacuations Officers sick 1 inj nil OR sick 6 inj nil	
			Remaining diseases influenza 2	
BLENDECQUES	17.12.18		6 OR proceeded to XIX Corps Regnl Camp for demobilization	
			Admissions Officers nil OR sick 4 inj nil	
			Evacuations Officers nil OR sick 5 inj nil	
			Remaining diseases Scabies 3	

WAR DIARY or INTELLIGENCE SUMMARY.

Army Form C. 2118.

Instructions regarding War Diaries and Intelligence Summaries are contained in F. S. Regs., Part II. and the Staff Manual respectively. Title pages will be prepared in manuscript.

(Erase heading not required.)

Place	Date	Hour	Summary of Events and Information	Remarks and references to Appendices
BLENDECQUES	18/12/18		2 OR having been evacuated to the 3 Conv. Decot. WD on 16/12/18 are struck off the strength. Admissions Officers nil OR Sick 4 and nil. Evacuations Officers nil OR Sick 4 and nil. Prevailing disease Influenza 3	
BLENDECQUES	19/12/18		Capt. T. J. LLOYD having reported his return from temporary duty with 31st D.A.D. is posted for duty with R.O.D. Malhove & struck off the strength accordingly. Admissions Officers sick 1 and nil OR sick 2 and nil. Evacuations Officers sick 1 and nil OR sick 1 and nil. Prevailing disease ILD Influenza 2	
BLENDECQUES	20/12/18		Admissions Officers nil OR sick 8 and nil. Evacuations Officers nil OR sick 9 and nil. Prevailing disease Influenza 6	
BLENDECQUES	21/12/18		Admissions nil. Evacuations nil.	
BLENDECQUES	22/12/18		Admissions nil. Evacuations nil.	

WAR DIARY
or
INTELLIGENCE SUMMARY.

(Erase heading not required.)

Army Form C. 2118.

Place	Date	Hour	Summary of Events and Information	Remarks and references to Appendices
Blendecques	23.12.18		Admissions Officers nil. O.R. Sick 5. wd nil Evacuations Officers nil. O.R. Sick 5. wd nil	
Blendecques	24.12.18		Capt. J.A. Ryle RAMC. SR yesterday reported his departure from Headquarters. Prevailing disease, dysentery, I.C.T. proceeded to U.K. for special duty at the 1st Eastern General Hospital Cambridge & struck off the strength accordingly. Admissions. Officers nil. O.R. Sick 8. wd nil Evacuations Officers nil. O.R. Sick 8. wd nil	
Blendecques	25.12.18		Visit by A.D.M.S. who addressed the men at their Xmas dinner. Admissions Officers nil. O.R. Sick 5. wd nil Evacuations Officers nil. O.R. Sick 5. wd nil Prevailing disease I.C.T. 2.	
Blendecques	26.12.18		Lieut Col. E.C. Lang, D.S.O. RAMC. today reported his departure from Headquarters to proceed to U.K. on leave from 27.12.18 to 10.1.19. Admissions. Officers nil O.R. Sick 3. wd nil Evacuations Officers nil O.R. Sick 3. wd nil	

WAR DIARY
or
INTELLIGENCE SUMMARY.

(Erase heading not required.)

Army Form C. 2118.

Place	Date	Hour	Summary of Events and Information	Remarks and references to Appendices
Blendecques	27/12/18		Admissions Officers nil O.R. Sick 6 wd. nil	
			Evacuations Officers nil O.R. Sick 6 wd nil	
Blendecques	28/12/18		Admissions Officers nil O.R. Sick 2 wd nil	
			Evacuations Officers nil O.R. Sick 2 wd nil	
Blendecques	29/12/18		Admissions Officers nil O.R. Sick 8 wd nil	
			Evacuations Officers nil O.R. Sick 8 wd nil	
Blendecques	30/12/18		Admissions Officers nil O.R. Sick 3 wd nil	
			Evacuations Officers nil O.R. Sick 3 wd nil	
Blendecques	31/12/18		Admissions Officers nil O.R. Sick 6 wd nil	
			Evacuations Officers nil O.R. Sick 6 wd nil	
			Prevailing disease Dental Caries (3) Graham Major RAMC T A/OC 94th Field Ambulance	
Blendecques			Admissions Officers nil O.R. Sick 5 wd nil	
			Evacuations Officers nil O.R. Sick 5 wd nil	

Jan 1919

31st DIV
Box 2131

140/3524

No. 94 Field Ambulance

COMMITTEE FOR THE
MEDICAL HISTORY OF THE WAR
Date

31

WAR DIARY
or
INTELLIGENCE SUMMARY.
(Erase heading not required.)

Army Form C. 2118.

94 Fld Amb

Vol 34

Place	Date	Hour	Summary of Events and Information	Remarks and references to Appendices
Blendecques	1.1.19		Admissions Officers nil. O.R. Sick 5 wd nil Evacuations Officers nil O.R. Sick 5 wd nil	
Blendecques	2.1.19		Under orders from A.D.M.S. 31 Div. 1 N.C.O & 24 men proceeded for duty to 3rd Can. S.H. By request of O.C. 4 Stat. Hosp. Longuenesse 1 N.C.O & 12 men were sent there for temporary duty. Admissions Officers nil O.R Sick 4 wd nil Evacuations Officers nil O.R Sick 4 wd nil	
Blendecques	3.1.19		Admissions Officers nil O.R Sick 2 wd nil Evacuations Officers nil O.R Sick 2 wd nil	
Blendecques	4.1.19		Admissions Officers nil O.R Sick 4 wd nil Evacuations Officers nil O.R Sick 4 wd nil	

WAR DIARY or INTELLIGENCE SUMMARY.

Army Form C. 2118.

(Erase heading not required.)

Place	Date	Hour	Summary of Events and Information	Remarks and references to Appendices
Steenbecque	5.1.19		In accordance with 31 Div RAMC order No 59 by Lt Col R.E. Drake-Brockman. DSO. RAMC. temp. comdg RAMC 31 Div the 94th Fd. Amb. moved today to Steenbecque (Map reference Hazebrouck 5A - F.4.80.10.) & took over the field ambulance site there, opening a hospital to deal with units of XIX Corps in that area.	
			Admissions Officers nil O.R. Sick 3. Wd. nil	
			Evacuations Officers nil O.R. Sick 3 Wd nil	
Steenbecque	6.1.19		Lt. Heacock C.H. M.C. USA (and four nursing orderlies) today proceeded for temporary duty with I.W.T. at Aire	
			Admissions Officers Sick 1 O.R. Sick 2. Wd. nil	
			Evacuations Officers Sick 1 O.R. Sick 2 Wd nil	
Steenbecque	7.1.19		Admissions Officers nil O.R. nil Wd. nil	
			Evacuations Officers nil O.R. nil Wd nil	
Steenbecque	8.1.19		Admissions & Evacuations nil	
Steenbecque	9.1.19		Admissions Officers nil O.R. Sick 2 Wd. nil	
			Evacuations Officers nil O.R. nil Wd nil	

WAR DIARY
or
INTELLIGENCE SUMMARY.
(Erase heading not required.)

Instructions regarding War Diaries and Intelligence Summaries are contained in F. S. Regs., Part II. and the Staff Manual respectively. Title pages will be prepared in manuscript.

Army Form C.

Place	Date	Hour	Summary of Events and Information	Remarks and references to Appendices
STEENBECQUE	10.1.19		Admissions. Officers nil. OR Sick 1 wd nil. Evacuations Officers nil OR Sick 1 wd nil	
STEENBECQUE	11.1.19		No 60684 Sgt Webber F. awarded the Belgian Croix de Guerre. Admissions. Officers nil. OR wd 8 wd nil. Evacuations Officers nil OR Sick 7 wd nil. Prevailing disease I.C.T. 2	
STEENBECQUE	12.1.19		1 OR. RASC having been admitted to 4 Stat Hosp 4.1.19 is Struck off the Strength. 2 OR RAMC having proceeded to UK for demobilisation are Struck off the Strength. Admissions Officers nil. OR Sick 4 wd nil. Evacuations Officers nil OR Sick 2 wd nil	
STEENBECQUE	13.1.19		4 OR RAMC having proceeded to UK for demobilisation are Struck off the Strength. 4 OR RASC having rejoined their unit on demobilisation are taken on the Strength. Admissions. Officers nil OR Sick 4 wd nil. Evacuations Officers nil OR Sick 1 wd nil	

WAR DIARY or INTELLIGENCE SUMMARY.

(Erase heading not required.)

Army Form C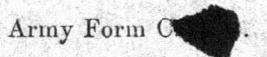

Instructions regarding War Diaries and Intelligence Summaries are contained in F. S. Regs., Part II. and the Staff Manual respectively. Title pages will be prepared in manuscript.

Place	Date	Hour	Summary of Events and Information	Remarks and references to Appendices
STEENBECQUE	14.1.19		Admissions Officers nil OR Sick 6 wd nil (includes 2 ? P.O.W.) Evacuations Officers nil OR Sick 2 wd nil No 63811 Pte Ashworth F Roused is appointed ?/H/Cpl with pay vice A/Cpl F McGrath demobilised. Pk	
STEENBECQUE	15.1.19		Admissions Officers nil OR Sick 2 wd nil Evacuations Officers nil OR Sick 3 wd nil Discharges OR Sick 2 Pk	
STEENBECQUE	16.1.19		Admissions Officers nil OR Sick 8 wd nil (includes 2 ? P.O.W.) Evacuations Officers nil OR Sick 3 Pk	
STEENBECQUE	17.1.19		Admissions Officers nil OR Sick 4 wd nil Evacuations Officers nil OR Sick 4 wd nil (includes 1 ? P.O.W.) Pk	
STEENBECQUE	18.1.19		4 OR (3 RAMC & 1 RASC MT) having proceeded to U.K. for demobilisation are struck off the strength. 1 OR Rand having been admitted to 4 Stat H on 11.1.19 is struck off the strength from that date. Admissions Officers nil OR Sick 10 wd nil Evacuations Officers nil OR Sick 9 wd nil (includes 3 ? P.O.W.) Disch to duty OR Sick 2 Prevailing diseases Diarrhoea 2 I.C.T. 2 Pk	

A5834 Wt. W4973/M687 750,000 8/16 D. D. & L. Ltd. Forms/C.2113/13.

WAR DIARY or INTELLIGENCE SUMMARY.

(Erase heading not required.)

Army Form C.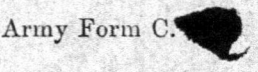

Place	Date	Hour	Summary of Events and Information	Remarks and references to Appendices
STEENBECQUE	19.1.17		Information has been received from the Major that the Hospital equipped by this unit was required for the use of the civil population application has already been put in asking the accommodation to his own use. 3 Standard huts 60 ft × 20 ft have arranged for by DDMS XIX Corps to be drawn & arrangements made with Area Commandant to dismantle Iunal & all Nissen huts in vicinity and erect them near present site where there is already a large Hospital Nissen hut wanted. Admissions officers nil OR Regt 4 and nil Evacuations officers nil OR Regt 3 and nil Sick to duty OR R 2	
STEENBECQUE	20.1.17		7 OR Rank having proceeded to UK for demobilisation and struck off his strength. 6 OR Rank MT which has arrived his taken on the strength from this date. Admissions officers nil OR Regt 3 and nil Evacuations officers nil OR Regt 3 and nil Sick to duty O.R. Regt 3	

WAR DIARY or INTELLIGENCE SUMMARY.

Army Form C.

(Erase heading not required.)

Instructions regarding War Diaries and Intelligence Summaries are contained in F. S. Regs., Part II. and the Staff Manual respectively. Title pages will be prepared in manuscript.

Place	Date	Hour	Summary of Events and Information	Remarks and references to Appendices
STEENBECQUE	21.1.19		Admissions Officers nil. OR ReP 4 md nil. Evacuations Officers nil OR ScOR 4 md nil. Proceeding to rest M.T.D. Agency 2. 7 O.R. Ranks having proceeded to U.K. for demobilisation are Struck off the Strength. In accordance with orders from A.D.M.S. 2 Corps 4 H.D. horses class X were dispatched to Corps horse Concentration Camp for transfer to U.K.	
STEENBECQUE	22.1.19		3 O.R. Ranks having proceeded to U.K. for demobilisation are Struck off the Strength. Admissions Officers nil. OR ReP 4 md nil (1 civilian + 3 P.O.W). Evacuations Officers nil OR nil.	
STEENBECQUE	23.1.19		1 O.R. Rank having been demobilised whilst on leave in U.K. is Struck off the Strength from 15/1/19. Admissions Officers nil. OR ReP 1 md nil. Evacuations Officers nil OR ReP 1 md nil. Disch. to duty OR ReP 2.	

WAR DIARY
or
INTELLIGENCE SUMMARY.

(Erase heading not required.)

Army Form C.

Instructions regarding War Diaries and Intelligence Summaries are contained in F. S. Regs., Part II. and the Staff Manual respectively. Title pages will be prepared in manuscript.

Place	Date	Hour	Summary of Events and Information	Remarks and references to Appendices
STEENBECQUE	24.1.19		Admissions. Officers nil. OR sick 12 and nil. Evacuations Officers nil. OR sick nil eye nil. One complete Standard hut has been received from D.D.M.S. XIX Corps.	
STEENBECQUE	25.1.19		Admissions Officers nil. OR sick 3 and nil. Evacuations Officers nil. OR sick 1 and nil.	
STEENBECQUE	26.1.19		Admissions. Officers nil. OR sick 4 and nil. Evacuations Officers nil. OR sick 3 and nil. Quick to duty. OR sick 2.	
STEENBECQUE	27.1.19		Admissions Officers nil. OR sick 2 and nil. Evacuations Officers nil. OR sick 2 and nil.	
STEENBECQUE	28.1.19		2 OR Ranks having been sent to Clothes the sick in Bed. Communicants Officer in charge of the station. 1 OR Rank proceeded to "A" B south 31st D. H. for duty as clerk on station of the strength. Admissions. Officers nil. OR sick 5 and nil. Evacuations Officers nil. OR sick 1 and nil. Sent to duty, OR sick 1. Prevailing disease P.U.O. 3	

A5834 Wt. W4973/M687 750,000 8/16 D. D. & L. Ltd. Forms/C.2118/13.

WAR DIARY or INTELLIGENCE SUMMARY.

Army Form C.2118.

Instructions regarding War Diaries and Intelligence Summaries are contained in F. S. Regs., Part II. and the Staff Manual respectively. Title pages will be prepared in manuscript.

(Erase heading not required.)

Place	Date	Hour	Summary of Events and Information	Remarks and references to Appendices
STEENBECQUE	29.1.19		1 OR having been admitted to No 3 Can Stat Hosp on 24/1/19 is Struck off the Strength.	
			Admissions. Officers nil OR R&R 4 and nil	
			Evacuations Officers nil OR R&R 1 and nil	
			Back to duty OR R&R 2	
			Prevailing disease Bronchitis 12	R.B.
STEENBECQUE	30.1.19		Admissions Officers nil OR Sick 4 and nil	
			Evacuations Officers nil OR Sick 1 and nil	
			Back to duty OR Sick 3	
			Prevailing disease Influenza 2	R.B.
STEENBECQUE	31.1.19		1 OR having been discharged whilst on leave to UK is Struck off the Strength from 9/12/18	
			Admissions Officers nil OR S.R. 5 and nil	
			Evacuations Officers nil OR Sick 2 and nil	R.B.
			Total Admissions for January. Officers 1 OR R&R 111 and nil (includes G.P.O.W. 12)	
			Total Evacuations for January Officers R&R 1 OR R&R 74 and nil	
			Total Back to duty OR R&R 21	
			Prevailing diseases Influenza 6, P.U.O. 6	
			Rhoma W/Col Ramo O.C. 94th Fed Amb	

A5834 Wt. W4973/M687 750,000 8/16 D. D. & L. Ltd. Forms/C.2118/13.

Feb. 1919

140/3524

No 94 Field Ambulance

31   94th Fld Amb

WAR DIARY
or
INTELLIGENCE SUMMARY.
(Erase heading not required.)

Army Form C. 2118.

Vol 35

Place	Date	Hour	Summary of Events and Information	Remarks and references to Appendices
STEENBECQUE	1.2.18		The unit is still stationed in STEENBECQUE, drawing rations from 30th Div. Arty, M.G. Bn, and Corps Heavy Artillery. The erection of huts to replace the accommodation in the billets acquired by the French Civil authorities is being proceeded with. Admissions Officers nil OR Sick 4 wounded nil. Evacuations Officers nil OR Sick 7 wounded nil.	
STEENBECQUE	2.2.18		Admissions Officers nil OR Sick 1 wounded nil. Evacuations Officers nil OR Sick 4 wounded nil.	
STEENBECQUE	3.2.18		4 OR RASC MT being surplus to our establishment were transferred for duty to 31st Div. Train. Admissions Officers nil OR Sick 3 wounded nil. Evacuations Officers nil OR Sick 4 wounded nil.	
STEENBECQUE	4.2.18		Admissions Officers nil OR Sick 4 wounded nil. Evacuations Officers nil OR Sick 3 wounded nil.	

WAR DIARY or INTELLIGENCE SUMMARY.

Army Form C. 2118.

Instructions regarding War Diaries and Intelligence Summaries are contained in F. S. Regs., Part II. and the Staff Manual respectively. Title pages will be prepared in manuscript.

(Erase heading not required.)

Place	Date	Hour	Summary of Events and Information	Remarks and references to Appendices
STEENBECQUE	5-2-19		Admissions Officers nil. OR Sick 3 and nil. Evacuations Officers nil OR Sick nil and nil. Remaining under Tet 2	
STEENBECQUE	6-2-19		3 OR RASC MT for repatriation to Canada. 2 OR RAMC having proceeded to UK for demobilisation on strength on 1st Division. Admissions Officers nil OR Sick 1 and nil. Evacuations Officers nil OR Sick 2 and nil.	
STEENBECQUE	7-2-19		2 OR RAMC having proceeded to UK for demobilisation on strength on 1st Division ordinary leave. 1 OR RASC MT having been demobilised whilst on leave to UK on strength on 1st strength from 13/1/19. Admissions Officers nil OR Sick 2 and nil. Evacuations Officers nil OR Sick 1 and nil.	
STEENBECQUE	8-2-19		1 OR RAMC having proceeded to UK for demobilisation on strength of 1st Division. Admissions Officers nil OR Sick 2 and nil. Evacuations Officers nil OR Sick nil and nil.	

WAR DIARY
or
INTELLIGENCE SUMMARY.
(Erase heading not required.)

Army Form C. 2118.

Instructions regarding War Diaries and Intelligence Summaries are contained in F. S. Regs., Part II. and the Staff Manual respectively. Title pages will be prepared in manuscript.

Place	Date	Hour	Summary of Events and Information	Remarks and references to Appendices
STEENBECQUE	9.2.19		*[illegible handwritten entries regarding officers, OR, strength, D.D.M.S. XV Corps, STEENWERCK, 2/1 N. Midland Fld. Amb. at EBBLINGHEM]*	
STEENBECQUE	10.2.19		*[illegible handwritten entries; Major J.M. MOYES proceeded with advance party to take over S/K at STEENWERCK from 76th Fld. Amb.]*	
STEENBECQUE	11.2.19		*[illegible handwritten entries regarding officers, OR, strength, 73 Q.P.O.W.]*	
STEENBECQUE			*Major J. ??? proceeded with party of personnel in lorries to STEENWERCK. 1 OR RAMC being proceeded to UK for demobilisation is struck off the strength.*	

WAR DIARY
or
INTELLIGENCE SUMMARY.
(Erase heading not required.)

Army Form C. 2118.

Instructions regarding War Diaries and Intelligence Summaries are contained in F. S. Regs., Part II. and the Staff Manual respectively. Title pages will be prepared in manuscript.

Place	Date	Hour	Summary of Events and Information	Remarks and references to Appendices
STEENBECQUE	12.2.19		Remainder of unit moved to STEENWERCK personnel by motor lorry & transport by road, horses being provided by 30th DAC.	
			The site is a hutted camp, comprising 3 large hospital nissen huts and two double small nissen huts for German P.O.W. and one small nissen hut for British patients. There are various other huts for administration officers & personnel. The accommodation provided is sufficient for 200 patients sleeping on stretchers. 2 MAC cars are attached for evacuation to 54 CCS at REMY SIDING.	
			Admissions. Officers nil OR Sick 25 wd nil (Incl. 23 G.P.O.W.)	
			Evacuations Officers nil OR Sick 27 wd nil (" do ")	
			Prevailing diseases. I.C.T. 5. Influenza 4. Trench foot 5.	
			1 OR Rank having proceeded to UK for demobilisation is struck off the strength.	

WAR DIARY or INTELLIGENCE SUMMARY.

Army Form C. 2118

(Erase heading not required.)

Place	Date	Hour	Summary of Events and Information	Remarks and references to Appendices
STEENWERCK	12.2.19		As the result of a collision between a G.S. wagon belonging to this unit, and a light railway engine at No 2 level crossing BAILLEUL, Dvr ERRINGTON R.A.S.C. MT sustained injuries necessitating his evacuation and one 4.5 horse was killed.	
STEENWERCK	13.2.19		The ambulance site was visited today by Lieut General Sir H.E. WATTS, Commanding XIX Corps. Capt. H.W. TAYLOR R.A.M.C. T.F. having reported his arrival for duty from 10th Bn East Yorks Regt. is taken on the strength. 1 OR K.O.Y.L.I. attached and 1 OR R.A.S.C. MT having proceeded to U.K. for demobilisation are struck off the strength. Admissions. Officers nil. OR 2cR 26 2nd Red. (incl. 17 B.P.o.W) Evacuations. Officers nil. OR 2cR 26 2nd Red (incl. 20 B.P.o.W) Disch to duty. 1 OR 2cR Prevailing diseases. Influenza 6. Trench foot. 5. Diarrhoea 3.	

WAR DIARY
or
INTELLIGENCE SUMMARY.
(Erase heading not required.)

Army Form C. 2118.

Instructions regarding War Diaries and Intelligence Summaries are contained in F. S. Regs., Part II. and the Staff Manual respectively. Title pages will be prepared in manuscript.

Place	Date	Hour	Summary of Events and Information	Remarks and references to Appendices
STEENWERCK	14.2.19		Capt. J.M. McCORMACK reported his return from temporary duty with XIX Corps HQ.	
			1 OR RAMC & 1 OR RASC MT having proceeded to U.K. for demobilisation are struck off the strength.	
			Admissions: Officers nil, OR Sick 20 wd. nil. (Incl 13 G POW)	
			Evacuations: Officers nil OR Sick 22 wd nil (" 14 ")	
			Prevailing diseases: Influenza 5, Trench Feet 5, NYD pyrexia 3.	
STEENWERCK	15.2.19		Information was received from D.D.M.S. XIX Corps that the medical charge of outlying companies of 33rd & 34th Labour Groups was to be taken over by 94th Fd. Amb. and that OC 94th Fd. Amb. would act as S.M.O. Bailleul - Estaires Area.	
			The following arrangements were made with OC. these Labour Groups.	
			Capt. H.W. Taylor RAMC takes over from MO% 33 Labour Group the medical & Sanitary charge of 30th D.A.C.	

WAR DIARY or INTELLIGENCE SUMMARY.

(Erase heading not required.)

Army Form C. 2118.

Place	Date	Hour	Summary of Events and Information	Remarks and references to Appendices
STEENWERCK	15.2.19	Cont'd	199 P.O.W. Coy. G.R.U. near Armentières. 298 P.O.W. Coy. 321 P.O.W. Coy. 181 Chinese Labour Coy. 103 Labour Group. 1st Middlesex Labour Coy. Capt. J.M. McCORMACK takes over medical & sanitary charge from M.O. of 24th Labour Group of 185 P.O.W. Coy. 184 P.O.W. Coy. 123 G.R.U. & 242 P.O.W. Coy. 1 OR RAMC having proceeded to U.K. for demobilisation is Struck off his Strength. 1 OR RASC MT having been transferred to 22nd Aux. H.T. Coy. are Struck off his Strength. 1 OR RASC MT having been transferred to 31 Div. MT Coy. is Struck off his Strength. Admissions. Officers nil. OR sick 38 wd nil (incl. 24 G.P.O.W.) Evacuations. Officers nil. OR sick 16 wd nil (incl. 5 G.P.O.W.) Back to duty. 1 G.P.O.W. Sick. Prevailing diseases NYD pyrexia 4. Diarrhoea 4. I.C.T. 4. P.H.	

WAR DIARY or INTELLIGENCE SUMMARY

Army Form C. 2118.

Place	Date	Hour	Summary of Events and Information	Remarks and references to Appendices
STEENWERCK	16.2.19		Admissions. Officers nil. OR Sick 13. wd nil. (Inclusive 11 GPoW) Evacuations. Officers nil OR Sick 12 wd nil (8) Prevailing diseases. Debility 3. Diarrhoea 2. Scabies 2.	Ok
STEENWERCK	17.2.19		1 OR KOYLI attached to unit. proceeded to UK for demobilisation in other of the strength. Admissions. Officers nil OR Sick 37 wd nil (incl 2 GPoW) Evacuations. Officers nil OR Sick 8 wd nil (5) Back to duty. 1 OR Sick. Prevailing diseases. Influenza 12 Diarrhoea 3 P.U.T 5	Ok
STEENWERCK	18.2.19		2 OR RAMC having proceeded to UK for demobilisation are struck off the strength. Admissions. Officers nil. OR Sick 26 wd nil (incl 22 GPoW) Evacuations. Officers nil OR Sick 9 wd nil (2) Back to duty. OR Sick 2 (incl 1 GPoW) Prevailing diseases. Diarrhoea 4 Influenza 4 P.U.T 3	Ok
STEENWERCK	19.2.19		2 OR having proceeded to UK for demobilisation are struck off the strength. Admissions. Officers nil OR Sick 16 wd nil (incl 9 GPoW) Evacuations. Officers nil OR Sick nil wd nil Prevailing diseases. Diarrhoea 5. Influenza 3. Trench foot 3.	Ok

WAR DIARY or INTELLIGENCE SUMMARY

Army Form C. 2118.

Place	Date	Hour	Summary of Events and Information	Remarks and references to Appendices
STEENWERCK	20.2.19		1 OR. RASC HT having been evacuated to 54 CCS on 13/2/19 is struck off the strength from this date. 1 OR. RAMC having proceeded to UK for demobilisation struck off the strength. Capt (A/Major) J. GRAHAM RAMC TF and Temp Capt (A/Major) J.M. MOYES RAMC having proceeded to UK for demobilisation are struck off the strength. Temp Capt J.W. MACFARLANE M.C. RAMC and Lieut N.B. PEACOCK RAMC SR having reported for duty from 93rd & 95th Field Ambulances respectively are taken on the strength. 2 OR RAMC at present doing duty with ADMS office 31st Div are taken on the strength. The 94th Field Ambulance Est. was inspected by DMS 5th Army. Admissions Officers nil. OR Sick 27 wd nil (incl. 15 GPOW) Evacuations Officers nil. OR Sick 33 wd nil (incl. 22 GPOW) Prevailing diseases NYD pyrexia 4, Influenza 5, Diarrhoea 4	

WAR DIARY or INTELLIGENCE SUMMARY

Army Form C. 2118.

(Erase heading not required.)

Place	Date	Hour	Summary of Events and Information	Remarks and references to Appendices
STEENWERCK	21.2.19		2 OR RAMC having proceeded to UK for demobilisation are struck off the strength. 1 OR having died admitted to H Stat. Hp on 12/2/19 is struck off the strength. Admissions: Officers nil. OR sick 40 wd nil. (incl. 31 G.P.O.W.) Evacuations: Officers nil. OR sick 27 wd nil (" 9 ") Disch. to duty OR sick 3 (incl 3 G.P.O.W) Prevailing diseases Influenza 15. Diarrhoea 5. I.C.T. 5	A.b.
STEENWERCK	22.2.19		2 OR RAMC having proceeded to UK for demobilisation are struck off the strength. Admissions: Officers nil. OR sick 25 wd nil (incl 20 G.P.O.W) Evacuations: Officers nil. OR sick 30 wd nil (" 22 ") Disch. to duty OR sick 1. Prevailing diseases Diarrhoea 6. Scabies 2. I.C.T. 2	A.b.
STEENWERCK	23.2.19		Admissions: Officers nil OR sick 13 wd nil (incl 6 G.P.O.W) Evacuations: Officers nil OR sick 11 wd nil (" 4 ") Disch. to duty OR sick 18. (incl. 13 G.P.O.W.) Prevailing diseases Influenza 5. I.C.T. 4. Diarrhoea 3.	A.b.
STEENWERCK	24.2.19		Lieut H.B. PEACOCK has been granted special leave to UK from 25/2/19 to 11/3/19. 2 OR having proceeded to UK for demobilisation are struck off the strength. Admissions: Officers nil. OR sick 21 wd nil. (incl 10 G.P.O.W) Evacuations: Officers nil. OR sick 20 wd nil (" 12 ") Deaths 1 G.P.O.W (Diarrhoea). Disch. to duty 2 OR sick. Prevailing diseases Diarrhoea 4. Influenza 3. I.C.T. 2	A.b.

WAR DIARY or INTELLIGENCE SUMMARY.

Army Form C. 2118.

(Erase heading not required.)

Place	Date	Hour	Summary of Events and Information	Remarks and references to Appendices
STEENWERCK	25/2/19		Capt. H.W. Taylor RAMC TF proceeded on leave to UK from 25/2/19 to 12/3/19. Lieut. E.J.S. BONNETT RAMC SR resumed his ordinary duty from 25th bell amb. 2 OR RAMC having proceeded to UK for demobilisation. An officer off the strength Lieut ...... RAMC Admissions Officers nil. OR sick 20 wd nil (incl 13 & POW) Evacuations Officers nil OR sick 31 wd nil Disch. to duty. OR sick 11 (incl. 10 & POW) Prevailing diseases. Debility 5. NYD pyrexia 4. Influenza 2.	
STEENWERCK	26/2/19		1 OR RAMC having proceeded to UK for demobilisation. Struck off the strength. Admissions Officers sick 1 wd nil OR sick 21 wd nil (incl 10 & POW) Evacuations Officers sick 1 wd nil OR sick 26 wd nil Disch. to duty. OR sick 13 (incl. 7 & POW) Prevailing diseases. Diarrhoea 4. NYD pyrexia 3. Influenza 2.	
STEENWERCK	27/2/19		Admissions Officers nil OR sick 18 wd nil (incl. 7 & POW) Evacuations Officers nil OR sick 25 wd nil (incl. 15 & POW) Disch. to duty. OR sick 9 (incl. 3 & POW) Prevailing diseases. Influenza 2. Gonorrhoea 2. Bronchitis 2.	

WAR DIARY or INTELLIGENCE SUMMARY

Army Form C. 2118.

Place	Date	Hour	Summary of Events and Information	Remarks and references to Appendices
STEENWERCK	28.2.19		1 OR RAMC having proceeded to UK for demobilisation is struck off the strength.	
			Admissions. Officers nil. OR sick 16 wd nil (incl. 11 G.P.o.W.)	
			Evacuations Officers nil. OR sick 17 wd nil (incl 15 G.P.o.W)	
			Disch. to duty. OR sick 19. (incl 14 G.P.o.W.)	
			Prevailing diseases NYD pyrexia 4. Diarrhoea 2. Debility 2	
			Total admissions during the month of February 1919.	
			Officers sick 1. wd nil. OR sick 519. wd nil. (incl 346 G.P.o.W.)	
			Total Evacuations Officers sick 1 wd nil. OR sick 293. wd nil (incl 244 G.P.o.W)	
			Total Discharged to duty. OR sick 84. (incl 52 G.P.o.W.)	
			Prevailing diseases Influenza 40. Diarrhoea 63. I.C.T. 34 NYD pyrexia 35. Trench feet 33. Debility 10.	
			A. H. Laing Lt-Col R.A.M.C. O.C. 94th Field Amb.	

Mar. 1919

160/3551

92ⁿᵈ 7.a

17 JUL 1919

WAR DIARY or INTELLIGENCE SUMMARY

Army Form C. 2118.

94 Fd Amb

Place	Date	Hour	Summary of Events and Information	Remarks and references to Appendices
STEENWERCK	1.3.19		The 94th Field Ambulance is still situated at Steenwerck treating SICK from 33rd & 34th labour groups. 1 OR RAMC having proceeded to UK for demobilisation is struck off the strength. Admissions Officers nil OR SICK 11 and nil (incl. 6 G.P.O.W.) Evacuations Officers nil OR SICK 8 and nil (" 3 ") Back to duty OR SICK 4 (incl 3 G.P.O.W.) Prevailing diseases, Diarrhoea 3 Influenza 3.	
STEENWERCK	2.3.19		Admissions Officers SICK 1 and nil OR SICK 14 and nil (incl 12 G.P.O.W.) Evacuations Officers SICK 1 and nil OR SICK 14 and nil (" " ") Back to duty OR SICK 4 (incl 4 G.P.O.W.) Prevailing diseases Diarrhoea 5 NYD pyrexia 3 I.C.T. 2.	
STEENWERCK	3.3.19		3 OR RASC HT & 2 OR RAMC having proceeded to UK for demobilisation are struck off the strength. Admissions Officers nil OR SICK 17 and nil (incl 12 G.P.O.W.) Evacuations Officers nil OR SICK 12 and nil (incl 11 G.P.O.W.) Back to duty OR SICK 2. Prevailing diseases Scabies 4 Influenza 3 NYD pyrexia 3	

WAR DIARY or INTELLIGENCE SUMMARY

Army Form C. 2118.

Place	Date	Hour	Summary of Events and Information	Remarks and references to Appendices
STEENWERCK	4.3.19		4 O.R. R.A.M.C. having proceeded to U.K. for demobilisation are Struck off this Strength.	
			Admissions. Officers nil. O.R. Sick 11 and nil (Incl. 5 a.P.O.W)	
			Evacuations. Officers nil. O.R. Sick 6 and nil (" 4 ")	
			Disch. to duty. O.R. Sick 2. (Incl. 2 a.P.O.W)	
			Prevailing diseases N.Y.D. Pyrexia 6. Influenza 1.	
STEENWERCK	5.3.19		Temp. Capt. J.W. MACFARLANE. M.C. R.A.M.C. having proceeded to U.K. for demobilisation is Struck off this Strength.	
			3 O.R. R.A.M.C having proceeded to U.K. for demobilisation are Struck off this Strength.	
			Admissions. Officers nil. O.R. Sick 14. and nil (Incl. 8 a.P.O.W)	
			Evacuations. Officers nil. O.R. Sick 14 and nil (Incl. 10 ")	
			Disch. to duty. O.R. Sick 5. (Incl. 3 a.P.O.W)	
			Prevailing diseases. Influenza 3. Trench fever 2. debility 2.	

WAR DIARY or INTELLIGENCE SUMMARY.

Army Form C. 2118.

(Erase heading not required.)

Place	Date	Hour	Summary of Events and Information	Remarks and references to Appendices
STEENWERCK	6-3-19		RAMC. 1 OR having proceeded to U.K. for demobilisation is struck off the strength.	
			Admissions. Officers nil. OR SicR 18 ind nil (incl. 18 @ PoW)	
			Evacuations. Officers nil. OR SicR 21 ind nil (" 19 ")	
			Disch. to duty. OR SicR 1 (incl. 1 @ PoW.)	
			Prevailing diseases. Debility 4. NYD pyrexia 4. Scabies 1.	
STEENWERCK	7-3-19		3 OR RAMC having proceeded to U.K. for demobilisation are struck off the strength.	
			Admissions. Officers nil. OR SicR 20 ind nil (incl. 15 @ PoW)	
			Evacuations. Officers nil. OR SicR 11 ind nil (" 8 ")	
			Disch. to duty. OR SicR 11 (incl. 11 @ PoW)	
			Prevailing diseases. NYD pyrexia 5. Debility 5. Diarrhoea 4.	
STEENWERCK	8-3-19		9 OR RAMC (non-releasable) proceeded to report to ADMS 3rd Div. for duty with Army of the Rhine	
			1 OR RAMC & 2 OR RASC. HT. proceeded to U.K. for demob- -ilisation & are struck off the strength.	
			Admissions. Officers nil. OR SicR 15 ind nil (incl. 11 @ PoW)	

WAR DIARY or INTELLIGENCE SUMMARY.

Army Form C. 2118.

(Erase heading not required.)

Place	Date	Hour	Summary of Events and Information	Remarks and references to Appendices
			Evacuations. Officers nil. OR Sick 19 wd. nil (incl 16 @ P.o.W.)	
			Disch. to duty OR Sick 3. (incl 2 Q.P.O.W)	
			Prevailing Diseases. Debility 3. N.Y.D pyrexia 2. Sunburst 1.	
STEENWERCK	9.3.19		1 OR RAMC having been demobilised while on leave he OR is struck off the Strength from 3/1/19.	
			Admissions. Officers nil. OR Sick 5. wd. nil (incl 4 @ P.o.W.)	
			Evacuations. Officers nil. OR Sick 7 wd. nil (" 2 ")	
			Disch. to duty OR Sick 6. (incl 4 @ P.O.W)	
			Prevailing disease N.Y.D pyrexia 2.	
STEENWERCK	10.3.19		3 OR RAMC having proceeded to U.K. for demobilisation are struck off the Strength.	
			Admissions. Officers nil. OR Sick 26 wd. nil (incl 9 @ P.o.W)	
			Evacuations. Officers nil OR Sick 9 wd nil (" 7 ")	
			Disch. to duty OR Sick 1. (incl. 1 @ P.O.W.)	
			Prevailing diseases N.Y.D pyrexia 6. Debility 5. Scabies 2.	

WAR DIARY or INTELLIGENCE SUMMARY.

Army Form C. 2118.

(Erase heading not required.)

Place	Date	Hour	Summary of Events and Information	Remarks and references to Appendices
STEENWERCK	11.3.19		2 OR RAMC having proceeded to U.K. for demobilisation are struck off the Strength.	
			Admissions. Officers nil OR Sick 24 and nil (incl 13 (P.O.W.))	
			Evacuations Officers nil OR Sick 24 and nil (" 13 (P.O.W.))	
			Disch. to duty nil.	
			Prevailing diseases. Diarrhoea 6 NYD pyrexia 4, Debility 4.	
			The following promotions have been authorised by Officer i/c RAMC Section to complete to cadre establishment	
			60658 Q.M.S. Marshall F.L. to be A/Sergt-Major, vice 30403 Sergt Major Crossley A.	
			60628 Cpl. Sopp W.E. to be A/Sergt. vice 29051 Sgt. Maghud S.H.	
			60900 L/Cpl McNee A. to be A/Cpl. vice 60628 Cpl. Sopp W.E.	
			301523 L/Cpl Leith J. to be A/Cpl. vice 67775 Cpl. Munro J.	
STEENWERCK	12.3.19		9 OR RAMC having proceeded to UK to demobilisation are struck off the Strength. 1 OR RAMC having surrendered while in transit to UK is struck off the Strength from 14/1/19.	

WAR DIARY or INTELLIGENCE SUMMARY.

Army Form C. 2118.

(Erase heading not required.)

Place	Date	Hour	Summary of Events and Information	Remarks and references to Appendices
			2 OR RASC HT having been transferred from 31 Div. Train are taken on the strength.	
			Admissions. Officers nil OR Sick 18 wd nil (incl. 12 GPoW)	
			Evacuations Officers nil OR Sick 11 wd nil (" 6 ")	
			Disch. to duty. OR Sick 3 (incl. 0 GPoW)	
			Prevailing diseases. NYD. pyrexia 4 debility 2.	
STEENWERCK	13.3.19		3 OR RAMC having proceeded to UK for demobilisation are struck off the strength.	
			Admissions. Officers nil OR Sick 8 wd nil (incl 6 GPoW)	
			Evacuations Officers nil OR Sick 7 wd nil (" 3 ")	
			Disch to duty OR Sick 2 (" 2 ")	
			Prevailing diseases. Debility 2. ? Influenza 2.	
STEENWERCK	14.3.19		2 OR RAMC having proceeded to UK for demobilisation are struck off the strength.	
			Admissions Officers nil OR Sick 15 wd nil (incl 11 GPoW)	
			Evacuations Officers nil OR Sick 11 wd nil (" 8 ")	

WAR DIARY
or
INTELLIGENCE SUMMARY.

Army Form C. 2118.

(Erase heading not required.)

Instructions regarding War Diaries and Intelligence Summaries are contained in F. S. Regs., Part II. and the Staff Manual respectively. Title pages will be prepared in manuscript.

Place	Date	Hour	Summary of Events and Information	Remarks and references to Appendices
STEENWERCK	15.3.19		Disch to duty OR Sick 2 (Incl. 2 @ POW)	
			Prevailing diseases Tonsillitis 3 I.C.T. 2	R.h
			2 OR RAMC having proceeded to the Rhine army to duty with 3rd Div. are struck off the strength	
			4 OR RASC MT having proceeded to UK for demobilisation are struck off the strength	
			Admissions Officers nil OR Sick 11 wd nil (Incl 7 @POW)	
			Evacuations Officers nil OR Sick 12 wd nil (" 7 ")	
			Disch to duty. OR Sick nil.	
			Prevailing diseases. Debility 2 Scabies 2	R.h
STEENWERCK	16.3.19		Lieut H.B PEACOCK RAMC SR having proceeded to duty with the Rhine army is struck off the strength	
			Admissions Officers nil OR Sick 6 wd nil (Incl. @POW 3)	
			Evacuations Officers nil OR Sick 11 wd nil (" " 8)	
			Disch to duty. OR Sick 9 (Incl. @POW 9)	
			Prevailing diseases. NYD Pyrexia 4 Tonsillitis 1	R.h

WAR DIARY or INTELLIGENCE SUMMARY.

Army Form C. 2118.

(Erase heading not required.)

Place	Date	Hour	Summary of Events and Information	Remarks and references to Appendices
STEENWERCK	17.3.19		2 OR RAMC on detached duty at 4 Stat. Hosp. having proceeded to UK for demobilisation are struck off the Strength.	
			2 OR RASC MT having proceeded to UK for demobilisation are struck off the Strength.	
			Admissions Officers nil. OR Sick 14 wd nil (incl QPoW 9)	
			Evacuations Officers nil OR Sick 6 wd nil (" " 6)	
			Back to duty OR Sick 2 (incl 0 QPoW)	R.H.
			Prevailing diseases N.Y.D. pyrexia 4.	
STEENWERCK	18.3.19		Capt. R.G. BATTERSBY RAMC SR. 93rd Fld. amb. is transferred to 94th Fld. amb. remaining on detached duty with ADMS 81 Div.	
			Admissions Officers nil OR Sick 9 wd nil. (incl 6 QPoW)	
			Evacuations Officers nil OR Sick 11 wd nil (" " 6 ")	
			Back to duty OR Sick 4 (incl 2 QPoW)	R.H.
			Prevailing diseases Defective vision 2. Tonsillitis 2.	
STEENWERCK	19.3.19		1 OR RASC MT having proceeded for duty with the Rhine Army is struck off the Strength.	
			Admissions Officers nil OR Sick 10 wd nil. (incl 4 QPoW)	

WAR DIARY or INTELLIGENCE SUMMARY.

Army Form C. 2118.

(Erase heading not required.)

Place	Date	Hour	Summary of Events and Information	Remarks and references to Appendices
STEENWERCK	30.3.19		Evacuations. Officers nil. OR Sick 31 wd. nil (incl. 23 @ POW) Disch. to duty OR Sick 11 (incl. 10 @ POW) Prevailing disease NYD pyrexia 5. Orders were received from DDMS XIX Corps to evacuate or discharge as many patients as possible as 11 CCS had been ordered to take over the site on 30/3/19. Advance party from 11 CCS. arrived to take over. 2 officers (Capt McCormack & Lieut Bonnett) with 7 OR and 2 ambulance cars were left to carry on duties until completion of relief. 7 patients remaining. Remainder of personnel proceeded by lorry & cars to St Omer, being accommodated in WATTS CAMP with 93rd Fld. Amb. Horses provided by 19th Aux. M.T. Coy. Mess transport provided by road staging for the night at Hazebrouck. 1 OR RAMC on temp. duty at No 4 Stat. Hp. is posted to that unit & struck off strength accordingly. R.L.	

WAR DIARY or INTELLIGENCE SUMMARY.

Army Form C. 2118.

(Erase heading not required.)

Place	Date	Hour	Summary of Events and Information	Remarks and references to Appendices
ST. OMER	21.3.19		Horse transport arrived from Hazebrouck by road. 1 CAPT. A.B.R. SWORN R.A.M.C. having proceeded for duty with the Rhine Army is struck off the strength from 10/3/19. Admissions nil. Evacuations nil.	
ST. OMER	22.3.19		2 OR. RASC MT from 31st Div. MT. Coy. having reported their arrival for duty are taken on the strength. 2 OR. RAMC (non-releasable) transferred to 95th Fd Amb. Admissions nil. Evacuations nil.	
ST. OMER	23.3.19		Admissions nil. Evacuations nil.	
ST. OMER	24.3.19		Admissions nil. Evacuations nil.	
ST. OMER	26.3.19		1 OR RAMC on detached duty at XIX Corps Concentration Camp having proceeded to Rhine Army on 20/3/19 is struck off the strength. 1 OR RASC MT. having proceeded to U.K. for demobilisation is struck off the strength. G.O.C. 31st Div. has granted permission to Capt. R.G. BATTERSBY to wear the badges of Major pending notification appearing in the Gazette. Admissions nil. Evacuations nil.	

WAR DIARY or INTELLIGENCE SUMMARY.

Army Form C. 2118.

(Erase heading not required.)

Place	Date	Hour	Summary of Events and Information	Remarks and references to Appendices
ST. OMER	26.3.19		Admissions nil. Evacuations nil.	
ST. OMER	27.3.19		Admissions nil. Evacuations nil.	
ST. OMER	28.3.19		Orders were received that all officers on strength of units were to be struck off strength from 29.3.19 except one per cadre. Major J.G. FRASER being the officer detailed to take over cadre of 94th Fld Amb to vice Lieut Col E.O. LANG on transfer to 95th Fld, and handed over command to Major J.G. FRASER	
ST. OMER	29.3.19		Took over command of Cadre Establishment of 94rd Ambulance correct.	J.G. Fraser
ST. OMER	30.3.19		1 O.R. (W.O. RASC H.T.) transferred to 30 Gen H, Calais, sick (? VD).	J.G.F.
ST. OMER	31.3.19		Inspected Personnel & Horse Lines. Satisfactory.	J.G. Fraser Lt & QrMr RAMC A/O C 94 Field Amb.

Apr 1919

No. 94. 7. a.

17 JUL 1919

WAR DIARY or INTELLIGENCE SUMMARY.

(Erase heading not required.)

Army Form C. 2118.

94 Fd Amb

Place	Date	Hour	Summary of Events and Information	Remarks and references to Appendices
St. Omer	1/4/19	—	Unit still at ST. OMER. Capt R.G. BATTERSBY, granted leave to U.K. 2/4/19 to 16/4/19. Capt R.G. BATTERSBY, RAMC, Capt J.M. McCORMICK, RAMC & 1st Lieut C.H. HEACOCK. M.C. U.S.A. struck off strength of Unit, & transferred to ADMS 5th Area. J.G.J.	
ST. OMER	2/4/19	—	Capt. E.P. HARDING, RAMC posted to Unit from No4 Stationary Hospital but remaining with latter Unit for temporary duty. J.G.J.	
ST. OMER	3/4/19	—	Inspected Unit. satisfactory. J.G.J.	
ST. OMER	4/4/19	—	NIL. J.G.J.	
ST. OMER	5/4/19	—	1 OR (WO RASC HT) returned to duty from 30 General Hospital. J.G.J.	
ST. OMER	6/4/19	—	NIL. J.G.J.	
ST. OMER	7/4/19	—	Capt. E.P. HARDING RAMC taken off strength; reposted to No4 Stationary Hospital. Major R.G. BATTERSBY, RAMC SR, reposted to 94 Fd Amb Cadre Establishment. 1 OR RASC HT transferred to 31st Div Train for duty. J.G.J.	
ST. OMER	8/4/19	—	Inspected Unit: satisfactory J.G.J.	
ST. OMER	9/4/19	—	NIL. J.G.J.	
ST. OMER	10/4/19	—	2 OR RASC MT transferred to 31st Div M.T. Coy. Two Ambulance Cars withdrawn from Unit by 31st Div M.T. Coy. J.G.J.	

WAR DIARY or INTELLIGENCE SUMMARY.

Army Form C. 2118.

Instructions regarding War Diaries and Intelligence Summaries are contained in F. S. Regs., Part II. and the Staff Manual respectively. Title pages will be prepared in manuscript.

(Erase heading not required.)

Place	Date	Hour	Summary of Events and Information	Remarks and references to Appendices
ST. OMER	11/4/19	—	NIL. JGF.	
ST. OMER	12/4/19	—	Inspected Mobilization Equipment. Satisfactory JGF.	
ST. OMER	13/4/19	—	Inspected Unit. Satisfactory JGF.	
ST. OMER	14/4/19	—	1 OR RASC HT (W.O.) transferred to 93 Field Amb. Sick (N.Y.D.N.) JSF	
ST. OMER	16/4/19	—	1 OR RASC MT transferred to 31st Div M.T. Coy for duty with Motor Cycle. JGF	
ST. OMER	19/4/19	—	Inspected Unit Satisfactory JGF.	
ST. OMER	21/4/19	—	8 OR posted temporarily to No 4 Stat'y HP for duty. JGF	
ST. OMER	22/4/19	—	1 OR (W.O. RASC HT) struck off strength not having returned from Hospital JGF	
ST. OMER	25/4/19	—	Inspected Unit. – Satisfactory. JGF.	
ST. OMER	27/4/19	—	Mobilization Equipment inspected by DADOS – Satisfactory JGF	
ST. OMER	30/4/19	—	Inspected Unit Satisfactory. JGF.	

www.ingramcontent.com/pod-product-compliance
Lightning Source LLC
Chambersburg PA
CBHW081432300426
44108CB00016BA/2354